Understand Those Financial Reports

Understand Those Financial Reports

Question-and-Answer Guide for Investors and Nonfinancial Managers

RAYMOND J. LIPAY

JOHN WILEY & SONS

New York   Chichester   Brisbane   Toronto   Singapore

Library of Congress Cataloging in Publication Data:

Lipay, Raymond J.
    Understand those financial reports.

    Includes index.
    1. Financial statements. 2. Corporation reports.
I. Title.

HF5681.B2L5852 1984   657'.33   83-16652
ISBN 0-471-86571-0

Printed in the United States of America

10 9 8 7 6 5 4 3 2 1

For my loving wife, Marguerite,
my most precious investment

Preface

If you own or intend to own stocks or bonds of one or more publicly listed corporations, you have an obligation to yourself to keep tabs on those companies that will be using your hard-earned invested dollars. Also, if you are a nonfinancial manager or executive who seeks advancement and opportunity within the corporate hierarchy in order to become an integral part of the organization, you want to gain more insight into your company's financial health and operating performance. The most readily available means for maintaining a vigilant eye on your investee and/or employer companies are the financial reports those companies issue for the benefit of their stockholders. Most important, you do not have to be a certified public accountant or a financial analyst to understand the meaning and significance of financial reports.

Nonfinancial persons often regard financial reports in the same way as they regard income tax returns. Too many numbers! Too technical! Confusing! The question and answer format of this book has been designed to soften such criticisms. Questions addressed in this book are those that might arise in the minds of present and potential corporate investors and managers when they turn the pages of a financial report. Answers have been designed in such a way as to enable a reader to appreciate, comprehend, and interpret the meaning and significance of the various types of financial reports issued by publicly listed corporations. In general, this book contains questions and related answers that should fulfill the needs of investors and nonfinancial managers, regardless of their level of knowledge concerning financial reports.

The guts of all financial reports are the financial statements, related notes, and other supplementary financial information that accompany those financial statements. This book will help to dispel any mystique that shrouds such financial data so that investors and nonfinancial managers may get the message behind the numbers. As a result, you will learn how to measure a corporation's performance, recognize red lights or warning signals concerning troubled situations, and interpret financial accounting and reporting terms as they are used throughout financial statement related data.

A special chapter is devoted to the audit reports that accompany financial statements. Their meaning and significance are explored.

Financial reports also contain financial and related narrative data that are not covered by audit reports. These include financial highlights, the president's letter, and the management report. The importance of these and other nonaudited items are covered in a separate chapter.

A unique feature of this book is a separate chapter on those financial reports filed by publicly listed companies with the Securities and Exchange Commission (SEC). The purpose of these reports and the ways they differ from the conventional annual and interim financial reports issued to stockholders are described.

In order to obtain a clear picture as to how financial reports are packaged and presented to shareholders, illustrations of financial statements, related notes, supplementary financial information, audit reports, and other related data are provided in designated chapters. These illustrations were taken from the 1982 annual reports of certain well-known publicly listed corporations. A glossary of 100 key terms and phrases that might be helpful in reading and analyzing financial reports is also provided as a reference aid at the end of this book.

For you as an investor, an understanding of financial reports issued by publicly listed corporations will provide you with a twofold advantage: (1) you will feel as though you are taking an active part in your investment, and (2) you will derive investor confidence in assessing your investment risk. For you as a nonfinancial manager, an understanding of financial reports issued by your employer corporation will enable you to be more aware of your company's past, present, and future. The question and answer format of this book will provide that essential understanding. Reading financial reports will then become a pleasure rather than a chore.

RAYMOND J. LIPAY

New York
November 1983

Contents

Understand Those Financial Reports

Chapter One

Overview of Financial Reports

1

INTRODUCTION

The majority of investors in publicly listed corporations are not directly involved or affiliated with their investee companies. Therefore, they cannot visualize on a day-to-day basis how those companies conduct their business operations. Financial reports help to resolve this obstacle by serving as the primary channel of communication between corporate management and owners (i.e., investors). Millions of dollars are spent annually by publicly listed corporations to produce and distribute financial reports in order to keep investors informed as to their investee companies' financial health and progress in an economic and competitive environment. This chapter covers the purpose and importance of financial reports, the basic types issued to stockholders, their overall content, and the frequency of their distribution.

PURPOSE AND IMPORTANCE

Q: What is the purpose of financial reports?

A: Financial reports are documents used by corporations to report information concerning corporate management's stewardship function to stockholders and other interested parties, such as creditors, suppliers, and financial analysts. In this way users of financial reports are able to judge management's philosophy, performance, goals, and future prospects.

Q: How does information concerning management's stewardship function benefit investors?

A: Such information enables investors to assess the risks and returns of their investment dollars. In this way, investors can ascertain whether or not management is fulfilling its assigned responsibility, that is, managing and implementing the corporation's resources effectively.

Q: What types of companies issue financial reports?

A: Generally financial reports are issued by those companies that are considered to be publicly listed or publicly traded. In other words, such companies have their debt (i.e., bonds) or equity (i.e., stock) securities traded in a public market on a domestic stock exchange (e.g., the American Stock Exchange and the New York Stock Exchange) or in the domestic over-the-counter stock market. Publicly listed companies are also required to file their financial statements with the Securities and Exchange Commission (SEC), a regulatory agency of the federal government. Once a business enterprise issues its financial statements in preparation for the sale of any class of securities (i.e., bonds or debentures, preferred or common stock), that enterprise or company is considered to be a "publicly traded" or "publicly listed" company.

Q: As a potential shareholder, why should I look at financial reports when I can easily get a broker to advise me as to what companies I might invest in?

A: Investing in the securities of a particular company through a broker is like buying property through a real estate agent. Although a real estate agent will advise you to buy a particular piece of property that is within your financial means, you would generally inspect the property to determine its condition before actually purchasing it. The same should hold true for a purchase of a company's securities. A careful reading of that company's financial report prior to making an investment decision will give you some indication as to the company's operating condition and financial health.

Q: Now that I own shares in a particular company, why should I read the financial reports issued by that company? My broker will advise me as to whether I should continue to maintain the investment or sell out.

A: That's true! However, investing in a public company is similar to being a landlord of rental property. As a landlord, you would make periodic visits to the rented property to see that everything is in working order. In like manner, as an investor (or partial owner) of a company you should be inclined to "check up" periodically on your investment. Financial reports provide an opportunity for this periodic "checkup" on your investment.

TYPES OF FINANCIAL REPORTS

Q: What are the most common forms of financial reports issued by publicly traded companies?

A: The two most common types are annual reports and interim reports. Annual reports present financial information covering an operating cycle of a corporation's business, which is generally one full year. Interim reports present financial information covering three months, or a quarter of a year, for example, January 1, 19X2 through March 31, 19X2. Two other types of financial reports issued by publicly traded companies that must be filed with the SEC are:

1. SEC Form 10-K, an expanded version of the annual report.
2. SEC Form 10-Q, an expanded version of the interim report.

Although SEC Forms 10-K and 10-Q are similar in most respects to annual and interim reports issued to stockholders, both forms contain additional financial and nonfinancial information that might interest readers of financial reports.

Q: When comparing annual with interim reports, which is more important in terms of credibility?

A: Annual reports might be considered more important in terms of credibility because the financial statements included within annual reports are audited or examined by independent certified public accountants (CPAs). Although financial information included within interim reports is not audited or examined by CPAs, interim reports are important to investors because the information contained therein is part of a total and continual flow of information to the investment community.

Q: Should an investor refer to both interim and annual financial reports, or is the information provided within annual reports sufficient for keeping tabs on an investee company?

A: An investor should have access to both interim and annual reports of an investee company. Although the annual report provides information regarding a company's history and operating performance throughout the past year, interim reports can serve as a timely progress report to an investor regarding investee company activities during the course of a year.

CONTENT OF FINANCIAL REPORTS

Basic Information

Q: What kinds of information does a typical annual report include?

A: An annual report typically includes such data as:

Description of the company's business (products or services).
Objectives, philosophy, and strategy of the business.
Explanations of current developments that might affect the business, such as conditions existing within the industry, legislative and foreign policies that affect the operation of the company, the labor–management situation, and economic conditions that affect the company (e.g., inflation).
An indication of the company's future outlook.

Programs the company has undertaken to fulfill its social responsibility (e.g., environmental protection or aid for the handicapped).
The company's financial results for the current and preceding years.

Method of Presentation

Q: How is all of this information presented within an annual report?

A: Annual report information is presented through a combination of the following:

Narrative material, such as a letter from the company's president to its shareholders, company description and statement of philosophy.
Pictures of operating locations, plants, and offices.
Highlights or review of financial results.
Charts and graphs that illustrate certain financial results by product lines and/or service, as well as trends over past years.
Audited financial statements and other supplementary financial information.

Charts and Graphs

Q: How important are the colorful and often impressive charts and graphs in annual reports?

A: Graphics alone are not important as a means of understanding a company's activities in order to assess investment risk. Graphics are important only when they are an integral part of the entire company story. In other words, elaborate artwork should complement the narrative and financial information.

Overall Review of Annual Report

Q: Since there appears to be a great deal of information within an annual report, how might a prospective investor obtain an overall view of a company's operations from reading the report?

A: In order to obtain an overall or "summary-type" review of a particular company, a prospective investor might look at:

>*The president's letter.*
>*Financial highlights or review section.*
>*Selected financial data.*
>*Management's discussion and analysis of financial condition and results of operations.*
>*Report of management.*

Q: Would the above information be adequate for a prospective investor to make an investment decision?

A: Not necessarily, because such information is unaudited. When making an investment decision, a prospective investor should rely primarily on the audited financial statements contained within an annual report.

Audited Versus Unaudited Financial Information

Q: Why should a prospective investor rely on the audited financial statements rather than the unaudited information? What is the basic difference?

A: The unaudited information (e.g., president's letter, financial highlights) is usually not verified or examined by a party outside the particular company. On the other hand, audited financial statements are examined by CPAs who are independent of the company that issues such statements. As a result, the annual report will contain an independent auditor's report, which will indicate that:

Certain auditing steps were undertaken to verify the items contained in the financial statements, and to make certain that these steps met standards of practice approved by the public accounting profession.

The financial statements covered by the independent auditor's report have been prepared by the company's management in conformity with generally accepted accounting principles.

In other words, if the annual report contains financial statements that have been audited or examined by public accountants who are independent of the company in question, a prospective investor can be reasonably assured that the figures within those financial statements have a certain degree of credibility.

Q: What is the general purpose of these audited financial statements, and what are they comprised of?

A: Audited financial statements represent a progress report and a summation of the current financial condition of a business. They serve as a measure of management's past performance and are presented in conformity with generally accepted accounting principles on a comparative basis with prior years. Audited financial statements found in annual reports include:

Balance sheet.

Income statement or statement of earnings.

Accumulated retained earnings statement, which may often be combined with the income statement, or a statement of changes in stockholders' equity.

Statement of changes in financial position.

Footnotes, which clarify and explain certain items in the actual financial statements.

Basis for Financial Statements

Q: How do financial statements actually develop from a company's accounting records?

A: Like living organisms, financial statements undergo a growth process from an embryonic stage to full development. The preparation of financial statements encompasses five stages of growth. They are as follows:

1. **Transactions Take Place in the Business.** A company orders and eventually receives materials and merchandise from other companies and suppliers. The materials ordered may then be refined through the company's manufacturing process in order to produce a salable product. Orders from customers are received and subsequently filled. The final product is then shipped to customers and distributors, such as retail outlets. Afterward, proceeds from the sale of the product are received by the company. If the demand for the product increases, additional facilities, such as a factory or a warehouse, may be needed to accommodate increased production and storage. As a result, those added facilities will be purchased or leased by the company. These are all "transactions," the lifeblood of any business, which will ultimately find their way into the company's financial statements in the form of income, expense, asset, liability, and equity items.

2. **Transactions Are Recorded on Source Documents.** All transactions that take place on a daily basis involving the company business are recorded on source documents. These include purchase orders, purchase invoices, checks for payment of purchases, sales orders, sales receipts, etc. These source documents are indicators of the activity that has transpired throughout the company.

3. **Transactions Are Summarized and Classified.** Accountability for all transactions that have taken place in the company is now firmly established. All source documents that evolved

from the transactions are now maintained in accounting records, where they are summarized and classifed in various journals or registers. These include purchase journals, sales journals, check registers, bank statements, etc. The extent of such records will vary with the size and complexity of the business operation.

4. Transactions Are Recorded in a Final Summary. The various journals and registers are summarized into the original books of account, which are often referred to as the general ledger.

5. Presentation of Financial Statements. Financial statements are then prepared from the general ledger and other accounting records, after which they are audited or examined by a CPA.

Generally Accepted Accounting Principles

Q: What are generally accepted accounting principles?

A: Generally accepted accounting principles, which CPAs often refer to as GAAP, can be considered ground rules for financial accounting. These ground rules address the following issues:

The types of economic resources that are recorded as assets and the obligations that are recorded as liabilities on a company's books of account.

The nature of changes in assets and liabilities that are recorded on a company's books of account.

Timing considerations for revenue and expense items (i.e., the period or year when revenue and expense items are recorded on the company's books).

Methods of measuring assets and liabilities (e.g., historical cost, current value).

The types of financial statements prepared by company management (e.g., balance sheet, income statement, statement of changes in financial position).

Amount of information required to be disclosed in the financial statements.

Methods of disclosing financial statement information (either directly on the financial statements or within the footnotes).

In general, GAAP encompasses accounting principles and practices as well as the methods used to apply those principles and practices.

Q: What are the implications of GAAP for investors?

A: GAAP provides a common denominator, or universal accounting language, in financial statement presentation. In this way, readers of financial statements are able to compare balance sheets, income statements, and statements of changes in financial position from one company to another. Financial statements prepared in accordance with GAAP imply that the company is measuring and reporting asset, liability, income, and expense items with methods identical to those of other companies. For example, GAAP requires the implementation of the accrual basis of accounting by reporting companies. According to the accrual basis, revenues are recorded when realized, and expenses are recorded when incurred, regardless of the date when cash is received for revenues of disbursed for expenses. Another example is the required use of historical cost, rather than current or appraised value, to reflect fixed assets on the balance sheet, such as property, plant, and equipment. Historical cost is the original cost used for recording goods and services in a company's financial records at the time of acquistion. It is considered to be the primary measurement basis in financial accounting.

Financial Accounting Standards Board

Q: Sometimes a note to the financial statements will refer to a specific accounting rule issued by the Financial Accounting Standards Board. What is the Financial Accounting Standards Board?

A: The Financial Accounting Standards Board (FASB) is an organization that is responsible for establishing standards of financial accounting and reporting. The standards that are developed by the Board consist of generally accepted accounting principles (GAAP), which govern the preparation of all financial reports for publicly listed companies and private companies. The FASB operates as an organization that is independent of all other business and professional organizations, such as corporations and public accounting firms. The FASB has seven members who serve on a full-time basis. They come from diverse backgrounds, which include public accounting, industry, and academe. Each of the Board members possesses knowledge of accounting, finance, and business, and shares a common concern for the public interest in matters relating to financial accounting and reporting. In addition, the FASB is assisted by technical specialists with expertise in various areas of financial accounting and reporting, as well as by administrative, secretarial, and clerical staff.

Q: How are standards of financial accounting and reporting established by the FASB?

A: The FASB issues statements of financial accounting standards, statements of concepts, and interpretations. Statements of financial accounting standards establish new standards or amend those previously issued. Statements of concepts serve as a guide for the FASB in solving problems and enable those who use financial reports to better understand the context in which financial accounting standards are formulated. Statements of concepts do not establish new standards or require any change in existing accounting principles. Interpretations clarify, explain, or elaborate on existing standards. Also, the FASB staff issues technical bulletins to provide guidelines for applying existing standards to certain financial accounting problems and for reporting problems on a timely basis.

Before it issues a statement, the Board is required to follow extensive due process procedures. In connection with each of its major projects, the Board does the following:

Appoints a task force of technical experts representing a broad spectrum of preparers, auditors, and users of financial information to advise on the project.

Studies existing literature on the subject and conducts such additional research as may be necessary.

Publishes a comprehensive discussion memorandum of issues and possible solutions as the basis for public comment.

Conducts a public hearing.

Gives broad distribution to an exposure draft of the proposed statement for public comment.

The FASB technical staff works directly with the Board and task forces, conducts research, participates in public hearings, analyzes oral and written comments received from the public, and prepares recommendations and drafts of documents for considerations by the Board. The Board deliberations are open to the public, and a complete public record is maintained.

Prior Years' Financial Statements

Q: How many financial statements from prior years are generally included within an annual report?

A: Usually two, that is, the current year and the year immediately preceding. However, the income statement and statement of changes in financial position are presented for three years.

Financial Information Based on Estimates

Q: Are the dollar amounts shown in financial statements the actual amounts related to the specific item, such as cash, accounts receivable, and inventory?

A: There is a certain amount of uncertainty regarding the outcome of future events that affects the measurement of a company's earnings for a particular period of time (e.g., one year or operating period) and the measurement of its assets and liabilities on a particular date (e.g., December 31, 19X2). Therefore a certain degree of imprecision is reflected in some of the amounts found on the financial statements. For example, assets generally include accounts receivable, for which an estimate of the amount that may be uncollectible is required. Also, liabilities may include estimates of claims to be paid under warranties. In general, financial statement amounts are often determined on the basis of the best or most realistic estimates that corporate management can make at the time financial statements are issued.

Consolidated Financial Statements

Q: Most annual reports refer to consolidated financial statements such as consolidated balance sheet, consolidated income statement, etc. What does "consolidated" mean as it relates to financial statements?

A: Consolidated financial statements report the financial condition and operating results of a parent company together with the condition and results of its subsidiary companies. Thus parent and subsidiary companies appear as if they were one organization.

Q: What is a subsidiary company?

A: A subsidiary company is a corporation owned or controlled by another company (the parent company). This ownership or control is usually through the voting stock of the subsidiary company and must represent more than 50% of that voting stock.

Q: When financial statements are presented on a consolidated basis, do those statements also include transactions between a parent company and its subsidiaries, or between subsidiaries? For example, are sales revenues obtained by a parent company when it makes sales to its subsidiary reported on the financial statements?

A: No. Consolidated results include only transactions between the parent company and/or its subsidiaries with companies outside, and independent of, the organization. The results of any material transactions, such as sales, between a parent company and one or more of its subsidiaries or between subsidiaries are eliminated in arriving at the consolidated results.

Interim Reports

Q: Do interim reports include the same type of information as annual reports?

A: Interim reports, which are generally issued by companies on a quarterly basis, do not contain all of the information generally found in annual reports. Since interim reports serve as timely progress reports to shareowners, their content is restricted to information that affected the company during the past quarter, such as sales and earnings, new accounting pronouncements, actions of the board of directors, capital expenditures, dividend declarations, and financial statement data.

Q: Do interim reports contain financial statement data identical to those included within annual reports, such as the balance sheet, income statement, statement of changes in financial position, and related notes?

A: Some publicly listed companies may provide one or more complete financial statements with a limited number of footnotes. However, as a minimum, publicly traded companies are required by an accounting rule to provide at least the following summarized financial statement information within interim reports:

Sales or gross revenues.
Provision for federal income taxes.
Extraordinary items, including related income tax effects.
Cumulative effect of a change in accounting principle or practice.

Net income.

Primary and fully diluted earnings per share for each period presented.

Seasonal revenue costs or expenses.

Any significant changes in estimates or provisions for income taxes.

Disposal of a business segment.

Contingent items (e.g., pending lawsuits).

Changes in accounting principles or estimates.

Significant changes in financial position, such as with respect to liquid assets (e.g., cash, marketable securities), net working capital, or long-term liabilities.

Such information is generally provided in a combined tabular and narrative form.

Q: Do publicly traded companies present the required minimal financial statement information within their interim reports on a basis that can be compared with similar information contained within prior interim reports?

A: If a publicly traded company presents summarized financial statement information on a regular basis, generally quarterly, in interim financial reports, that information is usually presented either for the current quarter and the current year-to-date or for the last twelve months with comparable financial data for the preceding year.

FREQUENCY OF FINANCIAL REPORT DISTRIBUTION

Q: When are financial reports published by publicly traded companies?

A: Annual reports are usually published two to three months after a company's calendar or fiscal year ends. For example, a company operating on a calendar year basis (January 1 through December

31, 19X2) generally issues its annual report in February or March of the following year. Interim reports are usually issued one month following the quarter or interim period.

Q: Where might an investor obtain copies of the latest interim and annual reports of various companies?

A: If you are already an investor or shareowner in a particular company, you should be receiving interim and annual reports directly from your investee company. Otherwise, copies of financial reports can be obtained by writing to a corporation's Public Relations or Treasury Department. Stockbrokers and business libraries are another source for obtaining financial reports.

Q: Why do some publicly traded companies have their financial statements presented as of the end of the calendar year (December 31, 19X2), while other companies indicate a year ending on the last day of another month, such as January, February, or October?

A: A company closes its books at the end of its natural business year, which signifies the lowest point of business activity. This is referred to as a company's fiscal year end. The calendar year end (December 31) is the fiscal year end most companies use for closing their books, and is therefore most frequently used for presenting financial statements. However, companies that operate in the retail industry usually have a fiscal year end on January 31. Sales and inventory are at their lowest level right after Christmas; thus January 31 is the natural end of their business year.

Chapter Two

Financial
Statements

INTRODUCTION

Financial statements are considered to be the most important facet of financial reports. Business transactions have become complex because companies operate in various industries, merge with other companies, divest themselves of portions of previously acquired companies, and change their financing through creative and innovative methods. While accounting is the method used to record business transactions on a company's books, financial statements are the vehicles used to disclose complex business transactions to investors. Thus, financial statements are a concise way to provide investors with information concerning a public company's financial health.

The purpose of this chapter is to provide investors with some insight as to the nature, purpose, content, and interpretation of the basic types of financial statements that are included within the financial reports of public companies. These are the balance sheet, the income statement, the statement of retained earnings, the statement of changes in financial position, and related notes. Illustrations of these items, reproduced from the 1982 annual reports of certain well-known public companies, are provided at the end of this chapter.

BALANCE SHEET

Purpose

Q: What is the purpose of the balance sheet?

A: The balance sheet is designed to represent a company's financial position as it stands on a particular day, for example, as of December 31, 19X2. It is a form of scorecard that reveals the fundamental financial strength of a company and its capability for financing continued operations at a particular point in time.

Content

Q: The balance sheet refers to assets, liabilities, and stockholders' equity. How do these categories differ from one another?

A: Assets are those items a company *owns*, while liabilities represent the money a company *owes* to its creditors. The difference between assets and liabilities is the equity (i.e., stockholders' equity). Equity represents the remaining interest in a company's assets, or the ownership interest (i.e., stockholders' interest). Assume, for example, that a corporation goes out of business on the date of the balance sheet (e.g., December 31, 19X2). In that situation, equity would represent what the stockholders might expect to receive as their portion of the business.

Q: Certain assets on the balance sheet are referred to as current assets and certain liabilities are referred to as current liabilities. What does the term *current* imply?

A: Current assets are those assets that are likely to be coverted into cash or consumed in operations in the normal course of business, usually within one year. They generally include cash, marketable securities, accounts and notes receivable, and inventory. Current liabilities represent those amounts that are due to be paid to creditors within one year. They generally include the current portion of long-term debt, amounts due on short-term notes (notes payable), amounts due to suppliers and vendors (accounts payable), and income taxes due to federal, state, and local governments.

Cash

Q: What does cash on the balance sheet specifically include?

A: Cash, the most liquid of all assets, generally includes currency, checks, money orders, bank drafts, and any other instrument that a bank will immediately recognize as cash, as well as a company's balances in bank accounts that are payable on demand. In order to be classified as a current asset, cash or items similar to cash must be available for use in normal business operations. Most companies have more than one account that relates to cash on the balance sheet, such as cash in banks, cash on hand, and petty cash (small amounts of cash that are maintained in order to pay minor expenses).

Q: What are the sources from which a corporation obtains its cash?

A: The most common sources of cash include the following:

Normal operations, which comprise the excess of cash collected from sales and other revenues earned over the cash used to pay operating expenses, and which usually comprise the major source of cash.

Direct investments by stockholders.

Short-term or long-term borrowing.

Sale of assets other than through normal operations.

Q: Is cash ever excluded from current assets on the balance sheet?

A: In some cases, a corporation might restrict a certain amount of available cash for a specific purpose, such as the purchase or construction of property, plant or equipment, or the retirement of long-term debt. If cash is restricted, it is not available for normal operations and will be classified in the investments category of the balance sheet.

Q: Why is cash on the balance sheet an important item to investors?

A: Cash might be considered the most important item on a corporation's balance sheet because it is the prime source for payments of dividends to stockholders.

Marketable Securities

Q: What are marketable securities?

A: These current assets represent a temporary investment of excess or idle cash that is not immediately needed by the company. They usually comprise investments in commercial paper or government securities (e.g., U.S. Treasury notes).

Q: When presenting marketable securities on the balance sheet, some companies show certain amounts for the current year and prior year in the column of figures at cost. Larger dollar amounts appear in parentheses as market values. For example:

	19X2	19X1
Marketable Securities, at Cost (Market value: 19X2, $6,800,000; 19X1, $5,600,000)	$5,000,000	4,000,000

How do cost and market amounts differ, and why are they shown this way?

A: The cost of marketable securities includes all costs incurred by the company when those temporary investments were first acquired. These include brokerage costs and taxes. Market value is the value of those securities on the balance sheet dates (e.g., December 31, 19X1), or the value of those securities as determined on the balance sheet date by a recognized stock exchange (American Stock Exchange or New York Stock Exchange). If there is a large difference between the cost of those securities and their market value, an accounting rule requires that such temporary investments be valued at cost or market, whichever is lower, as a conservative measure of value. The higher value, in this case market value, is shown parenthetically to provide information for investors.

Q: What does the term *marketable* imply?

A: *Marketable* means that the sales prices or bid and asked prices of the securities are currently available on a national securities exchange (either the American Stock Exchange, or the New York Stock Exchange), or in the over-the-counter market. Marketable also implies that the securities can be readily sold if cash is needed by the company on short notice and that those securities are subject to minimal fluctuation in price.

Marketable Equity Securities

Q: Companies often present an item called *marketable equity securities* on the balance sheet. Many present amounts with current assets, while other amounts, are included with noncurrent assets. Are they the same as marketable securities?

A: When marketable equity securities are presented with current assets, they are similar to marketable securities in that they can be readily sold for cash if the need arises. Marketable equity securities relate specifically to those types of securities that represent ownership shares in other companies such as common stock and preferred stock. They also include the right to acquire stock (e.g., warrants, rights, and call options), and the right to dispose of stock (e.g., put options). That is where the term *equity* comes into play in reference to ownership. Those marketable equity securities included with noncurrent assets are not intended by the company to be readily converted into cash. They represent a long-term form of investment in the equity securities of other enterprises. While marketable securities refer to investments in commercial paper or government securities, marketable equity securities refer to the shares of securities of other companies.

Receivables

Q: What is the difference between notes receivable and accounts receivable?

A: Both are current asset items that represent amounts due from customers for goods delivered or services rendered that have not been paid for. In most cases customers are given 30, 60, or 90 days in which to pay. Notes receivable differ from accounts receivable in two respects:

1. Notes receivable represent a form of promissory note from a customer that is payable to the company within a certain period of time, usually with interest.
2. Notes receivable are more "liquid" than accounts receivable in that notes receivable can be transferred or sold to a third party (e.g., a bank) before it is due at face or maturity value. The sale price often includes a discount that represents interest for the unexpired term of the note.

Q: Accounts receivable are usually presented on the balance sheet "net" or "less" an amount described as allowance for bad debts or allowance for doubtful accounts. What does that "allowance" represent?

A: Some customers often fail to pay their bills on time because of either financial problems or catastrophic events, such as a flood, hurricane, or tornado. In order for companies to reveal a figure as their accounts receivable balance that properly reflects economic reality, an estimated allowance for doubtful accounts is made. This figure is based on a particular company's experience, and is deducted from accounts receivable or the amounts due from customers. Allowance for doubtful accounts is sometimes referred to as a "reserve for bad debts." Doubtful accounts, or bad debts, represent those amounts or receivables that will probably never be collectible from customers.

Q: Is the allowance for doubtful accounts something on which investors should focus their attention, since it is basically an estimated amount?

A: An allowance for doubtful accounts, or reserve for bad debts, is important to investors because it is an indicator of management performance. For example, if a company has maintained a substantial amount in its allowance or reserve account over the years, and if that amount decreases substantially in a current operating period or year, a cutback in dollar amount may have been made to make the company appear more profitable than it actually was in a true economic sense. In most cases, a company's accounts receivable will increase each year. The related allowance for doubtful accounts will generally increase on a proportional basis.

Q: What causes a company's accounts receivable to grow at a faster rate than sales? And what are the consequences?

A: When receivables outrun sales growth, the reason could be inefficient collection policies or extension of credit to customers with greater credit risk. This type of situation may lead to a future cash squeeze on a company, or a large writedown of receivables by the company, or possibly both.

Q: When comparing the balance sheets of a company over a period of years, is an increase in accounts receivable with a related increase in sales revenues a good sign of a profitable company?

A: Not necessarily. Increased accounts receivable balances, or a higher accounts receivable balance relative to sales, could be interpreted as a sign of trouble. For example, when year-to-date sales lag behind and a company needs an immediate increase in sales to improve profits, the company may grant a customer generous credit terms and thereby load the customer with products that he or she does not necessarily need. Although the company has recorded a sale to this effect, and therefore increased its accounts receivable, it has really only shifted inventory from the company's inventory to the customer's inventory. In effect, these are nonrecurring sales that are made at the expense of future sales.

Q: Are there any indicators or yardsticks an investor might refer to in order to determine whether or not a company's receivables are being converted into cash within a reasonable amount of time?

A: There are two indicators of receivable performance investors can use:

     1.   Determine the company's receivable turnover by dividing net sales, or credit sales, by the total of accounts and notes receivable. This ratio measures the number of times accounts and notes receivable turn over during the year. A high turnover of receivables generally indicates a more rapid collection of sales during the period and a greater liquidity of receivables (i.e., conversion of receivables into cash). In other words, a high turnover reflects a short time period between actual sales to, and collection of cash from, customers. For example, a company with sales of $810,000 and receivables of $90,000 would have a sales/receivable ratio of 9.0 ($810,000 divided by $90,000). This means that receivables turn over nine times during the year. This turnover rate should then be compared with companies in similar industries.

     2.   Determine the average collection period of receivables by either of the two methods:

     a.   Receivables times days in year (i.e., 365) divided by annual credit sales

     b.   365 days divided by receivable turnover (as determined in number 1 above)

         Each method will provide the same result, that is, the average time in days that receivables are outstanding. The final result will indicate the efficiency of a company's cash collection practice. In general, the greater the number of days outstanding, the greater the probability of delinquencies a company will experience in collecting cash from its customers.

Inventory

Q: Some companies that are heavily engaged in manufacturing certain products have inventory broken down in the balance sheet according to raw materials, work in process, and finished goods. How do these three categories of inventory differ?

A: Raw materials are those goods purchased for use as an ingredient or a component of a product that is ready for sale. Raw materials generally comprise either (1) goods or items in a natural state (e.g., wood from a tree, iron ore from a mine) that requires further treatment, or (2) completed parts that can be assembled without further processing. Work in process, or work in progress, are partially finished products that require further processing. Finished goods are ready to be sold to customers.

Q: Is there any way to tell whether or not a company's inventory is actually being sold on a regular basis?

A: This can be determined by computing a company's inventory turnover. This is done by dividing the cost of sales or cost of goods sold (which usually appears on the face of the income statement) by the average inventory. The average inventory is computed by totaling the beginning and ending inventory and dividing that figure by two. Beginning and ending inventories can be obtained from the face of comparative balance sheets. For example, if comparative balance sheets are presented for December 31, 19X2 and 19X1, the beginning inventory would be that presented for 19X1 and the ending inventory would be that presented for 19X2. The higher the inventory turnover, the more efficient the inventory management of the company. The ratio tells us how quickly inventory is converted into sales and accounts receivable. For example, if a company's inventory turnover is 5.1, that means that on the average inventory goods are bought and sold out approximately five times per year. The ratio of turnover, like other ratios, must be compared either with those of similar companies or with the industry average, since it varies widely from industry to industry. For example, turnover is usually higher in food than in tobacco. Although a high ratio generally indicates efficient inventory management, it may also be the result of too low a level of inventory and frequent stockouts. A relatively low inventory turnover may indicate slow-moving inventory or obsolescence of some of the stock. A low inventory turnover may also indicate that sales efforts should be more aggressive or that goods have not been sold because of changes in style or public taste. In this regard, it may be helpful to compute the turnover ratio for major categories of inventory to help pinpoint potential problem areas. However, most annual reports do not provide breakdowns of inventory by major category.

Prepaid Expenses

Q: Some balance sheets often include an item called other assets among their current assets. What do other assets generally comprise?

A: Other assets generally comprise prepaid expenses, which represent amounts paid in advance by a company for benefits or services to be received in the future, such as insurance premiums, rent, commissions, and real estate taxes. These are unexpended items which will be used up or charged to income in future years. For example, three years of insurance premiums or two years of rent paid in advance. If these advance payments for future expenses were not made, the company would have either maintained the cash on hand or deposited it in a bank. Prepaid expenses, or prepayments, are therefore presented as assets because they are payments made in advance; the company has yet to receive the benefits from those payments. In other words, prepayments are benefits that a company will receive in the future, usually within one to three years.

Working Capital

Q: When making an investment decision, what should investors look for in a balance sheet to determine whether or not a particular company is solvent?

A: Investors should look at the working capital of a company, which is the difference between total current assets and total current liabilities. In other words, working capital represents the amount that is free and clear after all the current debts of the company are paid. A company's working capital often determines its ability to meet its obligations when due and to expand its volume. A growing company usually has a larger working capital for the present year (e.g., December 31, 19X2) than for the past year (e.g., December 31, 19X1).

Q: What might a prospective investor consider to be an adequate or conservative working capital?

A: Although various methods are used by financial analysts for evaluating the working capital position of companies in different industries, a prospective investor will find the current ratio of a company more helpful than the total dollar value of working capital. The current ratio is determined by dividing total current assets by total current liabilities. Analysts generally agree that current assets should be at least twice as large as current liabilities. In other words, a typical industrial company should have $2 in current assets for every $1 of current liabilities as a safety cushion to meet debts when they are due. Therefore, an adequate working capital ratio should be 2 to 1. In this way, a company will be able to meet its obligations over the coming year and still maintain ample funds to run an effective business operation.

Q: Does working capital vary among companies?

A: The amount of a company's working capital will vary with the type of business as well as between companies in the same business.

Variance will depend upon the size of the company, geographic location, and the general nature of the business. For example, a manufacturer generally maintains a substantial amount of accounts receivable and inventory in proportion to its total debt because it engages in the manufacture and sale of a product. As a result, working capital requirements are generally high for manufacturing companies. On the other hand, supermarket chain stores do not have accounts receivable and do not have to maintain a substantial inventory in proportion to their current debt because of rapid turnover of inventory goods. Therefore, companies engaged in retail supermarkets require less working capital than companies engaged in manufacturing. In general, companies that have (1) a small amount of inventory and accounts receivable, and (2) a high rate of collectibility from customers, are able to conduct operations with a lower current ratio than those companies that have a greater proportion of their current assets tied up in inventory and that sell their products on credit.

Q: Can it be assumed that a gradual increase in the current ratio over the years is a healthy sign of improvement in a company's financial strength?

A: Not necessarily. A current ratio of more than 4 to 1 or 5 to 1 may be regarded as excessive, and may therefore indicate any or all of the following:

> *Contraction in the business operation.*
> *Underutilization of cash to expand operations.*
> *Increasing or mounting of inventories that are not being readily sold.*

Q: What if a company needed cash for a sudden emergency? Is the current ratio the only way to measure a company's solvency?

A: There is another indicator investors can use, which is referred to as the *quick ratio* or *acid test ratio.* This is determined by dividing *quick* assets by current liabilities. Quick assets are those assets that a company could immediately turn into cash during an emergency. These include cash, marketable securities, and receivables. Inventories are excluded because they would have to be sold before cash can be obtained. A quick or acid test ratio of 1 to 1 or better is an indicator of a company's short-term or immediate ability to meet its debt without depending on inventory sales to pay off creditors.

Accumulated Depreciation

Q: An amount called *accumulated depreciation* is always deducted from property, plant, and equipment on the balance sheet. What is accumulated depreciation?

A: Property, plant, and equipment include land, buildings, machinery, furniture and fixtures, and motor vehicles. Except for land, these fixed assets are subject to depreciation over their estimated useful life. Depreciation is the decline in the useful life or value of a fixed asset (i.e., property, plant, and equipment) as a result of wear and tear, passage of time, or obsolescence due to new and advanced inventions and techniques. Unlike those costs which usually require a cash outlay when incurred, depreciation represents a portion of the original cost of a fixed asset, which is allocated to future years based on the estimated service life of the asset. In other words, the depreciable cost of a fixed asset is matched against the income that is generated from the fixed asset during the estimated service life, or future years of the asset. Depreciation is like any other cost of conducting a business, such as paying for heat and light. Depreciation might be illustrated by the following example. A company purchases a machine for $40,000 to be utilized in the manufacturing process. Based on studies conducted by engineers, the company estimates that the machine has a useful life of 20 years before it becomes obsolete as a result of normal wear and tear due to usage. In this situation, $2,000 of the cost of the machine will represent depreciation expense or a charge to income over 20 years ($40,000 ÷ 20 years = $2,000). Each year the depreciation expense charged to income is accumulated as a balance sheet account, in other words, accumulated depreciation. This accumulated amount is subtracted from the original cost of the machine on the balance sheet in order to reflect the unexpired cost or present worth of the machine. For example, referring to our illustration, at the end of year 2 in the useful life of the machine, the unexpired cost reflected on the balance sheet will be $36,000, which represents $40,000 original cost less two years' accumulated depreciation of $4,000.

Accumulated Depletion

Q: The balance sheets of companies involved in mining and oil production include "accumulated depletion." Is depletion the same as depreciation?

A: Depletion is the same as depreciation in that depletion is a periodic assignment of cost to future years. In the case of depletion, the cost relates to a natural resource, such as coal, oil, or timber. Depletion is a reduction in the value of such natural resources as they are used. Depletion differs from depreciation in that depletion comprises the removal of a natural resource, or an actual physical shrinkage of an estimated quantity of coal, gas, or timber. Depreciation is an estimated reduction in the service capacity of an asset, such as a building or a machine, as a result of usage.

Intangible Assets

Q: What are intangible assets?

A: Intangible assets are assets that have no physical existence but have value to a company. Such value is limited by certain rights and benefits that possession of the intangible asset confers upon the owner (i.e., the company or corporation). Examples include patents, trademarks, franchises, and goodwill.

Q: What is goodwill?

A: When a company purchases another company, the difference
between what the company paid to acquire the other company
and the fair value of its net assets at the time of acquisition is
referred to as goodwill. For example, if the fair market value of the
net assets of the acquired company is $3 million and the company
has to pay $5 million to get the shareholders of the acquired
company to sell, the $2 million difference represents goodwill.
Goodwill is a form of premium or dollar amount paid by a company
(e.g., a parent company) for certain shares of stock of another
company (e.g., a subsidiary company) that exceeds the book value
of the assets of the subsidiary company on the dates the shares
were acquired by the parent company.

Net Book Value/Net Asset Value

Q: Is it possible to determine from the balance sheet whether or not
the company's assets are being properly managed?

A: Proper management of company assets can be determined by
focusing on a company's net book value or the net asset value of a
company's securities. This is determined by dividing the difference between total assets and total liabilities by the number of
shares of the outstanding common stock. Net book value represents the amount of corporate assets protecting shareholders'
securities. A net book value that is significantly higher than the
market price of a company's securities is generally an indication
that a company's assets are poorly managed. However, investors
should not be misled by net asset value or net book value figures.
For example, many profitable companies often present a low net
book value and high substantial earnings. On the other hand,
some companies may reflect a high net book value for their common stock and low or irregular earnings figures, which may result
in the market price of the common stock being much less than its
apparent book value. This latter situation often prevails with
railroad companies and airlines. In some cases, the net book value

of common stock for certain companies may be a fair indicator of the market value of that common stock. This is true with banks, insurance companies, and investment companies whose assets are predominantly liquid in nature, such as cash, accounts receivable, and marketable securities.

Q: The balance sheets of many publicly listed companies reflect three separate classes of securities: bonds, preferred stock, and common stock. Can a determination be made for a net asset value as to each class of security?

A: Yes. Net asset value or net book value can be determined for each class of security with a simple calculation. In each calculation, the values of any intangible assets (e.g., patents, goodwill) are subtracted from total assets under the assumption that these intangibles will have no value upon liquidation of the company. Net asset values for bonds, preferred stock, and common stock are described as follows:

Bonds.   Total assets less intangible assets are reduced by current liabilities. The result is then divided by the number of bonds outstanding, which can be found on the face of the balance sheet or within the notes to the financial statements. This calculation is illustrated as follows:

Total assets	$10,000,000
Less: intangible assets	200,000
Total tangible assets	9,800,000
Less: current liabilities	1,000,000
Net tangible assets that are available to meet the claims of bondholders	$ 8,800,000

$$\frac{\$8,800,000}{2,200 \text{ bonds outstanding}} = \$4,000 \quad \text{net asset value per } \$1,000 \text{ bond}$$

In this case, there is a $4,000 net asset value protecting each $1,000 bond.

Preferred Stock.   Total assets less intangible assets are reduced by the total of current liabilities and long-term liabilities. The result is then divided by the number of outstanding shares of preferred stock, which can usually be found within the stockholders' equity section on the face of the balance sheet. This calculation is illustrated as follows:

Total assets		$10,000,000
Less: intangible assets		200,000
Total tangible assets		9,800,000
Less: current liabilities	$1,000,000	
long-term liabilities	2,200,000	
Total liabilities		3,200,000
Net tangible assets that are available to meet the claims of preferred stockholders		$ 6,600,000

$$\frac{\$6,600,000}{6,000 \text{ outstanding shares of preferred stock}} = \$1,100 \quad \text{net asset value per share of preferred stock}$$

In this case, there is a $1,100 net asset value protecting or supporting each outstanding share of preferred stock.

Common Stock.   Net asset value or net book value per common share of stock is basically calculated in the same manner as was done for net asset value per share of preferred stock. However, in this case the liquidation rights of bondholders and preferred stockholders would have to be satisfied. This calculation is illustrated as follows:

Total assets		$10,000,000
Less: intangible assets		200,000
Total tangible assets		9,800,000
Less: current liabilities	$1,000,000	
long-term liabilities	2,200,000	
preferred stock	600,000	
Total liabilities and outstanding preferred stock		3,800,000
Net assets available for common stockholders		$ 6,000,000

$$\frac{\$6,000,000}{400,000 \text{ outstanding shares of common stock}} = \$15.00 \quad \text{net asset value per share of common stock}$$

In this case, the $15 net asset value per share of common stock can be considered as the amount of money stockholders would receive for each share of their common stock in the event that the company is liquidated.

Payables

Q: What are accounts payable?

A: They are liabilities that represent amounts that a company owes to its regular business creditors on account. Accounts payable are similar to purchases made by consumers with credit cards. In other words, the cash will be paid to the company for the purchased goods at a later time, usually within 30, 60, or 90 days.

Q: What are notes payable?

A: They are liabilities that represent amounts owed to a bank or other lender of credit by a company. They indicate that some form of promissory note has been given by that company to the bank or lender.

Accrued Liabilities

Q: What does it mean when a liability is *accrued*, as in accrued liabilities?

A: Accrued liabilities represent expenses recognized in a determination of income but unpaid as of the balance sheet date. They represent moneys owed to parties other than regular business creditors, and might include interest on funds borrowed from a bank, fees to attorneys or accountants, wages to employees, and premiums owed to an insurance company.

Deferred Income Taxes

Q: Deferred income taxes appear to be included in most annual reports among the liabilities on the balance sheet. What are deferred income taxes?

A: Deferred income taxes are not liabilities in the true economic sense, such as amounts owed to others. They are amounts that result from timing differences in the recognition of income and expense for financial reporting purposes and income tax purposes. For many corporations, the amount of income or loss reported in financial statements usually differs from the amount of income or loss reported on the income tax return. For example, four types of transactions result in timing differences between the recognition of revenues and expenses as reported on the income statement and as reflected on the income tax return.

1. Revenues or gains are included on the income statement prior to their inclusion on the tax return. An example would be an installment sale in which the total sale price is reported as revenue on the income statement. However, for income tax purposes the seller would report as taxable income only the cash collected in each of the years in which collections are made if the transaction meets certain specified criteria.

2. Expenses or losses are recognized on the tax return prior to their inclusion on the income statement. For example, an accelerated depreciation method might be used for the tax return and straight line depreciation used for the income statement.

3. Revenues or gains are included on the tax return before they are recognized on the income statement. For example, the tax law may require that the total sales price be included on the tax return in the year of sale, although in cash basis accounting the sale may not yet be recognized on the income statement.

4. Expenses or losses are included on the income statement before they can be deducted on the tax return. These include estimated warranty expenses, which are recorded in the year of sale but which the tax law will not allow to be deducted until paid.

Since most companies generally conserve cash by taking advantage of the tax law that permits them to delay tax payments, the first two timing differences listed above are the most prevalent. These differences, which result from good tax planning, create a deferred tax liability. The latter two timing differences result in the payment of taxes before they are recognized as an expense on the income statement. These timing differences may lead to a deferred tax asset, which is similar to a prepaid asset.

Q: How does a timing difference in deferred income taxes actually work with an item such as depreciation?

A: Deferred income taxes are common with respect to depreciation expense. For example, depreciation of machinery may be recognized by a straight line method on the books of a company and by an accelerated method for income tax purposes. In an acclelerated method, more depreciation is deducted on the tax return than is deducted on the company's books. The resulting timing difference represents deferred income taxes to be paid in future years. In effect, a deferred income tax liability arises because the current tax liability, which is actually owed to the government, is less than the amount of income tax expense presented in the income statement. This can be illustrated with a hypothetical example. Assume a $20,000 excess depreciation deduction for tax purposes in the current year and a 50% tax rate. Income tax expense for financial reporting purposes would include the tax effect of the excess depreciation (i.e., $20,000 \times 50\% = $10,000). The $10,000 would also be presented as a deferred tax liability on the balance sheet. In accounting terms, this is often referred to as comprehensive income tax allocation. This method assumes that almost all timing differences reverse within a definite period of time and that the tax effect of an item of accounting income or expense should be matched with that item and recorded in the same period. In most cases, the reversal of certain timing differences is offset in the period of reversal by similar originating differences. For example, reversal of the excess depreciation deduction relating to old equipment may be offset by the originating excess depreciation deduction relating to new equipment.

Q: How should an investor analyze deferred income taxes?

A: Because deferred income taxes are not actual liabilities in the true economic sense, they should be eliminated, or "backed out," of any computation in which a measurement includes liabilities owed to creditors, such as working capital and debt to equity ratio.

Long-Term Debt

Q: How does long-term debt differ from the debt figures shown under current liabilities?

A: Long-term debt represents liabilities due for payment more than 12 months from the balance sheet date, which may include bonds (i.e., debentures) or other borrowings payable over periods ranging up to 30 years or more. On the other hand, those debts included under current liabilities, such as accounts payable to vendors or federal income tax payable, are generally due for payment within 12 months of the balance sheet date.

Q: All companies have a certain amount of long-term debt reflected as a liability on the balance sheet. How do you determine a company's ability to obtain additional credit, if needed?

A: An effective way to determine a company's ability to obtain credit is to figure out the ratio of debt to equity. Simply divide total current and long-term liabilities by total stockholders' equity. For a typical industrial company, a debt to equity ratio in excess of 25% should be cause for concern. In general, there is no correct ratio. However, an investor should be alert to a shift by the company toward more debt. This can be detected by studying five- or ten-year financial summaries, usually presented at the end of annual reports and referred to as selected financial data. Look at the long-term and/or total debt for each of the years presented to see if the amount accelerates with each succeeding year. During an uncertain economic period, lenders may be reluctant to extend additional credit to a company if there is a shift toward more debt. An ideal debt to equity ratio for most companies is 20% or less.

Capital Leases

Q: Some companies show *capital lease obligations* immediately after long-term debt on the balance sheet. Are capital lease obligations liabilities similar to other forms of long-term debt?

A: Capital lease obligations are considered to be long-term liabilities. In those cases where a lease arrangement transfers essentially all the benefits and risks of ownership associated with the leased property to the lessee, that lease arrangement is to be accounted for by the lessee company as the acquisition of an asset, or capital lease, and the incurrence of a liability for the leased property. A lessee company will include the amount of a capital lease as an asset with its property, plant, and equipment on the balance sheet, while the related lease obligation will be presented as a liability, provided that the lease arrangement meets any one of the following criteria:

1. The lease transfers ownership of the property to the lessee company by the end of the lease term.
2. The lease contains an option for the lessee company to purchase the leased property at a bargain price.
3. The lease term is equal to or greater than 75% of the estimated economic life of the leased property (i.e., the life of a similar piece of property owned by the lessee company or by other companies in the same industry).
4. The present value of rental and other minimum lease payments equals or exceeds 90% of the fair value of the leased property, less any investment tax credit retained by the lessor.

Q: What might constitute the fair value of leased property?

A: Fair value of leased property might be any one of the following: cash sales price of the asset, cost of property to the lessor, or current market price of the property.

Minority Interest

Q: Some balance sheets include an item termed *minority interest* between long-term liabilities and stockholders' equity. What is the nature of minority interest?

A: Minority interest represents the interest in a subsidiary company owned by stockholders other than the parent company when the parent company does not own 100% of the subsidiary company's voting stock. For example, if a parent company owns 90% of a subsidiary, the remaining 10% on the balance sheet represents minority interest. In other words, minority interest represents the minority ownership, or ownership outside the parent company, in a subsidiary company that is being consolidated. Minority interest is part of a consolidated company's capital structure since it is an outside source of funds for the company.

Preferred and Common Stock

Q: What does *cumulative* mean as it applies to preferred stock?

A: If the management of a corporation fails to pay preferred stockholders their dividends in any given year, then those dividends accumulate until such future time when those dividends are finally paid by the corporation. As indicated by the term *preferred,* dividends would have to be paid to preferred stockholders before any dividend distributions could be paid to common stockholders. Failure to pay dividends to preferred stockholders generally occurs if a company fails to earn enough income to pay the stipulated dividend amount.

Q: The stockholders' equity section of the balance sheet of many companies includes preferred stock and common stock. What are the similarities and differences between the two?

A: Both preferred stock and common stock represent the shares of stock investors hold in the ownership interest of a company. These shares are represented by stock certificates issued by a corporation to its shareholders or stockholders. Many companies issue different classes or types of shares, such as preferred stock and common stock. Each class usually has certain characteristics that differ from the other.

Holders of common stock have the remaining interest in the ownership of a company's assets after all liabilities and preferred stockholders claims have been paid. The rights to participation in a corporation's earnings in the form of dividends is neither limited nor preferred as is that of preferred stockholders. As a result, when the company's earnings are high, dividends paid to common stockholders may also be high. On the other hand, when earnings are low, dividends paid to common stockholders will also be low. Unlike preferred stockholders, holders of common stock do not have a voice in the management of a corporation.

Q: What is *par value* as it applies to common and preferred stock?

A: A par value is the face value or money value assigned to a share of stock. Par value, or stated value, is assigned to each share of stock within certain limits set by the laws of incorporation in the state in which a particular corporation is incorporated. The amount assigned to shares, which represents the legal capital of a corporation, may vary from state to state.

Q: What does it mean when a certain number of shares of stock are authorized, while a smaller number of shares are issued?

A: Authorized shares are those shares of stock that a corporation may issue under its articles of incorporation. Issued shares comprise that portion of a corporation's authorized shares of capital stock (common and/or preferred) represented by stock certificates that have been legally issued to stockholders for cash or some other form of consideration. For example, a corporation may have 1,000,000 authorized shares of common stock of which 700,000 have been issued to the public.

Surplus Accounts

Q: What is paid-in-surplus?

A: Paid-in-surplus, referred to in some balance sheets as capital surplus or capital paid in excess of par value, represents the amount paid in by stockholders over the par or legal value of each share of stock. For example, if a corporation has a $6 par value for each share of its common stock and sells a share for $10, then $4 represents the paid-in-surplus for each share of common stock sold.

Treasury Stock

Q: Some companies have an amount in stockholders' equity that is a negative balance noted parenthetically, called "cost of common shares held in treasury." What are these shares? Do they differ from regularly issued stock?

A: Treasury stock represents common stock that has been paid for by shareholders and has been reacquired by the corporation through gift, donation, or purchase. It is generally available either for resale to the public or for cancellation. Treasury stock is not considered a part of stock issued and outstanding, and that is why the related amount is presented as a negative figure subtracted from stockholders' equity. Treasury stock does not carry voting, liquidation, and dividend privileges as do outstanding common or preferred shares. However, when resold, treasury stock is again classified as outstanding stock.

Q: Why would a corporation want to purchase shares of its own stock after it has sold them to the investing public?

A: A corporation may purchase its own stock (i.e., treasury stock) for the following purposes:

1. To make an investment, since buying treasury stock is similar to investing in the stock of any company.

2. To buy out a particular stockholder or group of stock-holders.

3. To acquire shares for distribution to corporate employees under various compensation and profit-sharing plans.

Retained Earnings

Q: What are retained earnings?

A: Retained earnings represent undistributed profits (i.e., profits not distributed to stockholders in the form of dividends) that are reinvested in the business by the company in order to enable the company to continue to expand its operations. Retained earnings are the end result of undistributed profits from prior years, plus the current year's earnings, less dividends paid to stockholders during the current year.

Leveraged Companies

Q: Can an investor determine from a reading of the balance sheet, whether or not a company has an ideal capital structure?

A: There is no such thing as an ideal capital structure. However, an investor should be aware of whether or not the investee company has a large proportion of long-term debt (e.g., bonds) and pre-ferred stock in relation to common stock. Such companies are considered high leverage companies. For example, if Company A has $10 million in 5% bonds outstanding, and is earning $540,000 before bond interest, only $40,000 in earnings will remain for common stock dividends after the $500,000 in bond interest is paid to bondholders (i.e., $10 million at 5% = $500,000). Howev-er, an increase in earnings of 10% (i.e., $540,000 at 10%= $54,000) would provide $94,000 for common stock dividends (i.e., $540,000 + $54,000 = $594,000 net income − $500,000 bond interest = $94,000), or an increase of over 100% in earnings for common stockholders. On the other hand, a 10% decline in earnings would not only wipe out any earnings available for com-

mon stock dividends, but would also result in Company A being
unable to cover its bond interest payment. This illustrates a weak-
ness of high leverage companies that have a disproportionate
amount of debt or preferred stock over common stock. Conservative investors usually avoid investing in high leverage companies
because they are considered risky. Companies with one stock
capitalization (common stock) may be attractive to investors
because there are no prior claims ahead of the common stock. But
long-term debt and preferred stock add what is called leverage to a
company's capital structure. After bond interest and preferred
dividends are paid, any increased earnings benefit the common
stock. However, a high degree of leverage may be dangerous if a
company's earnings are irregular.

INCOME STATEMENT

Comparison to Balance Sheet

Q: What is the purpose of the income statement as compared to the
balance sheet?

A: The balance sheet reflects the financial position of a company on a
given date (e.g., December 31, 19X2), and the income statement
reveals the operating activities of a company for the entire year.
The income statement matches the revenues obtained from the
sale of goods or services and other income (e.g., interest income
from investments, sale of a plant or subsidiary) against all the costs
and expenses that were incurred in operating the business.

Q: Which financial statement is more important to investors for
analysis, the balance sheet or the income statement?

A: Although the balance sheet reveals the financial soundness of a
company by reflecting its financial position at a given date, the
income statement may be of greater interest to investors because
it reveals a record of a company's operating activities and prof-

itability for an entire year, and therefore serves as an invaluable source in anticipating how a company might perform in the future. However, both the balance sheet and the income statement are worthy of the attention of investors.

Sales

Q: Some companies show net sales on their income statements. What does *net* sales actually signify?

A: Net sales represents the amount left over after the deduction of (1) materials and merchandise returned to vendors because they were damaged during shipment or contained some kind of imperfection and (2) any allowance for reductions in sales price or sales discount in those cases in which the customer remitted the sales proceeds to the company within a designated period of time. An example of a sales discount is when a customer is allowed 2% off the sales price if proceeds are remitted to the company within 10 days. This is often referred to on a sales invoice as "2.10 n/30."

Q: Does the dollar amount for sales on the income statement reflect the actual cash received by the company from its customers in return for goods or services?

A: No. Revenues are recognized by companies during the period in which the revenues are actually earned, which may not necessarily be the same period in which cash is actually received. This is known as the accrual basis of accounting. For example, a company may sell an item during the year for $1,000. On the income statement, the $1,000 will represent sales revenues. If the item is sold on credit, the $1,000 will be listed under accounts receivable on the balance sheet, and will remain as such until the cash is actually remitted to the company by the customer—usually the following year. The accrual basis of accounting also applies to expenses, which are recognized when they are incurred rather than when they are paid by the company.

Cost of Sales

Q: What is cost of sales?

A: Cost of sales, also referred to in some financial statements as cost of goods sold, includes all the expenses incurred by a company in preparing its products or services for sale to customers. For example, cost of sales in a manufacturing company represents all the costs incurred when a factory converts raw materials into finished products for sale to customers. These costs include raw materials, labor (wages and salaries), freight, electricity, fuel, rent, supplies, maintenance, and repairs.

Operating Profit

Q: Which figure on the income statement indicates the profit (or loss) incurred by a company from its operations?

A: It is the operating profit or net profit, which is the difference between net sales or revenues and the sum of cost of sales and selling and administrative expenses. It does not include other income earned, such as interest income on investments, or gains on sales of a portion of a business, since those income items do not relate to normal operations.

Net Income (Loss)

Q: The news media often use the expression *bottom line* when referring to a company's income statement. What is the bottom line?

A: The bottom line is the net income (or loss) or net earnings (or loss). It is the final figure on an income statement which represents the difference between all revenue and income items (e.g., sales, interest income) and all costs and expenses (e.g., cost of sales and selling, administrative expenses, interest expense, and income taxes).

Determining Operating Efficiency

Q: How may an investor analyze a company's growth rate or operating efficiency from the income statement?

A: There are two indicators available to investors:

1. Operating profit margin or gross profit margin, which is computed by dividing operating profit by net sales. This ratio reveals the productivity of each dollar of sales. For example, if a company's net sales are $12 million and its operating profit is $1.2 million, the operating profit margin is 10% ($1.2 million ÷ $12 million). This means that there is an operating profit of 10 cents for each sales dollar.

2. Net profit margin, which is computed by dividing net income by net sales. For example, if net income is $600,000, the net profit margin is 5% ($600,000 ÷ $12 million). This means that for every sales dollar, the company made a net profit of 5 cents on each dollar.

Since the income statement is presented for three years in annual reports, both of these ratios should be computed for each year and analyzed for year-to-year increases or decreases. They should also be compared with those of other companies in the same business or in similar industries. For example, if the gross profit margin of the company appears to be low compared with other companies in the same industry, it may be an unhealthy sign for the company.

Q: How might an investor compare growth rates or operating efficiency indicators, such as gross profit margins or net profit margins, with those of companies in similar industries?

A: Various business ratios pertinent to the balance sheet (e.g., working capital ratio) and income statement (e.g., gross profit margin) are provided in publications issued by such organizations as Dun & Bradstreet, Robert Morris Associates, Accounting Corporation of America, Bank of America, and various trade associations. For example, Robert Morris Associates publishes an annual financial statement study which contains composite balance sheets and income statement data on approximately 320 industries. This book serves as a reference source for accountants, analysts, bankers, and others interested in comparing financial statement ratios within specific industries. It enables an investor to compare a particular company with a general nationwide profile of the industry. Also, Dun & Bradstreet's business economic division publishes a yearly analysis of key business ratios pertinent to 400,000 retailers, wholesalers, and manufacturers in a publication entitled *Dun's Review*. These types of publications are generally available in the business sections of most public libraries.

Q: What might be considered a good operating profit margin for most companies?

A: This figure depends on the industry. For example, an adequate measure of operating profit margin should be 15% to 30% for companies in a growth industry, 20% for a supermarket chain, and 60% for a drug company.

Q: What does a decrease in operating profit margin and net profit margin tell an investor about a company?

A: A decrease may be caused by one or more of the following: costs increasing in relation to sales, costs rising faster than prices, changes in the company's marketing strategy, or increased competition in the company's business. A decrease tells an investor that the management of the company is doing a poor job of controlling those costs required to run the company, or that the investor's investment in the business is not generating a satisfactory return.

Amortization

Q: Is amortization expense similar to depreciation?

A: Amortization is similar to depreciation in that both represent a tax write-off each year of a portion of the cost of an asset. However, depreciation relates to a write-off of tangible, fixed assets, such as plant and equipment, while amortization is a write-off of a portion of an intangible asset, such as goodwill, or a write-off of a discount or premium on debentures sold to investors. Like depreciation, amortization is also an expense of conducting business that is charged annually to a company's earnings or income.

Managing Costs

Q: How much attention should investors pay to the various expenses noted on the income statement?

A: Clues to particular problem areas of a troubled company can be determined from ratios of major expense items to sales. Major expense items for most companies generally include cost of goods sold, selling and administrative expenses, interest, and taxes. Divide each of these major expense items by total sales for the current year, then compare their current year percentages with percentages from prior years. If the percentages appear to be increasing while sales appear to remain relatively stable, it is a sign that management may not be doing an adequate job of managing company costs.

Times Interest Earned

Q: For a company with a substantial amount of long-term debt on the balance sheet that is due many years in the future, such as bonds, how can an investor determine whether or not the company has put the borrowed money to good use so that earnings are available to meet interest payments due to bondholders?

A: The investor can determine the number of times bond interest is earned by dividing the company's profit or income before interest expense and income taxes paid by interest expense. For example, assume that Company A's income before interest and income tax expenses is $2.5 million and that interest expense is $500,000. In this case, annual interest expense is covered five times. A high ratio means that a company should have little difficulty paying the interest due on a loan. Most analysts agree that a company's bonds are a safe investment, provided the company can earn its bond interest requirement at least three times over. This is especially important to investors during periods of inflation, when interest rates on borrowed funds run excessively high. When the earning power of a company has a high and stable nature, the company is able to (1) obtain new debt, (2) refinance old debt, (3) pay off old debt, and (4) generate cash for interest payments. Two prime examples of companies for which this is considered to be of great concern are public utilities and airlines. When viewed over a period of time, the "times interest earned" indicates the safety of interest payments as well as the stability of a company's earnings.

Extraordinary Items

Q: Some income statements show an amount called an *extraordinary item* before arriving at net income or the *bottom line*. What is the nature of an extraordinary item and how does it differ, if at all, from operating profit?

A: An extraordinary item is a gain or loss that arises in those situations in which an event or transaction affecting a company has *both* of the following characteristics:

1. It is unusual in nature, in that the event or transaction is abnormal in the normal course of business and is clearly unrelated to, or only incidentally related to, the ordinary and usual business activities of the company.
2. It occurs infrequently in the course of business operations and the event or transaction would not be expected to recur in the foreseeable future.

Because of their unusual nature and infrequent occurrence, extra-ordinary items are not a part of the scope of a company's regular or typical activities that generate operating profit. Therefore, they are treated as a separate item on the income statement in order to highlight the fact that they are significantly different from custom-ary business activities.

Accounting Changes

Q: Is an accounting change the same as an extraordinary item?

A: Although an accounting change is singled out or presented sepa-rately on the income statement, as is an extraordinary item, it is not the same as an extraordinary item because it does not have the same characteristics (i.e., unusual nature and infrequency of occurrence). An accounting change involves a change from one accounting principle to another accounting principle that is pre-ferred by the company. An accounting change will either increase or decrease net income. The nature and reason for the change is usually disclosed in a note to the financial statements. Typical changes in accounting principle include:

A change in the method of pricing inventory, such as LIFO (last-in, first-out) to FIFO (first-in, first-out) or FIFO to LIFO. (LIFO and FIFO are explained in the section on notes to finan-cial statements later in this chapter.)

A change in the method of depreciating previously recorded assets, such as from a straight line to an accelerated method or from an accelerated to a straight line method.

A change in the method of accounting for long-term construc-tion-type contracts, such as from the percentage-of-completion method to the completed-contract method or from the com-pleted-contract method to the percentage-of-completion method.

The important thing with regard to an accounting change is to concentrate on the current year's impact and subsequent years' impact on earnings as a result of the change. Those numbers will be the key as to why the accounting change was made.

Discontinued Operations

Q: Some companies show a separate figure on their income statements called "loss from discontinued operations." Does such a figure mean that a company is going under?

A: Such an item on the income statement should not necessarily be interpreted as an indication that a company is in trouble. Discontinued operations usually refer to the operations of a segment of a business that has been sold or abandoned by the company. Occasionally the term refers to the operations of a segment that continues to operate but is subject to a formal plan for disposal. The segment may be in the form of a subsidiary, division, or department. A company will usually discontinue operations of a segment because it believes that it is no longer profitable to operate the segment, for whatever reason. Continuing with an unprofitable enterprise can only damage the overall profitability of a company. On the other hand, a reference to actual and expected discontinued operations might be a signal of future declines in earning power or an indication of poor management planning in moving the corporation into areas of deficient business activity. The notes to the financial statements or the president's letter within an annual report usually explain the reason for discontinuing operations on a business segment.

Effective Tax Rate

Q: How might an investor determine the effective tax rate for a company?

A: The effective tax rate can be determined by dividing the provision for income tax by income before taxes.

Earnings Per Share

Q: What do earnings per share reveal about a company?

A: Earnings per share indicate whether or not a company is earning money for its stockholders by revealing (1) the profit earned on each share of outstanding stock and (2) the ability of the company to pay dividends to its stockholders. If a company is doing well, the trend of earnings per share usually goes up. An ideal increase is 15% or more a year. Earnings per share usually influence the market price of a company's common stock.

Q: How is the earnings per share figure determined?

A: Earnings per share are generally computed by dividing net income by the number of shares of common stock that are out-standing. A note to the financial statements generally explains the computation of earnings per share. That note should be read care-fully because it will highlight any attempts by management to manage the earnings per share number by such devices as the reacquisition of voting common stock.

Q: What is the difference between primary earnings per share and fully diluted earnings per share?

A: Primary earnings per share is determined by dividing net income by the number of outstanding shares of common stock plus com-mon stock equivalents. Common stock equivalents are those types of securities that enable their holders to convert or exchange those securities for common stock at their discretion. Common stock equivalents include convertible preferred stock, convertible bonds, stock options and stock warrants. These are basically one step short of common stock, and are equivalent in substance to common shares because of their convertible nature. Primary earnings per share may be illustrated by the following example: Company A has 200,000 shares of common stock outstanding and 100,000 shares of preferred stock that is convertible into common stock on a basis of two shares of common for one share of preferred. This convertible feature makes the preferred stock a common stock equivalent. If net income for 19X1 was $800,000, earnings per share would be computed as follows:

$$\frac{\$800,000 \text{ net income}}{400,000 \text{ adjusted shares outstanding}} = \$2.00 \text{ earnings per share}$$

The number of adjusted shares outstanding is the sum of 200,000 shares of common stock outstanding and 200,000 common equivalent shares (i.e., 100,000 shares of preferred stock outstanding times 2). The number of fully diluted earnings per share is determined by dividing net income by the total of (1) the number of shares of common stock outstanding, (2) common stock equivalents, and (3) all other types of securities that are convertible into common shares even though, for whatever reason, they are not common stock equivalents. An example of (3) above might prevail under a contract that calls for the issuance of additional shares of common stock when certain conditions are met, such as the attainment or maintenance by the company of either a specified level of income or market value of outstanding shares. The purpose of presenting fully diluted earnings per share is to reflect the possible dilution of earnings that would result if all contingent issuances of common stock had occurred at the beginning of the company's fiscal or calendar year.

Common Stock Equivalents

Q: How is a common stock equivalent actually determined?

A: A convertible security is considered to be a common stock equivalent when, based on its market price upon issuance, the rate of return is less than two-thirds of the prime interest rate charged by banks at that particular point in time.

Q: What is the advantage to an investor of having convertible-type securities, such as bonds or preferred stock, that can be exchanged for common stock?

A: Convertible securities, such as convertible bonds or convertible preferred stock, offer an investor a twofold advantage: (1) a guaranteed rate of interest from bonds or a specified dividend rate from preferred stock and (2) an option to participate in the potential increase in earnings of common stock upon conversion of the convertible security.

Price Earnings Ratio

Q: Is price earnings ratio the same as earnings per share?

A: No, but the two are interrelated. Price earnings ratio is calculated by dividing the market price of a share of a company's common stock on a certain date by the earnings per share. For example, if the market price of Company A's common stock is $50 on December 31, 19X2 and earnings per share are $2, the price earnings ratio is 25 to 1. This means that the stock is selling at 25 times earnings. The price earnings ratio figure can be used by investors to view the record of a particular company's stock over a period of years and can be used in comparisons with the common stocks of similar types of companies.

Determining Profitable Growth

Q. Which figures on the income statement indicate whether or not the company is a growing and profitable enterprise?

A. Sales, net income, dividends, and earnings per share should be scrutinized or studied for increases and decreases from year to year. Although the income statement provides this information for three years, other parts of the annual report usually provide these figures within five- or ten-year capsules of selected financial data. In general, net income and dividends for most growing companies should have doubled during the previous five to eight years.

Return on Investment

Q. The news media often refer to a company's return on investment. What does that term mean to an investor? Is it something that can be determined from the income statement?

A. Return on investment represents the rate earned by management on all of the resources (i.e., assets) committed to the company. It is a prime indicator of management's ability to conduct profitable operations and is related to the earning power of a company's investment. Return on investment is determined from the income statement and balance sheet and is calculated by dividing the sum of net income plus interest expense by total assets. Return on investment is also referred to as a capital yield, return on assets employed, return on capital, or rate of return. It should generally increase from year to year.

STATEMENT OF RETAINED EARNINGS

Purpose

Q. Some companies present a statement of retained earnings with the other financial statements in their annual report. What is the purpose of that statement?

A. A statement of retained earnings is designed to inform readers of (1) the amount of dividends paid to stockholders and (2) the amount of money the company has retained or placed back into company operations for future growth. A statement of retained earnings is basically a reconciliation of the balance at the beginning of the period (e.g., January 1, 19X2) with the balance at the end of the period (e.g., December 31, 19X2). It explains the change from the initial balance to the ending balance, and therefore reconciles the changes between the two amounts, which usually consist of dividends paid to stockholders (decreases) and net income (increases) or net loss (decreases).

Dividends Per Share

Q. How might an investor relate the amount of dividends received to each share of common stock owned?

A. This can be determined through a simple calculation of dividends per share. Divide the amount of dividends paid to common stockholders, as obtained from the statement of retained earnings, by the number of common shares outstanding, as obtained from the balance sheet. For example, if the dividends paid to common stockholders are $250,000 and 500,000 common shares are outstanding, dividends per common share are 50 cents.

Net Income (Loss)

Q. Why is net income reflected in the statement of retained earnings?

A. Net income (loss) is the lifeblood of retained earnings. For example, the net income from each year is what causes retained earnings to accumulate from one year to another. Since net income is reflected on the income statement, and since the closing balance of retained earnings is reflected on the balance sheet, the statement of retained earnings serves as a catch-all between the income statement and the balance sheet. In other words, the statement of retained earnings draws net income from the income statement to the balance sheet.

Determining Dividend Payout

Q. How can an investor tell whether or not a corporation is paying too little or too much in dividends to common stockholders?

A. An investor should determine the corporation's dividend payout ratio. This can be calculated by dividing the amount of dividends paid to common stockholders, which can be obtained from the statement of retained earnings, by net income, which can be obtained from the income statement. For example, if net income is $750,000 and dividends paid to common stockholders amounts to $250,000, the dividend payout ratio is 33 1/3%. The average for most U.S. corporations varies from 40% to 50%. A low dividend payout ratio may mean that a company is retaining most of its income and putting it back into the business. If so, the reason for such a course of action should be explained within the annual report, usually in the president's letter.

Q. What about those corporations that continue to operate at a loss and still pay dividends to common stockholders? What does that indicate to an investor?

A. Corporations that show decreases in earnings and yet continue to pay dividends could be in trouble. In such cases, dividends are being paid from the corporation's capital in order to appease stockholders. This is dangerous because while the company is tapping its reserves, no earnings are being reinvested in the company to ensure its continued existence as a viable entity.

Significance of Bottom Line

Q. What is the significance of the ending balance or bottom line of a statement of retained earnings?

A. The bottom line figure tells a reader that if a company has some future years with poor earnings, it will still be able to pay dividends to stockholders as well as continue operating as an enterprise. Of course, if the bottom line is a negative figure, the company is operating at a loss with no reserves to fall back on, and is basically in trouble as a viable enterprise.

STATEMENT OF CHANGES IN FINANCIAL POSITION

Purpose

Q. What is the purpose of the statement of changes in financial position?

A. The statement of changes in financial position, also referred to as the funds statement, reveals how a company obtained or received funds either duing the year or during the company's accounting period. It also indicates how the funds were used or disposed of during that year. The funds statement shows where the money come from and where it went. It also reveals the causes of the changes in working capital (i.e., the difference between current assets and current liabilities) between the current year and the prior two years. The extent to which the souces of working capital are greater than or less than the uses of working capital explains the net increase or decrease in working capital.

Relationship to Other Financial Statements

Q. How does the statement of changes in financial position relate to the income statement and balance sheet?

A. The statement of changes in financial position provides an explanatory link between reported earnings on the income statement and changes in assets, liabilities, and equity on the balance sheet. The amounts displayed on the statement of changes in financial position can be derived from the income statement and the balance sheet. However, the statement of changes in financial position accumulates and presents the appropriate amounts in one complete summary type of financial statement.

Q. How does the statement of changes in financial position differ from the balance sheet, the statement of retained earnings, and the income statement?

A. While the balance sheet reports a company's financial position as of a given date (e.g., December 31, 19X3), the statement of changes in financial position reports the causes of changes in financial position from one period to another (e.g., December 31, 19X1 to December 31, 19X2 to December 31, 19X3). On the other hand, although the income statement reports changes as a result of operations, and the statement of retained earnings reports certain changes in owners' equity, neither of these statements reflects all the changes in financial position between two consecutive balance sheets, as does the statement of changes in financial position.

Importance to Investors

Q. How can the statement of changes in financial position specifically aid investors?

A. It helps investors to understand the relationships between cash flows associated with the three basic activities of most businesses: operating, investing, and financing. For example, changes in the relationship between cash flow from operations and income over time might indicate changes in management's policies or changes in the characteristics of the business. This can be illustrated in a situation where management decides to extend more credit terms to customers in an effort to increase market volume. As a result, the amount of cash taken in from operations in relation to income from operations might decline. In a similar manner, cash from operations would be relatively low in those cases where a company is expanding and investing in additional inventory. The statement of changes in financial position also provides the following to investors:

A basis for assessing a company's future cash flows.
Feedback for making earlier assessments of future cash flows.
A basis for assessing income and the quality of a company's performance.

Noncash Items

Q.   In arriving at working capital derived from operations on the statement of changes in financial position, why are certain expense items, such as depreciation and amortization, added back to net income?

A.   Items such as depreciation expense, depletion expense, and amortization of intangibles, are all examples of expenses that are subtracted on the income statement in order to arrive at net income, but that do not involve an outflow of working capital. Therefore, in computing working capital provided by operations, these noncash expenses are added back to net income. Similarly, amortization of discounts on bonds payable, which increases interest expense but does not involve an outflow of funds, and amortization of premiums on bond investments, which decreases interest income but does not reduce the cash interest income receipts realized during an accounting period, are added back to reported net income. Conversely, amortization of premiums on bonds payable, and amortization of discounts on bond investments are subtracted from net income.

It is important to bear in mind that these noncash items are either added back to or deducted from net income to arrive at working capital derived for the period of the financial statements. For example, the working capital effect of depreciation occurs when the asset involved (e.g., a machine or a truck) is initially acquired and paid for by the company, not when the estimate for depreciation is recorded.

Finance and Investment Activities

Q. If the funds statement is designed to reflect changes in working capital, why does it also present transactions that do not affect working capital, such as the conversion of long-term debt into common stock?

A. In order to meet its objectives, a funds statement will disclose separately any financing and investing activities of all significant transactions that affect the financial position of a company. These include conversion of long-term debt or preferred stock to common stock, or the issuance of securities in exchange for property, even though such transactions do not affect working capital directly. For instance, a financing and investing transaction, such as the acquisition of land and buildings by a company in exchange for issuing common stock, does not affect cash or working capital. However, such transactions are presented separately in the funds statement as a source of working capital (i.e., issuance of common stock in exchange for property) and as a use of working capital (i.e., acquisition of property in exchange for common stock).

Cash Flow

Q. If cash flow relates to the actual money or cash a company takes in from revenues and pays out for expenses, how does cash flow differ from net income?

A. Net income represents increases in net assets (i.e., assets less liabilities) that are derived from a company's operating and non-operating activities as accounted for on the accrual basis of accounting, while cash flow represents the cash inflows and outflows that are generated by those activities. For example, Company A sells a machine that costs $3,000 to Company B for $8,000. Assuming a 50% income tax rate, net income would be computed on the accrual basis of accounting as follows:

Sales	$8,000
Cost of sales	3,000
Income	5,000
Income tax	2,500
Net income	$2,500

An account receivable for $8,000 would be recorded on Company A's books at the time of sale. During the year, Company B sends Company A a check for $4,000. Although Company A's net income for the year is $2,500 from the sale of the machine, its cash flow from that sale is $4,000. In general, the recognition of revenue becomes further removed from the receipt of cash in those cases in which credit terms are longer and more complex.

Q. Is a company's cash flow position more important to an investor than a company's net income position?

A. Information about a company's earnings or net income, and the components of net income (e.g., cost of sales and interest expense), as measured by the accrual basis of accounting, provides a better measure of a company's performance than does information about that company's current cash receipts and cash disbursements (i.e., cash flow). Financial information that recognizes the financial effects of transactions when they actually occur, rather than when cash is received or paid, is generally considered a better basis for determining the ability of a company to operate as an ongoing entity, as well as its ability to continue to obtain future cash than are cash receipts and disbursements. However, information on cash flow is often considered by financial analysts as information on the quality of income. A basic determinant of the quality of income is the extent to which a company is able to turn its income into cash, or the relationship between cash flow from operations and earnings.

Q.   If net income is a more important parameter for measuring a company's performance than cash flow, why should an investor be concerned with a company's cash flow position?

A.   Net income or earnings figures have certain limitations that are not present in cash flow figures. For example, in an inflationary economy, the use of historical cost figures as a basis for calculating depreciation and inventory continually exaggerates reported earnings by publicly listed companies. On the other hand, cash flow, which represents the actual dollars a company uses to expand its operations, is not affected by inflation. Also, stock market quotations on every major stock exchange generally correlate closely with a company's cash flow and liquidity position (i.e., working capital), and seldom, if ever, correlate with earnings figures, which are usually distorted by inflation. Most important, a company's ability to generate favorable cash flows will affect its ability to:

Reward investors in the form of dividends.
Maintain its current productivity by replacing property, plant and equipment.
Make repayments on loans and related interest.
Accept new investment opportunities.

Q.   Has the effect of inflation on the economy contributed to the importance of cash flow information?

A.   The effect of inflation has increased the importance of information concerning cash flow. As prices increase, companies require more funds to finance holdings of higher priced inventories, as well as property, plant, and equipment. Also, as prices increase, more funds are required to finance increased investment in accounts receivable. Since current-period income is calculated on the historical cost basis, reported income does not reflect the increased prices resulting from inflation. Therefore, reported income may be a poor indicator of the funds available to pay debt, expand operations, and distribute dividends to corporate shareholders. The effect on expansion of rising prices during an inflationary period can be illustrated by the following example. Assume an automotive dealer purchases a truck for $10,000 and expects to sell it for $15,000. Because demand for automotive equipment is low, the truck remains unsold and the dealer considers reducing the selling price by offering a discount from the $15,000 list price. During the time the truck remains in inventory, the dealer's purchase price for an identical vehicle increases by 20%, to $12,000. In this case, the maximum discount that the dealer can offer is $3,000 if the truck sold is to be replaced. At a discounted selling price of $12,000, the dealer would have no cash surplus available for expansion, debt payments, or dividend payments. Sole reliance on income, which would be $2,000, as an indicator of this dealer's residual cash would be misleading. Although the dealer began with $10,000 and now has $12,000, the high replacement cost of the truck requires that the $2,000 be reinvested in order for the dealer to maintain the same level of activity.

Q: If a company shows a favorable earnings picture, does that imply a favorable cash flow position?

A: Not necessarily. Some companies have reported earnings or net income figures on their income statements while lacking the necessary cash flows to continue day-to-day operations. For example, prior to its bankruptcy in 1975, W. T. Grant & Co. presented a favorable earnings picture on its income statements from 1966 to 1975. However, the company had a negative cash flow position from 1971 to 1974.

Q: Why does a company's cash flow position sometimes differ significantly from its net income or earnings positions?

A: Differences between a company's cash flow and earnings position most often depend on the company's typical expense and revenue patterns, namely, the length of time it usually takes the company to collect cash from its customers after the products or services are sold. A more specific example is when a company has a temporary shortage in its cash inflow because one or more of its products is not selling in the marketplace, for whatever reason.

Q: How can an investor determine a company's cash flow from the annual report?

A: Most annual reports provide specific cash flow information within the annual report other than the statement of changes in financial position, such as the financial highlights. If they do not, cash flow can be determined through shortcuts by adding to or subtracting from net income certain noncash items, such as the addition of depreciation expense and the subtraction of amortization of discount on bonds payable.

NOTES TO FINANCIAL STATEMENTS

Purpose

Q: What is the purpose of notes to financial statements?

A: Notes to financial statements, also referred to as footnotes, are designed to provide information that relates to, but is not visually understandable from, the face of the financial statements. For example, although the amount of a company's long-term debt may be displayed as a liability on the balance sheet, the related footnote will reveal information concerning the long-term debt that cannot be determined from the balance sheet. These include the terms of the debt; interest rates (i.e., the cost of financing); collateral pledged to cover the debt (e.g., property and equipment); and any restrictive covenants, such as minimum working capital requirements or limitations on the amount of retained earnings available for dividends to shareholders. Notes to financial statements also provide information that is not discernable from the face of the financial statements because no dollar amount is shown. This includes contingent liabilities and commitments. An example of a contingent liability might be a pending lawsuit or claim for damages against the company, the amount of which cannot be readily determined. In general, any explanatory matter that cannot be easily abbreviated or condensed on the face of the actual financial statements is set forth in greater detail in the notes.

Accounting Policies

Q: What are accounting policies?

A: Accounting policies are the ground rules and methodology used by a company to implement the specific accounting principles followed by that company. The accounting policies selected are judged by a company's management to be the most appropriate under the circumstances. For example, an accounting policy generally describes how a company values its assets; depreciates its property, plant, and equipment; amortizes intangible assets; recognizes revenues; accounts for investment tax credit; and other accounting practices.

Q: Is an accounting policy the same as an accounting principle?

A: An accounting policy is a specific accounting principle used by a particular company. An accounting policy is the adoption of a specific accounting principle from similar principles that have been selected by company management to meet the particular needs of the company. For example, companies use a number of accounting principles to compute depreciation, such as the straight line method and accelerated methods. If a company applies the straight line method for depreciating its plant and equipment, that accounting principle serves as the company's accounting policy for depreciation.

Q: Why are accounting policies important to an investor?

A: The accounting policies used by a particular company can have a significant effect on the presentation of that company's financial position, changes in financial position, and results of operations. For example, a company may have an accounting policy whereby revenues are recognized according to the installment method, that is, as cash collections are made rather than at the time of sale. As a result of that accounting policy, results of operations are affected by gross profit based on cash collections from installment sales. Also, the accounting policies footnote can reveal whether or not a company's accounting policies actually reflect economic reality and whether or not they basically conform to the accounting practice for that company's particular industry. For example, a company may reduce its provision for product warranty expense when there are continual deficiencies in the quality of the company's product line. This will result in an increase in product warranty costs. In this case, a significant variance between provisions (i.e., estimates) for product warranty expense and actual experience in product deficiency suggests that the company is not considering the economic realities of its business. It may also suggest that the company is intentionally understating provisions for expenses in order to overstate earnings. It is therefore useful for an investor to understand the accounting policies of a company when making an investment decision about that company (i.e., whether or not to invest or divest).

Revenue Recognition

Q: Some companies that engage in construction activities indicate in their accounting policies note to the financial statements that revenues are recognized according to a percentage of completion method, while other companies refer to a completed contract method. What is the difference between these two methods of revenue recognition?

A: Companies that engage in construction activities will often undertake a construction project that requires several years to complete, such as an office building constructed over a three- or four-year period. Two alternative methods are used to recognize revenue from long-term construction projects: the percentage of completion method and the completed contract method. Under the percentage of completion method, at the end of the accounting period (i.e., one fiscal year) an estimate is made of the percentage of the total construction completed during that period. The percentage is then applied to the total revenue to be derived from the construction project, as defined in the contract. As a result, the amount of profit estimated to be earned during a particular accounting period is the percentage of the revenue recognized less any costs incurred. In this way a certain amount of profit is recognized and therefore reported on the income statement for each year that the construction is in process. On the other hand, under the completed contract method, profit is not recognized and therefore not reported on the income statement until the year that the construction contract is completed or substantially completed and the sale is considered complete.

Q: In comparing the percentage of completion method with the completed contract method, why would a company choose one method of revenue recognition over the other?

A: The choice of one method of revenue recognition for construction contracts over another depends on the circumstances. For example, the percentage of completion method would be the preferred method when the following circumstances prevailed:

> *Based on past experience, the contractor has the ability to produce dependable estimates of the percentage of total construction completed during an accounting period.*
>
> *The construction contract contains provisions that specify the enforceable rights regarding goods and services to be provided and received by the parties to the contract, the consideration to*

be exchanged (e.g., amount of money), and the manner and terms of settling the contract.

The buyer can be expected to satisfy his or her obligations under the contract.

The contracting company can be expected to perform its obligations under the construction contract.

The percentage of completion method is considered to be more economically realistic because profit is recognized as work progresses on the construction project. However, in certain circumstances the completed contract method is the more practical method. For example, it can be used to recognize revenue if the estimated costs to complete the construction contract cannot reasonably be estimated. The problem with the completed contract method is that it does not reflect current performance (i.e., profit) in those cases in which the construction contract period extends over more than one accounting period.

Q: The accounting policies of some companies indicate that revenue is recognized on an installment sales basis. How does that basis differ from revenue recognized on regular sales?

A: For regular sales, revenue is recognized by a corporation when the sales transaction is completed (e.g., when title to the property sold passes to the customer or buyer). In this type of situation, revenue is recognized in the period of sale in light of the fact that collection of the sales price will be made by the company within a relatively short period of time. For installment sales, collection of the sales price is usually made over an extended period of time (e.g., two or more years from the date of sale). Also, the probability of loss resulting from uncollectible receivables is usually greater than for regular sales. Therefore, revenue is recognized on the dates cash collections are made by the buyer on the sales price rather than on the date of sale. For example, assume that a company sells a $3,000 product for $5,000. A cash downpayment of $1,000 is made, and there are to be 20 monthly payments of $200 each. The revenue to be recognized by the corporation in the year of sale would depend on the amount of cash collected from the sale. If three monthly payments are made at $200 each, the gross profit or revenue realized from the sale is $640 (i.e., $1,000 cash down payment plus $600 monthly installments times 40% gross profit on the sale).

Equity Method of Accounting

Q: What does it mean when a company accounts for its unconsolidated subsidiaries on the equity method?

A: The equity method of accounting is used by an investor company to record an investment in the common stock of an unconsolidated company or subsidiary company. The original investment is recorded at cost and increased (or decreased) by the investor company's share of annual earnings (or losses) of the unconsolidated subsidiary, and decreased for any dividends received by the investor company from that subsidiary. The investor company's share of the annual earnings (or losses) of its unconsolidated subsidiary is included in the net earnings on the income statement.

Compensating Balances

Q: Some notes to financial statements refer to compensating balances with respect to credit arrangements with banks. What are compensating balances?

A: Compensating balances comprise that portion of any demand deposit, time deposit, or certificate of deposit maintained by a corporation that constitutes support for that corporation's borrowing arrangements with a bank or some other credit-granting organization. In effect, a company agrees to maintain a certain amount of money (i.e., a compensating balance) on deposit with a bank that extends credit to that company. Under such an arrangement, the company (or borrower) agrees not to allow the amount on deposit to go below a specified limit. This type of arrangement must be disclosed; otherwise a reader of the financial statements may assume that the entire cash balance is available to meet current debts and expenses.

Depreciation Methods

Q: Some companies indicate that they follow a straight line method for depreciating plant and equipment, while other companies refer to an accelerated method, such as the sum-of-the-years method. What is the difference between these two depreciation methods?

A: The straight line method relates depreciation directly to the passage of time rather than to the specific use of the asset. It is referred to as "straight line" because equal charges for depreciation expense are made in each period or year of the asset's service life. In other words, the same amount of depreciation gets written off each year. For example, assume that a company pays $90,000 for a piece of equipment that has an estimated service life of three years. For each of those three years depreciation expense will be $30,000 ($90,000 ÷ 3 years).

An accelerated method relates depreciation to the early use of an asset. Companies use this method when the expected productivity or revenue earning power of a fixed asset appears to be greater in the early years of the asset's useful life and maintenance and repair charges tend to increase in the later years. In other words, depreciation charges increase dramatically in the early years of an asset's life, and then slow down with the passage of time. Using the previous illustration, under an accelerated method of depreciation, such as the sum-of-the-years method, depreciation expenses would be as follows: $45,000 in year 1, $30,000 in year 2, and $15,000 in year 3. Some companies will use the straight line method of depreciation for financial reporting or book purposes and use an accelerated method of depreciation for income tax purposes to improve their cash flow position.

Q: What effect is there on a company's earnings if it uses the straight line method rather than the accelerated method of depreciation?

A: In the early years of an asset's service life, earnings tend to be higher under straight line depreciation than under an accelerated method, because under an accelerated method more depreciation expense is charged against revenues in the early years of an asset's life. During an inflationary period, many corporations use an accelerated depreciation method in order to be more conservative in their financial reporting and therefore reflect a higher quality of earnings.

Q: Which depreciation method—straight line or accelerated—is the more practical approach for a corporation to follow?

A: An accelerated method is generally considered to be more practical in light of continued technological changes in machinery and equipment. A slower method of depreciation, such as the straight line method, might encourage corporate management to maintain a piece of equipment or machinery long after superior replacements become available. This fact became evident when the automobile and steel industries discovered that they needed to replace fixed assets that were technologically obsolete.

Investment Tax Credit

Q: What is an investment tax credit?

A: As an incentive for businesses to help stimulate the economy through the purchase of capital goods, the federal government allows companies to take 10% of the cost of certain types of business machinery and equipment and apply that amount as a credit against their federal income tax liabilities. The money is recovered by the government over a period of three or more years.

Q: Notes to financial statements of some companies state that the investment tax credit is accounted for by the flow-through method, while other companies use a deferred method. How are these methods similar and how are they different?

A: The methods are similar in that the investment tax credit on a plant or productive facility reduces a company's income taxes. The flow-through method reduces income taxes by the full amount of the allowable investment tax credit in the year the credit arises. The deferred method lowers income taxes by reducing depreciation expense over the years of the useful life of the productive facility. For example, assume a company has an allowable investment tax credit of $10,000. Under the flow-through method, the entire $10,000 would generally be applied as a reduction of the company's income tax liability for the year. Under the deferred method, the $10,000 would be applied as a reduction of depreciation over the useful life of the plant or productive facility. If the plant has a useful life of ten years, depreciation expense would be reduced by $1,000, each year for ten years.

FIFO and LIFO Inventory

Q: Some companies indicate within notes to financial statements that inventory is valued on a FIFO (first-in, first-out) basis, while other companies refer to a LIFO (last-in, first-out) basis. What is the difference between these methods?

A: FIFO is an inventory valuation method that uses the most recent costs of goods purchased and manufactured to assign values to items in the year-end inventory. It assumes that the costs of the oldest items are the first costs assigned to cost of goods sold. In other words, the costs of the first purchased or first manufactured inventory items are the first or initial inventory costs to be charged to revenues. The assumption is that the oldest inventory items are the first goods to be sold (i.e., first-in, first-out). On the other hand, LIFO is an inventory valuation method that charges the most recent costs of goods purchased and manufactured to the cost of goods sold. In this way, year-end inventory is valued using the costs of items included in the beginning inventory (i.e., the cost of the oldest inventory items) plus costs of quantities added or purchased during the year. The assumption is that the latest inventory items or those purchased during the year are the first inventory items to be sold (i.e., last-in, first-out).

Q: Which method of inventory valuation is more reflective of economic reality, FIFO or LIFO?

A: The LIFO method presents a more economically realistic income statement because it matches current inventory acquisition costs with inflated sales dollars. In this way, inventory profits caused by inflation are removed, and this improves the quality of reported earnings. However, the LIFO method does not produce a satisfactory result for the balance sheet in a period of rising prices, since it tends to value inventories at amounts that are substantially below current costs (i.e., inventory costs at the beginning of the year). Under the LIFO method, inventory is stated on the balance sheet on a conservative basis rather than on a more realistic economic or current basis.

Q: What effect does the adoption of LIFO have on earnings reported in the income statement?

A: Reported after-tax earnings under LIFO are reduced in periods of inflation but are usually increased (or losses are diminished) in periods of recession. Adoption of LIFO for tax purposes requires its adoption for external financial reporting purposes. Although LIFO may result is cash savings from taxes, the tradeoff is lower reported earnings and earnings per share and lower inventory valuation. This is offset to some extent by the lower interest costs resulting from reduced borrowing requirements.

Q: What is the effect on earnings of the FIFO method of inventory valuation compared to the LIFO method?

A: FIFO assumes that goods sold today are the earliest bought or made and therefore, during a period of rising prices, the cheapest. This results in higher operating profit. On the other hand, LIFO assumes that goods currently sold are the most recently purchased or made and thus, during a period of rising prices, shows a smaller operating profit. When prices are rising, a change by a company from FIFO and LIFO causes earnings to be less, compared with prior years, than they otherwise would be.

Q: How do the FIFO and LIFO methods of inventory valuation affect income taxes?

A: Under FIFO, the oldest costs (i.e., the first-in and cheapest goods in a period of inflation) are matched against current sales prices, thereby creating higher profits. On the other hand, the LIFO method matches the current replacement cost of inventory with current sales prices by assuming that the last inventory that came into the company is the first to be sold. As a result, lower earnings are recorded, and this produces lower tax payments than would be the case under FIFO. In other words, the LIFO method of inventory valuation helps companies save on taxes. In periods of rising prices, LIFO results in lower inventory values than the FIFO method does. Under FIFO, items unsold at the end of the year are carried at higher prices, and this results in payment of correspondingly higher taxes. Under LIFO, rises in cost of goods or products attributable to inflation are matched with current sales, thereby reducing income and the related taxes, and inventories are carried at the lower, earlier costs.

Q: If lower earnings are reported under the LIFO method of inventory valuation, why would a company use LIFO?

A: Among the benefits that stem from the LIFO method are improved cash flow, through permanent tax savings, and a decreased need for costly borrowing that might otherwise be necessary to finance payment of income taxes on inflated earnings determined on a non-LIFO basis. In effect, the payment of higher taxes on earnings computed on a non-LIFO basis depletes cash and/or borrowing capacity that would otherwise be available for a company's capital reinvestment program or for a dividend distribution to shareholders.

Compensation to Employees

Q: Is there any information within the notes to financial statements that indicates how a company treats its employees?

A: The notes on employee pension plans, profit sharing, and stock options provide some information on a company's employee benefit plans. Most progressive companies provide such compensation benefits for their employees and corporate officers as incentives for continued productive employment.

Research and Development

Q: Is there any specific information within the notes to financial statements that indicates whether or not a company in a high-technology type of industry is progressive?

A: Look for a note that refers to the amount of research and development expense incurred by a company during the year. Although the amount cannot indicate the quality of the research and development effort, it is an important indicator of a company's commitment to that effort. Such a commitment implies that a company is innovative and looks ahead to new products that will outperform competitors and increase profits.

Accounts Receivable

Q: Some companies disclose the nature and composition of their accounts receivable in a note to the financial statements. What should an investor look for in this type of footnote?

A: Look for amounts due from foreign countries that may be politically and economically unstable as indicated by news media. Also look for an indication as to whether a company might be factoring its accounts receivable, that is, selling its receivables may imply that a company has problems obtaining financing at reasonable rates or that is has a liquidity problem since it is obtaining advanced funds at higher financing rates through factoring. These types of receivables are considered risky, and if they comprise a significant portion of a company's receivables, a company's cash flow position may be jeopardized, despite a favorable earnings picture.

Related Party Transactions

Q: Some companies provide notes to their financial statements concerning transactions with affiliated companies, corporate officers, and major shareowners. What is the purpose of disclosing such information?

A: A fundamental precept of financial reporting is that financial statements should reflect arms-length transactions between buyers and sellers, as though such parties were independent of one another. In other words, when a buyer and seller enter into a transaction, each party to the transaction agrees to a particular price that meets their own individual economic interests. Transactions between related parties (e.g., corporate officers) may not necessarily be considered arms-length transactions by individuals outside the company, such as credit grantors and investors. Therefore, if transactions in a company between related parties occur, professional accounting standards require that certain disclosures regarding the nature and volume of such transactions be included within that company's financial statement.

Q: Why would a company get involved in transactions with so-called related parties?

A: Certain economic factors might cause a company to become involved in material transactions with its owners, members of management, and other employees. These include:

A need for a favorable earnings picture.
A lack of sufficient working capital to continue in business.
Inability to obtain additional credit to continue operations.
Dependence on a few outside customers.
The industry is characterized by numerous business failures as a result of inflation or an energy crisis.

However, for the majority of those publicly listed companies that are in sound financial health, related party transactions usually come about at the request of the company's related party, such as corporate officers or major stockholders. It is important to bear in mind that transactions between a company and its related parties may arise for a number of reasons, which are not necessarily limited to the previously described economic factors. As long as the nature of the related party and a description of the transaction are disclosed in the financial statements, investors can be reasonably assured that there are no significant problems in that regard.

Foreign Currency Transactions

Q: How do foreign currency transactions affect earnings of U.S. multinational companies?

A: Gains and losses that result from translating foreign balance sheet items into U.S. dollars are reflected in a separate section of the stockholders' equity, as required by an accounting rule of the FASB. However, in some cases foreign exchange gains and losses may be included in net income. This occurs when the economic effects of an exchange rate change on a foreign operation that is an extension of a parent company's domestic operations are related to individual assets and liabilities and affect the parent company's cash flow directly. The exchange gains and losses that result from the translation of such an operation are included in net income. An example would be a U.S. manufacturing company's subassembly plant operations in a foreign country. The factor that determines whether or not the results of foreign operations are to be included in net income or stockholders' equity depends on the effect of those results on the cash flow of the parent company. If cash flow is affected, translation gains and losses become part of net income. On the other hand, if the cash flow of the parent company is not affected, translation gains and losses are reflected in stockholders' equity.

Q: How does the impact of Statement of Financial Accounting Standards No. 52, the current accounting rule for foreign currency translation, differ from Statement of Financial Accounting Standards No. 8, the former accounting rule?

A: The current standard, FASB Statement No. 52, established by the Financial Accounting Standards Board, directs multinational businesses to eliminate most foreign currency translation fluctuations on assets and liabilities (representing either gains or losses) from their current income statements. In essence, under the former rule (FASB Statement No. 8), the effects of fluctuating foreign currency exchange rates on translating international balance sheets from local currencies into dollars were included in the income statement, sometimes causing wide swings in earnings that did not fairly reflect the economic performance of the company. Now these swings, whether favorable or unfavorable, are incorporated into the shareholders' equity section of the balance sheet. As a result, the earnings now present a truer indication of the economic operations of the company.

This can be illustrated by the following example. Assume that at the beginning of the year a company had one million German marks in assets, valued then at 20 cents each. These would be translated onto the balance sheet as $200,000. During the year the dollar grew stronger in relation to the mark, which fell to a value of 15 cents each. The original one million marks would then be translated onto the balance sheet as $150,000, an unfavorable adjustment of $50,000. Under the old accounting rule, this adjustment had already been reported on the income statement and therefore had an unfavorable impact on the year's current earnings.

Earnings Per Share

Q: Many notes to the financial statements indicate that earnings per share are based on the weighted average number of common shares outstanding for the year. What comprises a weighted average?

A: A weighted average is the total of those common shares outstanding at the beginning of a company's year (i.e., January 1, 19X2) plus increases and minus decreases in outstanding shares during the year. For example, increases may comprise additional shares issued during the year as a result of conversions of bonds or preferred shares into common shares, the sale of additional common shares, or dividends paid in common stock. Earnings per share are derived by dividing net income by the weighted average number of common shares outstanding. A weighted average is designed to show the effect of increases or decreases in outstanding shares on earnings per share information when related to the portion of the year during which the related consideration (e.g., conversion of bonds to common shares) affected operations. In other words, the weighted average number represents a more equitable basis for determining earnings per share as compared to an average of the beginning and end of year balances of common shares outstanding.

Q: Are increases in earnings per share from year to year a true measure of a company's profitability?

A: Not necessarily. Increases in earnings per share, based on net income, may often result from changes in accounting principles, extraordinary items, the sale of a major plant or securities, or various tax credits taken by the company, none of which has anything to do with a company's current operating performance. If net income happens to be affected by any such items, and this is usually indicated in the notes to the financial statements, compare both income from operations and income before taxes (i.e., pretax income) to sales for several years to obtain a true picture of whether or not the company is performing efficiently.

Net Operating Loss Carryforward

Q: Extraordinary items on the income statement are sometimes described in notes to financial statements as the "tax benefit of a net operating loss carryforward." What is the nature of such an item?

A: Federal tax laws allow corporations that sustain losses to carry back to three prior years and to carry forward to fifteen future years net operating losses. In this way the corporation may secure refunds of income taxes paid in the three prior years. If the loss is so large that even after adjustment it is not absorbed fully when offset against the profitable years to which it is carried back, it can be carried forward for as many as fifteen years, during which time it may serve to reduce taxes that would otherwise be owed on income for those years. In situations where an operating loss is carried forward, the tax effects may not be recognized because there is no assurance that they will be realized. For example, a loss carryforward would decrease the amount of taxes due in a certain future period, but if the company continues to lose money, there will be no profits to offset the carryforward and it may never be utilized. However, when the tax benefits of a loss carryforward are recognized, in full or in part, in subsequent periods, it is reported as an extraordinary item in accordance with an accounting rule in Accounting Principles Board Opinion No. 11, "Accounting for Income Taxes." The tax benefits of a net operating loss carryforward can be illustrated as follows. Assume that a company sustained a net operating loss of $100,000 during its first year of operation. If the corporate tax rate is 50%, the tax benefit of the net operating loss carryforward is $50,000 ($100,000 × 50%). This amount would be presented as an extraordinary item on the income statement.

Q: For purposes of financial reporting, under what circumstances may a company recognize the tax effects of an operating loss carryforward?

A: According to Accounting Principles Board Opinion No. 11, the realization of the tax effects or tax benefits is not ordinarily assured because a company cannot know with absolute certainty that it will have taxable profits in the future against which the loss carryforwards can be used. Therefore, tax benefits that arise from loss carryforwards cannot be recognized until they are realized, except in unusual circumstances when realization is assured beyond any reasonable doubt. In order for realization to be assured "beyond any reasonable doubt," the company must meet three conditions which relate to the character of the loss being carried forward, the character of the company, and the character of the taxable income expected. For example:

1. **Character of the Loss Being Carried Forward.** The loss must have resulted from an identifiable, isolated, and non-recurring cause.

2. **Character of the Company.** The company must have been profitable on a continuous basis over a long period of time. Or, if the company experienced occasional losses, such losses must have been more than offset by taxable income later in the company's existence.

3.   **Character of the Taxable Income Expected.**   The taxable income, based on a reasonable degree of certainty, must be large enough to offset the loss carryforward and must evolve in the near future in order to deliver the tax benefits within the carryforward period.

APB Opinions

Q: Is an Accounting Principles Board (APB) opinion the same as a statement of financial accounting standards?

A: APB opinions are similar to statements of financial accounting standards issued by the FASB in that APB opinions also represent generally accepted accounting principles. The Accounting Principles Board (APB) was a part of the American Institute of Certified Public Accountants, a professional association of CPAs, and was the predecessor of the public accounting profession's self-regulatory body, the current FASB. During its 15-year existence, the APB issued 31 opinions and four statements relating to generally accepted accounting principles.

Most Important Notes

Q: The annual reports of most publicly listed companies contain a great deal of information within the notes to the financial statements. What specific notes might an investor consider to be the most important?

A: Actually all notes are important because they provide information that cannot be readily understood from the face of the financial statements. However, an investor might concentrate on the accounting policies notes and those notes that provide information that is not found on the face of the financial statements. For example:

Commitments and contingencies, such as appropriation of assets, pending or threatened litigation, product warranties or defects, and claims and assessments of a governmental agency such as the Internal Revenue Service.

Events that may have occurred subsequent to the date of the financial statements, the effects of which have not yet been adjusted to the financial statements. These include sale of a bond or capital stock issue; purchase of a business; settlement of litigation; or loss of a company plant or inventories because of a fire, flood, or some other disaster.

This type of information, which cannot be readily seen from the financial statements, may be an important factor when an investor makes an investment decision concerning a particular company. For example, the loss of a major plant after the balance sheet date may raise a question as to how the company will continue to service its customers and thereby raise future sales revenues.

Contingencies

Q: Many companies have a note to their financial statements describing some form of contingency, such as pending litigation or federal tax assessments. How can an investor determine whether or not the contingency poses a problem for the company?

A: Read the independent auditor's report. If the opinion paragraph of the report refers to the contingency, that is an indication that the contingency matter may pose a problem for the company because its resolution appears to be uncertain.

Years Ended December 31	1982	1981	1980
Net Sales	$3,737,378	$4,004,027	$3,752,718
Cost of products sold......................	3,260,062	3,399,274	3,118,218
Selling, general, and administrative			
expenses	415,701	415,343	383,691
Income From Operations	61,615	189,410	250,809
Interest and debt expense (Note 5)	74,693	81,403	57,614
Other (income) expense – net (Note 13)	(50,277)	(47,473)	(30,846)
Income Before Income Taxes	37,199	155,480	224,041
Income Taxes (Note 14)	(2,451)	35,834	41,621
Income From Continuing Operations	39,650	119,646	182,420
Loss From Discontinued Operations, Net of Applicable Income Tax Benefit (Note 3)	–	(18,277)	(18,375)
Income Before Extraordinary Item ..	39,650	101,369	164,045
Extraordinary Item, Net of Applicable Income Tax Benefit (Note 20)	–	–	(16,977)
Net Income	$ 39,650	$ 101,369	$ 147,068
Average Number of Common Shares Outstanding	54,935	54,739	53,841
Earnings Per Common Share:			
Primary:			
Continuing Operations	$ .45	$ 1.91	$ 3.28
Discontinued Operations	–	(.33)	(.34)
Extraordinary Item....................	–	–	(.31)
Net Income	$ .45	$ 1.58	$ 2.63
Fully Diluted:			
Continuing Operations	$ .45	$ 1.88	$ 3.19
Discontinued Operations	–	(.32)	(.32)
Extraordinary Item....................	–	–	(.30)
Net Income	$ .45	$ 1.56	$ 2.57

Exhibit 2.1. Illustrated financial statements (Champion International Corporation). Reprinted by permission from the 1982 annual report of Champion International Corporation.

Assets December 31	1982	1981
Current Assets:		
Cash	$ 22,418	$ 19,425
Temporary cash investments	34,874	33,882
Receivables – net	314,069	321,667
Inventories (Note 2)	459,120	487,724
Prepaid expenses	11,107	14,163
Total current assets	841,588	876,861
Equity in and Advances to Unconsolidated		
Affiliates (Note 4)	72,876	64,827
Timber and Timberlands, at cost – less cost of		
timber harvested (Note 8)	485,024	464,659
Property, Plant, and Equipment, at cost		
(Notes 5, 8, and 9)	3,147,518	2,973,219
Less – Accumulated depreciation	1,245,052	1,119,070
	1,902,466	1,854,149
Other Assets and Deferred Charges	170,040	182,730
	$3,471,994	$3,443,226

Liabilities and Shareholders' Equity December 31	1982	1981
Current Liabilities:		
Notes payable (Note 6)	$ 9,162	$ 39,523
Current installments of long-term debt...................	26,766	22,563
Accounts payable and accrued liabilities (Note 7)	384,866	388,379
Income taxes (Note 14)	17,996	17,180
Total current liabilities...............................	438,790	467,645
Long-Term Debt (Note 8)...............................	1,007,950	924,884
Other Liabilities..	81,372	38,127
Deferred Income Taxes (Note 14)	172,411	219,425
Minority Interest in Subsidiaries	34,374	39,701
Commitments and Contingent Liabilities		
(Notes 9 and 19)	–	–
Capital Shares (Notes 10 and 11):		
Preference stock, $1 par value:		
$1.20 Cumulative convertible series (liquidation		
preference aggregates $25,952)	6,755	7,040
$4.60 Cumulative convertible series (liquidation		
preference aggregates $149,950)	145,152	145,152
Common stock, $.50 par value, authorized		
100,000,000 shares; in 1982, issued		
55,730,841 shares; in 1981, issued 55,681,757		
shares	383,611	383,341
Retained Earnings (Note 8)	1,228,391	1,240,735
	1,763,909	1,776,268
Less:		
Treasury shares, at cost (Note 10).......................	15,920	16,105
Cumulative translation adjustment (Note 12)	10,892	6,719
	1,737,097	1,753,444
	$3,471,994	$3,443,226

Years Ended December 31	1982	1981	1980
Source of Funds:			
Income from continuing operations	$ 39,650	$119,646	$182,420
Items not requiring outlay of working capital:			
Depreciation and cost of timber harvested	167,161	168,598	147,502
Deferred income taxes	(30,709)	20,939	23,920
All other – net	18,451	(6,636)	11,754
Working capital provided from continuing operations	194,553	302,547	365,596
Loss from discontinued operations	–	(18,277)	(18,375)
Items not requiring outlay of working capital:			
Deferred income taxes	–	(2,163)	12,671
Loss on disposition of discontinued operations.	–	26,952	45,200
Working capital provided from discontinued operations...................	–	6,512	39,496
Extraordinary item	–	–	(16,977)
Total working capital provided from operations	194,553	309,059	388,115
Proceeds from long-term debt	119,728	190,772	184,567
Decrease (Increase) in funds held for construction ...	9,114	(43,295)	12,906
Proceeds from preference stock	–	–	145,200
All other – net	15,772	12,303	6,690
Total funds provided	339,167	468,839	737,478
Application of Funds:			
Expenditures for property, plant, and equipment ...	214,057	245,038	273,306
Timber and timberlands expenditures	42,360	89,110	81,814
Cash dividends declared	51,994	96,439	83,670
Decrease in long-term debt	34,912	76,889	189,083
Increase in net assets of discontinued furnishings business	2,262	1,043	50,914
Total funds applied	345,585	508,519	678,787
Increase (Decrease) in Working Capital...........	$ (6,418)	$(39,680)	$ 58,691
Changes in Working Capital Consist of:			
Increase (Decrease) in current assets:			
Cash	$ 2,993	$(14,157)	$ 20,014
Temporary cash investments	992	147	16,172
Receivables	(7,598)	(33,066)	48,413
Inventories	(28,604)	(6,079)	20,867
Prepaid expenses	(3,056)	3,017	2,021
Total.......................................	(35,273)	(50,138)	107,487
Increase (Decrease) in current liabilities:			
Notes payable	(30,361)	21,413	(9,673)
Current installments of long-term debt	4,203	(13,086)	(2,949)
Accounts payable and accrued liabilities...........	(3,513)	(29,044)	68,649
Income taxes..	816	10,259	(7,231)
Total.......................................	(28,855)	(10,458)	48,796
Increase (Decrease) in Working Capital...........	$ (6,418)	$(39,680)	$ 58,691

Years Ended December 31	1982	1981	1980
Beginning Balance	$1,240,735	$1,234,684	$1,171,286
Adjustment to Beginning Balance From Change in Translation Method	–	1,121	–
Net Income	39,650	101,369	147,068
Cash Dividends Declared:			
$1.20 Convertible preference – $1.20 per share	(1,394)	(1,569)	(2,198)
$4.60 Convertible preference – $4.60 per share in 1982 and 1981; $1.252 in 1980	(13,795)	(13,798)	(3,757)
Common – $.67 per share in 1982; $1.48 in 1981; $1.44 in 1980	(36,805)	(81,072)	(77,715)
Ending Balance	$1,228,391	$1,240,735	$1,234,684

Note 1. Summary of Significant Accounting Policies:

A. Consolidation

The consolidated financial statements include the accounts of the company and all of its domestic and foreign subsidiaries, except for the real estate subsidiaries. Real estate subsidiaries and 50% or less owned affiliates are reflected on the equity method. The company's Brazilian subsidiary is included in the consolidated financial statements using years ended November 30.

Certain minor amounts have been reclassified to conform to the current year's presentation.

B. Translation of Foreign Currency

The company's consolidated financial statements for 1982 and 1981 comply with the provisions of Statement Number 52 issued by the Financial Accounting Standards Board in 1981. Prior period financial statements have not been restated. (See Note 12.)

C. Inventories

Inventories are generally stated at the lower of average cost or market (market approximates net realizable value). Certain inventories of the paper and packaging segments, which represent approximately 20% of total inventories, are stated on the last-in, first-out (LIFO) method. (See Note 2.)

D. Capitalization and Amortization of Certain Costs

Preoperating expenses and start-up costs incurred in connection with the construction of major properties are deferred until such properties become operational and are then amortized over a five-year period.

E. Fixed Assets

Property, Plant, and Equipment, which includes capitalized leases, is stated at cost. Timber and Timberlands, which includes original costs, road construction costs, and reforestation costs, such as site preparation and planting costs, is stated at unamortized cost. Property taxes, surveying, fire control, and other forest management expenses are charged to expense as incurred.

For financial reporting purposes, plant and equipment are depreciated on the straight-line method over the estimated service lives of the individual assets. Leasehold improvements are amortized over the lesser of the lives of the leases or estimated service lives. Cost of timber harvested is based on the estimated quantity of timber available during the growth cycle and is credited directly to the asset accounts. (See Notes 5 and 9.)

F. Pensions

The company and its subsidiaries have contributory and noncontributory employee pension and retirement plans covering salaried and hourly employees. Past service costs are amortized over periods up to 40 years. Actuarial gains and losses are amortized over a 10 or 15-year period. Accrued pension costs are generally funded currently. (See Note 15.)

G. Earnings Per Common Share

Primary earnings per common share is computed by dividing net income, after deducting dividends on preference shares, by the average number of common shares outstanding during the year. Fully diluted earnings per common share assumes the average number of common shares outstanding is increased by the conversion of securities having a dilutive effect, with the addition to net income of dividends and after tax interest on such securities.

Note 2. Inventories:

If the lower of average cost or market method (which approximates current cost) had been utilized for inventories carried on the last-in, first-out (LIFO) method, inventory balances would have been increased by $97,759,000 and $103,951,000 at December 31, 1982 and 1981, respectively.

Note 3. Discontinued Furnishings Business:

In 1977, the company announced a plan to discontinue its furnishings business. Through December 31, 1982, substantially all of those operations had been disposed of for aggregate proceeds of $123,584,000. The company is actively seeking a purchaser for the remaining furnishings operation, a carpet manufacturer in Belgium, with net assets at December 31, 1982 of $9,020,000.

In 1980, the sale of the British carpet operations, together with a favorable adjustment of the estimated pre-disposition operating income from the remaining Belgian carpet business, resulted in a pretax charge to discontinued operations of $45,200,000. The unusually high tax benefit ($26,825,000 or 59.3%) resulted principally from the fact that the tax basis of the assets of these operations was higher than the book basis.

In the fourth quarter of 1981, the company sold securities, for less than book value, which had been received in connection with the earlier disposition of its U.S. carpet operations. There was also a reduction in the estimated realizable value of assets associated with its discontinued Belgian carpet operation. These events resulted in a pretax charge to discontinued operations of $26,952,000 and a tax benefit of $8,675,000.

Note 4. Equity in and Advances to Unconsolidated Affiliates:

Equity in and advances to unconsolidated affiliates consists of the following:

December 31	(in thousands of dollars)	1982	1981
Real estate affiliates:			
Investments and advances		$118,106	$62,729
Deferred gain on land sold to real estate subsidiary		(78,729)	(35,561)
		39,377	27,168
50% or less owned affiliates		33,499	37,659
		$ 72,876	$64,827

The company has sold certain land (including 47,000 acres in 1982) at fair market value to one of its unconsolidated real estate subsidiaries and deferred the gain represented by the excess of fair market value over original cost. Gains are recorded in the company's consolidated income only as the land is sold to non-affiliated parties.

Note 5. Property, Plant, and Equipment:

Property, Plant, and Equipment is summarized by major classifications as follows:

December 31 (in thousands of dollars)	1982			1981		
	Total	Owned	Leased	Total	Owned	Leased
Land and land improvements	$ 108,274	$ 96,500	$ 11,774	$ 105,681	$ 93,954	$ 11,727
Buildings	508,711	458,744	49,967	501,764	449,683	52,081
Machinery and equipment	2,277,728	1,988,738	288,990	2,175,073	1,884,678	290,395
Construction in progress	252,805	252,805	–	190,701	190,701	–
	3,147,518	2,796,787	350,731	2,973,219	2,619,016	354,203
Less – Accumulated depreciation	1,245,052	1,092,964	152,088	1,119,070	982,901	136,169
	$1,902,466	$1,703,823	$198,643	$1,854,149	$1,636,115	$218,034

Interest capitalized during 1982, 1981, and 1980 was $30,107,000, $15,102,000, and $18,987,000, respectively.

Note 6. Notes Payable and Lines of Credit:

The following summarizes short-term borrowings and lines of credit:

December 31 (in thousands of dollars)	1982	1981
Notes payable to banks	$ 9,162	$ 8,904
Commercial paper	–	30,619
Total short-term borrowings	$ 9,162	$ 39,523
Unused lines of credit – U.S.	$560,000	$460,000
Unused lines of credit – foreign	$ 48,000	$ 85,000

Early in 1982, U.S. lines of credit were increased to $560,000,000. At December 31, 1982, interest rates on approximately 80% of U.S. lines of credit and all foreign lines were no higher than the prime rate or its equivalent. A commitment fee of up to $\frac{1}{8}$% is required on the $560,000,000 of U.S. currency lines, $160,000,000 of which are available through 1984 and $400,000,000 of which are available to March 31, 1986, all on a revolving basis. At maturity the company can convert borrowings under each revolving credit agreement to a term loan, repayable over a four-year period. Commitments under the revolving credit agreements cannot be withdrawn provided the company continues to meet required conditions.

Note 7. Accounts Payable and Accrued Liabilities:

Accounts payable and accrued liabilities consists of the following:

December 31 (in thousands of dollars)	1982	1981
Accounts payable	$167,959	$165,756
Dividends payable	9,290	24,120
Accrued liabilities:		
Payrolls and commissions	77,580	71,927
Employee benefits	53,355	56,296
Taxes, other than income taxes	29,671	29,220
Other	47,011	41,060
Total accrued liabilities	207,617	198,503
	$384,866	$388,379

Note 8. Long-Term Debt:

Long-Term Debt (exclusive of current installments) consists of the following:

December 31 (in thousands of dollars)	1982	1981
Secured Debt, 8.8% average rate, payable through 2004 (a)	$ 41,187	$ 47,303
Unsecured Debt, 10.3% average rate, payable through 2012 (b)	619,190	520,340
Lease Obligations, 6.3% average rate, payable through 2008 (Note 9)	218,252	224,530
Timber Cutting Obligations, 8.0% average rate, payable through 1997 (c)	95,543	98,315
Other Contractual Obligations, 6.4% average rate, payable through 1999	33,778	34,396
Total (d)	$1,007,950	$924,884

(a) Such debt is secured by certain assets with a net book value at December 31, 1982 of $315,273,000.

(b) Unsecured debt includes revolving credit borrowings which mature in less than one year. The company has the option to renew or convert these borrowings through the expiration dates of the credit agreements provided that the company continues to meet required conditions. The company also utilizes commercial paper in lieu of direct borrowings under the credit agreements. At December 31, 1982, $108,002,000 of commercial paper and $20,245,000 of revolving credit borrowings have been classified as long-term debt, since the company intends to renew these or similar obligations through 1983 and into future periods. (See Note 6.)

(c) These timber cutting contracts have current minimum annual interest and principal payments in the amount of $12,464,000. The company has the right to cut the timber and all future growth until the termination date of the applicable contract at which time the company has the right to purchase the remaining timber for a nominal amount.

(d) The annual principal payment requirements under the terms of all long-term debt agreements for the years 1983 through 1987 are $26,766,000, $110,090,000, $57,803,000, $79,817,000, and $131,580,000, respectively.

The indentures and agreements relating to long-term debt arrangements, as well as the company's Certificate of Incorporation, contain restrictions on the payment of cash dividends. Under the most restrictive of these provisions, approximately $321,000,000 of consolidated retained earnings at December 31, 1982 is free of such restrictions.

Note 9. Commitments:

At December 31, 1982, future minimum lease payments for all capitalized leases and non-cancellable operating leases (net of sublease income) are:

Period (in thousands of dollars)	Capitalized Leases	Non-Cancellable Operating Leases
1983	$ 18,196	$10,952
1984	21,284	8,116
1985	21,474	5,335
1986	22,267	3,204
1987	21,287	2,406
Thereafter	329,335	8,858
Total Payments	433,843	$38,871
Less: Amount representing interest	211,260	
Present value of capitalized lease payments ($4,331 current; $218,252 long-term)	$222,583	

Payments under non-cancellable and cancellable operating leases that were charged to rental expense in 1982, 1981, and 1980 were $26,207,000, $26,444,000, and $28,129,000, respectively.

Note 10. Capital Shares:

Preference Shares

Each $1.20 and $4.60 preference share is cumulative and is convertible into one share and 1.667 shares of common stock, respectively, unless called for redemption, in which case the right to convert may end several days prior to the redemption date.

Each $1.20 preference share may be redeemed for $22.50 plus accrued dividends. At December 31, 1982 and 1981, 1,416,842 shares were authorized, and 1,163,575 and 1,212,640 shares, respectively, were issued.

Changes in $1.20 preference shares during the three years ended December 31, 1982 are as follows:

(in shares and thousands of dollars, net of treasury)	Shares	Amount
Balance at December 31, 1979	2,373,555	$ 13,211
Conversion to common shares	(850,752)	(4,828)
Conversion of long-term debt	12,122	310
Balance at December 31, 1980	1,534,925	8,693
Conversion to common shares	(335,831)	(1,938)
Conversion of long-term debt	3,376	86
Balance at December 31, 1981	1,202,470	6,841
Conversion to common shares	(49,065)	(285)
Balance at December 31, 1982	1,153,405	$ 6,556

Each $4.60 preference share may be redeemed currently at $53.68 and thereafter at prices that decline to $50.00 at October 1, 1990, plus accrued dividends in each case. At December 31, 1982 and 1981, 3,000,000 shares were authorized and 2,999,000 shares were issued.

At December 31, 1982 and 1981, 8,531,431 preference shares, for which no series has been designated, were authorized and unissued.

Common Shares

Changes in common shares during the three years ended December 31, 1982 are as follows:

(in shares and thousands of dollars, net of treasury)	Shares	Amount
Balance at December 31, 1979	53,299,976	$350,531
Conversion of preference shares	850,752	4,828
Exercise of stock options	2,781	66
Conversion of long-term debt	29,962	779
Contingent compensation plan	5,541	100
Acquisition of timberlands	336,250	8,409
Balance at December 31, 1980	54,525,262	364,713
Conversion of preference shares	337,498	1,986
Exercise of stock options	3,469	83
Conversion of long-term debt	20,105	524
Contingent compensation plan	7,084	129
Balance at December 31, 1981	54,893,418	367,435
Conversion of preference shares	49,065	285
Exercise of stock options	1,200	14
Conversion of long-term debt	19	1
Contingent compensation plan	7,963	155
Balance at December 31, 1982	54,951,665	$367,890

At December 31, 1982, common shares of the company are reserved for:

Conversion of preference shares	6,226,555
Conversion of long-term debt	88,944
Stock options granted or available for grant	3,491,992
Contingent compensation plan	1,702,647
Conversion of preferred shares of subsidiary	36,511
	11,546,649

Note 11. Stock Options:

The company has granted to officers and key employees options, accompanied by stock appreciation rights, to purchase common shares at the market price of the shares on the date of grant. The options expire ten years from the date of grant. Certain options become exercisable in full, and certain options become exercisable in installments, beginning one year from the date of grant.

Transactions in 1982 under the plans are summarized below:

	Shares
January 1, 1982 – Shares under option	1,275,705
Options granted	205,100
Options exercised at $12.25 per share or stock appreciation rights exercised	(15,772)
Options surrendered or cancelled	(104,008)
December 31, 1982 – Shares under option	1,361,025
Options exercisable at December 31, 1982	863,946
Shares available for grant:	
January 1, 1982	779,650
December 31, 1982	2,130,967

At December 31, 1982, the option prices ranged from $12.25 to $27.50 per share with an aggregate option price of $30,975,000.

Note 12. Cumulative Translation Adjustment:

The cumulative translation adjustment reflects the following:

Years Ended December 31 (in thousands of dollars)	1982	1981
Beginning balance	$ 6,719	$ —
Aggregate adjustment as of January 1, 1981 from change in translation method	—	7,349
Current year adjustment	4,173	(630)
Ending balance	$10,892	$6,719

Note 13. Other (Income) Expense – Net:

Other (income) expense – net includes the following:

Years Ended December 31 (in thousands of dollars)	1982	1981	1980
Interest income	$(20,677)	$(18,977)	$(13,621)
Foreign currency losses – net	2,907	2,061	665
Minority interest in income of subsidiaries	(3,486)	1,165	4,125
Equity in net income of unconsolidated affiliates	(10,822)	(10,544)	(6,922)
Royalty, rental, and commission income	(4,237)	(4,728)	(4,829)
Net gain on disposal of fixed assets and timberlands	(12,390)	(8,189)	(3,362)
Miscellaneous – net	(1,572)	(8,261)	(6,902)
	$(50,277)	$(47,473)	$(30,846)

Note 14. Income Taxes:

The provision for income taxes includes the following components:

Years Ended December 31 (in thousands of dollars)	1982	1981	1980
Provision for income taxes currently payable:			
Federal	$ (1,573)	$ (5,927)	$ 5,416
State and local	801	1,143	4,216
Foreign	29,030	19,679	8,069
	28,258	14,895	17,701
Provision for deferred income taxes:			
Federal	(19,558)	19,275	6,682
State and local	1,362	3,512	3,791
Foreign	(12,513)	(1,848)	13,447
	(30,709)	20,939	23,920
	$ (2,451)	$ 35,834	$ 41,621

Domestic and foreign income before income taxes are as follows:

Years Ended December 31 (in thousands of dollars)	1982	1981	1980
Domestic	$ 1,117	$103,924	$166,262
Foreign	36,082	51,556	57,779
	$ 37,199	$155,480	$224,041

Principal reasons for the variation between the effective rate and the statutory Federal income tax rate were as follows:

	1982	1981	1980
At statutory rate	46.0%	46.0%	46.0%
Income taxed at capital gains rate	–	(11.3)	(14.1)
Investment credit (flow-through method)	(55.7)	(12.0)	(15.2)
State and local taxes, net of Federal tax effect	3.1	1.6	1.9
All other – net	–	(1.3)	–
Effective income tax rate	(6.6)%	23.0%	18.6%

Deferred income taxes result from timing differences in income and expense between financial and taxable income, as follows:

Years Ended December 31 (in thousands of dollars)	1982	1981	1980
Excess of tax over financial depreciation and cost of timber harvested	$ 29,610	$ 14,890	$ 14,792
Capitalization of interest and deferral of preoperating and start-up costs (net) – deductible for tax purposes as incurred	9,860	2,317	6,352
Provision for accrued liabilities – deductible for tax purposes when paid	(9,897)	1,654	(1,530)
Effect on deferred taxes of net operating loss and investment tax credit carryforwards	(66,667)	–	–
All other – net	6,385	2,078	4,306
	$(30,709)	$ 20,939	$ 23,920

As of December 31, 1982, the company had available, for income tax return purposes, net operating loss carryforwards of $81,000,000 in the United States and $16,000,000 in Canada which expire in 1997 and 1987, respectively. In addition, the company had United States investment tax credit carryforwards of $58,000,000 which expire from 1995 through 1997. For financial reporting purposes, these carryforwards have been used to reduce deferred income taxes that were provided in 1982 or prior years. Such deferred taxes will be reinstated as the carryforwards are utilized in future years.

It is the company's intention to reinvest undistributed earnings of certain of its foreign subsidiaries and thereby indefinitely postpone their remittance. Accordingly, no provision had been made for income taxes on these undistributed earnings of $231,000,000 at December 31, 1982.

Note 15. Pension and Retirement Plans:

The company's pension expense for contributory and noncontributory employee pension and retirement plans for 1982, 1981, and 1980 was $46,946,000, $42,966,000, and $41,133,000, respectively. A comparison of accumulated benefits and net assets for the plans is presented below. These amounts are based on actuarial valuations and plan net assets at January 1, 1982 and 1981, respectively.

The actuarial present value of accumulated plan benefits based upon assumed rates of return averaging approximately 10% and 9% in 1982 and 1981, respectively, is as follows:

(in thousands of dollars)	1982	1981
Vested	$330,424	$339,575
Nonvested	36,887	37,159
	$367,311	$376,734
Net assets available for benefits	$380,270	$363,288

Note 16. Business Segments:

Information about the company's operations in different businesses for the three years ended December 31, 1982 is as follows:

(in thousands of dollars)	Building Products	Paper	Packaging	Total
Net Sales to Unaffiliated Customers:				
1982	$1,354,465	$1,656,082	$ 726,831	$3,737,378
1981	1,540,554	1,672,470	791,003	4,004,027
1980	1,557,041	1,472,640	723,037	3,752,718
Segment Income from Operations:				
1982	$ (33,920)	$ 163,103	$ (2,373)	$ 126,810
1981	9,606	207,828	36,522	253,956
1980	65,677	204,914	46,364	316,955
Identifiable Assets:				
1982	$ 706,160	$1,377,937	$ 591,360	$2,675,457
1981	776,593	1,254,305	628,335	2,659,233
1980	815,527	1,158,315	620,345	2,594,187
Capital Expenditures:				
1982	$ 9,757	$ 173,484	$ 11,065	$ 194,306
1981	37,007	135,199	35,884	208,090
1980	56,236	56,943	98,399	211,578
Depreciation Expense and Cost of Timber Harvested:				
1982	$ 64,138	$ 60,032	$ 36,802	$ 160,972
1981	70,116	57,595	35,541	163,252
1980	65,452	54,426	25,295	145,173

Information about the company's operations in different geographic areas for the three years ended December 31, 1982 is as follows:

(in thousands of dollars)	U.S.	Canada	Brazil	Total
Net Sales to Unaffiliated Customers:				
1982	$3,254,332	$ 324,271	$ 158,775	$3,737,378
1981	3,463,326	387,923	152,778	4,004,027
1980	3,248,992	384,770	118,956	3,752,718
Segment Income from Operations:				
1982	$ 93,307	$ (17,711)	$ 51,214	$ 126,810
1981	195,593	11,481	46,882	253,956
1980	259,290	18,853	38,812	316,955
Identifiable Assets:				
1982	$2,222,633	$ 239,174	$ 213,650	$2,675,457
1981	2,189,705	270,438	199,090	2,659,233
1980	2,143,947	266,065	184,175	2,594,187
Capital Expenditures:				
1982	$ 177,296	$ 1,457	$ 15,553	$ 194,306
1981	179,563	11,315	17,212	208,090
1980	188,637	19,392	3,549	211,578
Depreciation Expense and Cost of Timber Harvested:				
1982	$ 143,495	$ 10,403	$ 7,074	$ 160,972
1981	146,215	10,671	6,366	163,252
1980	126,547	12,569	6,057	145,173

A reconciliation of segment information to consolidated amounts is as follows:

Years Ended December 31 (in thousands of dollars)	1982	1981	1980
Segment income from operations	$ 126,810	$ 253,956	$ 316,955
Corporate general and administrative expense	(65,195)	(64,546)	(66,146)
Consolidated income from operations	$ 61,615	$ 189,410	$ 250,809
Segment identifiable assets	$2,675,457	$2,659,233	$2,594,187
Timber, timberlands, corporate, and other assets	796,537	783,993	745,331
Consolidated assets	$3,471,994	$3,443,226	$3,339,518
Segment capital expenditures	$ 194,306	$ 208,090	$ 211,578
Timber, timberlands, and corporate capital expenditures	62,111	126,058	143,542
Consolidated capital expenditures	$ 256,417	$ 334,148	$ 355,120
Segment depreciation expense and cost of timber harvested	$ 160,972	$ 163,252	$ 145,173
Corporate depreciation expense	6,189	5,346	2,329
Consolidated depreciation expense and cost of timber harvested	$ 167,161	$ 168,598	$ 147,502

The company's timber and timberlands assets and related capital expenditures support all segments but were not allocated to the various segments because identification of the specific timber and timberlands assets associated with any one segment is impossible. The timber that has been harvested has been transferred to the various business segments at cost.

Note 17. Quarterly Results of Operations (Unaudited):

Quarterly results of operations of the company for 1982 and 1981 were:

(in millions of dollars, except per share)

		March 31	June 30	September 30(a)	December 31
Net Sales	1982	$ 905.9	$ 950.6	$ 950.6	$930.3
	1981	1,000.8	1,065.4	1,008.8	929.0
Gross Profit	1982	$ 114.1	$ 126.2	$ 112.6	$124.5
	1981	162.9	177.1	143.4	121.4
Income Taxes (b)	1982	$ 0.3	$ 1.1	$ (4.5)	$ 0.6
	1981	15.4	22.7	3.8	(6.1)
Income from Continuing Operations	1982	$ 0.6	$ 11.5	$ 16.6	$ 10.9
	1981	30.3	45.9	24.5	19.0
Loss from Discontinued Operations (c)	1982	$ –	$ –	$ –	$ –
	1981	–	–	–	(18.3)
Net Income	1982	$ 0.6	$ 11.5	$ 16.6	$ 10.9
	1981	30.3	45.9	24.5	0.7
Primary Earnings Per Common Share: Continuing Operations	1982	$ (.06)	$ .14	$ .24	$ .13
	1981	.48	.77	.38	.28
Discontinued Operations	1982	$ –	$ –	$ –	$ –
	1981	–	–	–	(.33)
Net Income	1982	$ (.06)	$ .14	$ .24	$ .13
	1981	.48	.77	.38	(.05)
Fully Diluted Earnings Per Common Share: Continuing Operations	1982	$ (.06)	$ .14	$ .24	$ .13
	1981	.48	.75	.38	.27
Discontinued Operations	1982	$ –	$ –	$ –	$ –
	1981	–	–	–	(.32)
Net Income	1982	$ (.06)	$ .14	$ .24	$ .13
	1981	.48	.75	.38	(.05)

(a) The results for the third quarter of 1982 include a $.13 per share gain from a sale of land in Texas.

(b) The company reported a benefit from income taxes for the third quarter of 1982 and the fourth quarter of 1981. These benefits were due primarily to a change in the estimated tax rates for each period as a result of reduced profit levels.

(c) See Note 3.

Note 18. Inflation Accounting (Unaudited):

The company's financial statements are supplemented with selected current cost information which addresses the effects of changes in the specific prices of resources used by the company on the company's financial position and results of operations. Since the company measures a significant part of its operations in a functional currency other than the U.S. dollar (the Canadian dollar), constant dollar information is not required to be presented. Adjustments to current cost information to reflect the effects of general inflation are based on functional currency general price level indices.

Current cost accounting is a method of measuring and reporting certain existing assets and expenses associated with the use or sale of those assets at their current cost at the balance sheet date or at the date of use or sale. The current cost of property, plant, and equipment has been determined by adjusting historical acquisition costs through the use of external price indices. Depreciation expense has been recomputed based on the indexed asset valuations, using the same methods applied in the historical dollar statements.

Inventories have been adjusted to reflect the current costs of production or purchase. Cost of products sold has been adjusted to reflect the prices in effect when the products were sold.

The current cost of standing timber, including timber held under capitalized cutting contracts, includes costs that are directly related to reforestation and forest management, whether or not those costs are capitalized in the historical dollar statements. Annual forest management expenses were capitalized over the growth cycle to maturity assuming that the company's timber is one-half mature on the average. In computing the annual cost of timber harvested on a current cost basis, total reforestation and forest management expenses over the growth cycle were treated as the cost base. This amount was divided by the estimated total yield during the growth cycle to develop a per unit cost. The unit cost was multiplied by the units harvested during the year to arrive at the cost of timber harvested on a current cost basis. Timberlands values were determined by applying the estimated fair market value per acre in various regions to the total number of acres in those regions.

The gain from the decline in purchasing power of net monetary liabilities is determined separately for each functional currency by restating the opening and closing balances of, and transactions in, monetary assets and liabilities in units of constant functional currency purchasing power. The results are then translated into U.S. dollars at average exchange rates.

The following statement reflects the effect of these limited restatements during 1982:

Year Ended December 31, 1982 (in millions of dollars)	As Reported in the Historical Dollar Statements	Adjusted for Changes in Specific Prices
Net sales	$3,737	$3,737
Cost of products sold (excluding depreciation and cost of timber harvested)	3,111	3,124
Depreciation and cost of timber harvested	167	266
Selling, general, and administrative expenses (excluding depreciation)	397	397
Interest and debt expense	75	75
Other (income) expense – net	(50)	(50)
	3,700	3,812
Income (Loss) before income taxes	37	(75)
Income taxes	(3)	(3)
Income (Loss) from continuing operations	$ 40	$ (72)
Gain from decline in purchasing power of net monetary liabilities		$ 51
Increase in specific prices of inventories, property, plant, and equipment, and timber and timberlands held during the year*		$ 135
Effect of increase in general price level		195
Excess of increase in general price level over increase in specific prices		$ 60
Net translation adjustment		$ 1

*At December 31, 1982 the current cost of inventories was $556,000,000 and the current cost of property, plant, and equipment, and timber and timberlands, net of accumulated depreciation and cost of timber harvested, was $4,464,000,000.

The above table does not reflect any adjustments to net sales and other operating income and expenses, because they are considered to reflect average price levels for the year. Also, no adjustment has been made to the income tax provision which normally has the effect of increasing the company's effective tax rate.

The company has also restated selected financial data into average 1982 dollars for the five years ended December 31, 1982. The restatements of net sales, cash dividends declared, and market price per common share were calculated by indexing the historical dollar amounts into average 1982 dollars. Income from continuing operations, income from continuing operations per common share (primary), and gain from decline in purchasing power of net monetary liabilities have been computed as previously described. Net assets at year-end is a restatement of Shareholders' Equity at December 31, 1982, adjusted to reflect only the excess of current cost amounts for inventories, property, plant, and equipment, and timber and timberlands over their respective historical dollar amounts.

Information for the comparison of certain selected financial data adjusted for the effects of changing prices for the five years ended December 31, 1982 is as follows (in average 1982 dollars):

(in millions, except per share)	1982	1981	1980	1979	1978
Average consumer price index	289.1	272.4	246.8	217.4	195.4
Net sales...	$3,737	$4,250	$4,396	$4,988	$5,142
Current cost information:					
Income (Loss) from continuing operations.	(72)	-0-	87	186	
Income (Loss) from continuing operations per common share (primary).............	(1.59)	(.30)	1.48	3.48	
Excess of increase in general price level over increase in specific prices...........	60	34	37	28	
Net translation adjustment	1				
Net assets at year-end.......................	3,911	4,157	4,321	4,183	
Gain from decline in purchasing power of net monetary liabilities	51	102	149	156	
Cash dividends declared per common share ..	.67	1.57	1.69	1.76	1.73
Market price per common share at year-end..	23.48	20.28	27.41	30.02	30.28

This inflation accounting presentation is an attempt to describe some of the distorting effects inflation has on the company's historical financial information. The results of the methodology used in calculating these amounts do not purport to represent an exact measure of the impact that inflation has had on the company. The company cautions investors, analysts, and other readers against any simplistic use of this information.

Note 19. Contingencies:

While the result of any litigation contains an element of uncertainty, management presently believes that, with respect to known contingent liabilities, including lawsuits, federal taxes, and claims, if the plaintiffs were to prevail, the aggregate amount of any liability would not have a material adverse effect on the company's consolidated financial position.

Note 20. Extraordinary Item:

The extraordinary charge in 1980 of $25,322,000 (reduced by a related tax benefit of $8,345,000) represents the provision for the settlements and related expenses of certain antitrust suits. The tax benefit differs from the statutory tax rate because portions of the settlements were not deductible for income tax purposes.

Income Statement

Honeywell Inc. and Consolidated Subsidiaries
For the Years Ended December 31

(Dollars in Millions Except Per Share Amounts)	1982	1981	1980
Revenue			
Sales.	$4,593.9	$4,472.1	$4,118.8
Computer rental and service revenue	896.5	879.1	805.9
	5,490.4	5,351.2	4,924.7
Costs and Expenses			
Cost of sales	3,053.6	2,917.0	2,712.3
Cost of computer rental and service revenue	488.0	505.2	464.0
Research and development	396.9	368.8	295.4
Selling, general and administrative	1,217.1	1,146.0	1,015.5
	5,155.6	4,937.0	4,487.2
Interest			
Interest charges	98.7	95.1	66.5
Fees paid to finance subsidiaries	46.4	55.1	53.0
Income before income taxes of finance subsidiaries	(27.0)	(27.1)	(28.5)
Interest income	(66.2)	(71.9)	(50.9)
	51.9	51.2	40.1
Gain on Sale of Interests in Cii-HB and GEISCO	90.8		
Income and Income Taxes			
Income before income taxes	373.7	363.0	397.4
Income taxes	112.8	107.1	158.5
Equity income	10.4	0.4	37.4
Income before extraordinary income	271.3	256.3	276.3
Extraordinary income	1.6	3.0	12.6
Net income	$ 272.9	$ 259.3	$ 288.9
Earnings per Common Share			
Income before extraordinary income	$ 12.09	$ 11.25	$ 12.36
Extraordinary income	.07	.13	.56
Net income	$ 12.16	$ 11.38	$ 12.92

See accompanying Notes to Financial Statements (Pages 33 to 40).

Exhibit 2.2. Illustrated statements (Honeywell, Inc.). Reprinted by permission from the 1982 annual report of Honeywell, Inc.

Balance Sheet

Assets	(Dollars in Millions) 1982	1981
Current Assets		
Cash ....$	42.6	$ 41.3
Time deposits and marketable securities	273.7	249.9
Receivables...	1,180.4	878.2
Inventories	937.2	982.3
	2,433.9	2,151.7
Investments and Advances		
Finance subsidiaries	203.7	285.0
Other companies	205.7	329.8
	409.4	614.8
Property, Plant and Equipment		
Equipment for lease to others	810.2	1,005.5
Less accumulated depreciation	440.0	545.8
	370.2	459.7
Other property, plant and equipment......................................	1,636.1	1,395.0
Less accumulated depreciation	614.3	518.0
	1,021.8	877.0
	1,392.0	1,336.7
Other Assets		
Long-term receivables....	33.0	44.4
Goodwill..	118.3	102.0
Other...	84.3	81.2
Total Assets............. ....$	4,470.9	$4,330.8

See accompanying Notes to Financial Statements (Pages 33 to 40).

Liabilities and Stockholders' Equity	1982	1981
Current Liabilities		
Accounts payable.	$ **245.5**	$ 226.5
Short-term debt.	**115.9**	115.0
Customer advances	**121.4**	117.3
Income taxes.	**95.3**	119.3
Other accrued liabilities	**688.4**	621.4
	1,266.5	1,199.5

Other Liabilities		
Long-term debt.	**676.3**	605.8
Obligation for rental contracts conveyed to finance subsidiaries.	**14.0**	57.9
Deferred income taxes.	**307.0**	282.6
Other.	**63.7**	87.0

Stockholders' Equity		
Common stock—$1.50 par value		
Authorized—60,000,000 shares		
Issued—1982—23,191,168 shares		
1981—23,173,999 shares.	**34.8**	34.8
Additional paid-in capital	**659.1**	661.6
Retained earnings	**1,596.1**	1,401.6
Treasury stock—1982—463,309 shares.	**(32.0)**	
Accumulated foreign currency translation.	**(114.6)**	
	2,143.4	2,098.0

Total Liabilities and Stockholders' Equity.	**$4,470.9**	$4,330.8

Changes in Financial Position

Honeywell Inc. and Consolidated Subsidiaries
For the Years Ended December 31

(Dollars in Millions)	1982	1981	1980
Funds Provided			
Net income	$272.9	$259.3	$288.9
Items not affecting funds—			
Depreciation	299.7	300.0	256.2
Deferred income taxes	24.4	26.6	44.8
Equity income, including finance subsidiaries (less dividends received: 1982, $11.2; 1981, $14.2; 1980, $13.4)	(17.8)	(5.6)	(51.8)
	579.2	580.3	538.1
Funds Used			
Working capital—			
Receivables	84.2	53.2	138.1
Inventories	(45.1)	57.1	174.2
Accounts payable and accrued liabilities	(86.0)	(77.5)	(68.3)
Customer advances	(4.1)	(21.8)	(18.3)
Income taxes	24.0	59.0	(48.4)
	(27.0)	70.0	177.3
Increase (decrease) in investments and advances	(133.2)	16.1	(5.7)
Increase in property, plant and equipment	355.0	506.2	422.7
Increase (decrease) in long-term receivables	(31.7)	(43.0)	10.1
Increase (decrease) in goodwill	16.3	(0.5)	14.7
Dividends paid to stockholders	78.4	73.0	62.7
Accumulated foreign currency translation	114.6		
Other	26.4	15.4	(2.9)
	398.8	637.2	678.9
Net funds provided (used)	180.4	(56.9)	(140.8)
Financing Activities			
Debt transactions—			
Issuance of long-term debt	131.3	181.6	81.6
Reduction of long-term debt	(60.8)	(48.1)	(51.0)
Increase in short-term debt	0.9	8.7	24.7
Finance subsidiary transactions—			
Increase (decrease) in receivables sold to finance subsidiaries	(238.3)	43.5	85.6
Increase (decrease) in obligation for rental contracts conveyed to finance subsidiaries	(43.9)	2.5	53.6
(Increase) decrease in capital notes receivable from finance subsidiaries	90.0	(125.0)	(15.0)
Purchase of treasury stock	(108.9)		
Treasury stock reissued	31.5		
Exercise of stock options	42.9	37.7	30.9
	(155.3)	102.9	210.4

Notes to Financial Statements

1. Accounting Policies

Consolidation—The consolidated financial statements and accompanying data include Honeywell Inc. and subsidiaries except finance and real estate subsidiaries, whose operations are dissimilar to the manufacturing operations of the consolidated group. All material transactions between the consolidated companies are eliminated.

Revenue—Revenue from product sales is recorded when title is passed to the customer. This usually occurs at the time of delivery or acceptance. Revenue from cost reimbursement-type contracts is recorded as costs are incurred. Revenue from long-term contracts is recorded on the percentage-of-completion basis.

Revenue from most computer lease contracts is recorded as earned over the lives of the contracts. A portion of future rental receipts under such contracts is sold to Honeywell's finance subsidiaries and classified as "obligation for rental contracts conveyed to finance subsidiaries." Long-term lease contracts that qualify as sales-type leases are recorded as sales when the equipment is installed.

Tax Credits—U.S. tax credits are included in income as a reduction of the federal income tax provision in the year the credits are realized for tax purposes.

Earnings Per Common Share—Earnings per share amounts are based on the average number of common shares outstanding during the year.

Marketable Securities—Marketable securities are carried at cost, which approximates market.

Inventories—Inventories are valued at the lower of cost or market. Cost is determined using the weighted-average method. Market is based on estimated realizable value.

The cost of manufactured products is based on standards developed for individual items from current material, labor and overhead costs at normal activity levels. Standard costs are adjusted to actual by application of manufacturing variances.

Payments received from customers on uncompleted contracts are deducted from applicable inventories.

Investments—Investments in nonconsolidated subsidiaries and companies owned 20 to 50 percent are valued at cost, adjusted for Honeywell's cumulative share of the undistributed earnings since acquisition.

Property—Property is carried at cost and depreciated over estimated useful lives using the straight-line method. Equipment for lease to others is depreciated over a five-year life.

Goodwill—Goodwill is amortized over not more than a forty-year period.

Reclassifications—Certain amounts in the 1981 and 1980 financial statements have been reclassified to conform with the presentation of similar amounts in the 1982 financial statements.

2. Accounting Change

Honeywell adopted Statement of Financial Accounting Standards No. 52, "Foreign Currency Translation," in the second quarter of 1982, retroactive to January 1, 1982. Financial statements for 1981 and 1980 were not restated.

Following is a summary of the changes in accumulated foreign currency translation:

Adjustment at January 1, 1982	$(64.1)
Translation adjustments	(50.5)
Balance December 31, 1982	$(114.6)

Foreign currency exchange gains (losses), net of income taxes were as follows:

	1982	1981	1980
Honeywell and subsidiaries	$ 1.5	$16.8	$10.3
Equity companies	(0.4)	65.2	7.2
	$ 1.1	$82.0	$17.5

3. Changes in Investments

In the first quarter of 1982, Honeywell sold its 16-percent interest in GE Information Services Co. (GEISCO) to General Electric Co. This resulted in a gain of $51.6, increasing net income $36.0 ($1.60 per share).

On January 1, 1982, Honeywell discontinued using the equity method of accounting for its investment in Cii Honeywell Bull. In the second quarter of 1982, Honeywell entered into an agreement with Cii Honeywell Bull for a new 10-year technical and commercial association between Cii Honeywell Bull and Honeywell Information Systems. The agreement covers distribution arrangements for the two companies' common product line, technology exchanges and cooperative development. At the same time, Compagnie des Machines Bull purchased 27.1 percent of Cii Honeywell Bull common stock held by Honeywell Information Systems for $150 million. This reduced Honeywell's ownership in Cii Honeywell Bull to 19.9 percent from 47 percent. The Cii Honeywell Bull sale resulted in a gain of $39.2, increasing net income $30.3 ($1.35 per share).

4. Acquisitions

During 1982 Honeywell acquired four companies in exchange for 482,925 treasury shares and $19.7 in cash. During 1981 Honeywell acquired five companies for $35.6 in cash. During 1980 two companies were acquired for $24.6 in cash.

The acquisitions were accounted for as purchases, and the resultant goodwill amounted to $25.0 in 1982, and $16.3 in 1980. Goodwill in 1981 was not material. The operations of the companies have been included in the consolidated financial statements from the dates of acquisition. The proforma results for 1982, 1981 and 1980, assuming the acquisitions had been made at the beginning of each year, would not be significantly different from reported results.

Notes to Financial Statements

5. Income Taxes

1982	U.S. Federal	Foreign	State	Total
Current	$ 45.7	$ 29.0	$ 12.1	$ 86.8
Deferred	9.2	16.4	(1.2)	24.4
Tax effect of foreign operating loss carryforwards		1.6		1.6
	$ 54.9	$ 47.0	$ 10.9	$112.8

1981				
Current	$ 40.1	$ 29.0	$ 9.5	$ 78.6
Deferred	18.9	5.0	2.7	26.6
Tax effect of foreign operating loss carryforwards		1.9		1.9
	$ 59.0	$ 35.9	$ 12.2	$ 107.1

1980				
Current	$ 51.5	$ 53.4	$ 5.6	$ 110.5
Deferred	49.7	(6.1)	1.2	44.8
Tax effect of foreign operating loss carryforwards		3.2		3.2
	$ 101.2	$ 50.5	$ 6.8	$ 158.5

Amounts shown above for U.S. Federal—Current have been reduced by U.S. tax credits of $41.7 in 1982, $33.4 in 1981 and $23.3 in 1980.

Deferred tax expense results from timing differences between income for tax and for financial statement purposes. Sources of these differences and their tax effects were:

	1982	1981	1980
Excess of tax over book depreciation	$ (18.5)	$ 30.0	$ (2.8)
Gain on installment sales, conversion sales, sales-type leases and long-term contracts deferred for tax purposes	38.9	8.7	32.7
Undistributed earnings of Domestic International Sales Corporations	10.0	6.1	6.3
Accruals	(13.7)	(13.5)	4.4
Other	7.7	(4.7)	4.2
	$ 24.4	$ 26.6	$ 44.8

The combined effective income tax rate differed from the U.S. federal statutory rate as follows:

	1982	1981	1980
U.S. federal statutory rate	46%	46%	46%
U.S. tax credits	(11)	(9)	(6)
UK tax credits related to inventories		(4)	
Variation in tax rates on foreign income		(3)	(2)
Capital gain and tax exempt income	(7)	(3)	(1)
Other	2	3	3
Effective rate	30%	30%	40%

Income before income taxes consists of the following:

	1982	1981	1980
Domestic	$225.3	$241.8	$249.8
Foreign	134.1	114.7	160.0
Intercompany eliminations	14.3	6.5	(12.4)
	$373.7	$363.0	$397.4

Foreign subsidiaries had operating loss carryforwards approximating $29.8 at December 31, 1982.

6. Extraordinary Income

Extraordinary income consists of tax benefits of operating loss carryforwards as follows:

	1982	1981	1980
Foreign subsidiaries	$ 1.6	$ 1.9	$ 3.
Equity in extraordinary income of Cii Honeywell Bull		1.1	9.
	$ 1.6	$ 3.0	$12.

7. Leasing Arrangements

As Lessor—Receivables from sales-type lease contracts for computer equipment are as follows:

	1982	1981
Total minimum lease payments to be received	$ 81.5	$ 97.7
Less: Unearned income	22.5	23.8
Allowance for doubtful accounts	0.4	0.6
Net investment in sales-type leases	$ 58.6	$ 73.3

Minimum future rentals to be received as of December 31, 1982, under noncancellable leases for computer equipment are as follows:

	Sales-Type Leases	Operating Leases
1983	$ 99.7	$254.7
1984	75.4	136.1
1985	62.3	101.1
1986	43.5	55.2
1987	23.0	13.5
1988 and beyond	19.0	14.4
	322.9	575.0
Less amounts sold to finance subsidiaries	241.4	14.0
	$ 81.5	$561.0

As Lessee—Minimum lease commitments outstanding at December 31, 1982, with the majority having initial lease periods ranging from one to thirty years, are as follows:

	Capital Leases	Operating Leases
1983	$ 2.4	$ 79.7
1984	2.3	65.3
1985	1.6	51.1
1986	1.2	39.5
1987	1.0	24.4
1988 and beyond	12.7	115.1
	21.2	$375.1
Less interest	9.7	
Present value of net minimum lease payments	$ 11.5	

Rent expense for operating leases was $104.0 in 1982, $89.8 in 1981 and $77.1 in 1980.

Substantially all leases are for plant, warehouse, office space and automobiles. A number of the leases contain renewal options ranging from one to thirty years. Certain operating lease contracts grant Honeywell the option to purchase the leased assets at prices reduced by a portion of prior rental payments.

8. Receivables

Receivables have been reduced by an allowance for doubtful accounts as follows:

	1982	1981
Receivables—current	$ 31.1	$ 24.4
Long-term receivables	1.0	1.1

Receivables include approximately $27.5 in 1982 and $22.8 in 1981 billed to customers but not paid pursuant to retainage provisions in construction contracts. These balances are due upon completion of the contracts, generally within one year.

9. Inventories

Payments received from customers on uncompleted contracts are deducted from applicable inventories in the amounts of $289.5 at December 31, 1982 and $207.5 at December 31, 1981.

10. Finance Subsidiaries

Honeywell's nonconsolidated finance subsidiaries, located in the United States and Canada, purchase customer obligations under lease and sales contracts for computer systems, related products and computer services from Honeywell. As consideration, Honeywell pays a fee based upon the finance subsidiaries' expenses and interest income. In the United States fees are paid under a formula providing fixed charge coverage of 150 percent. All administrative functions relating to the receivables are performed by Honeywell.

Following are the summary of operations and condensed balance sheet of the finance subsidiaries.

Summary of Operations

	1982	1981	1980
Fees from Honeywell	$ 46.4	$ 55.1	$ 53.0
Interest income	41.3	40.0	38.8
	87.7	95.1	91.8
Interest and other expenses	60.7	68.0	63.3
Income before income taxes	27.0	27.1	28.5
Income taxes	8.4	8.8	10.1
Net income	$ 18.6	$ 18.3	$ 18.4
Dividends paid to Honeywell	$ 10.0	$ 5.0	$ 5.0

Condensed Balance Sheet

Cash and marketable securities	$ 0.1	$ 5.0
Receivables, including amounts due beyond one year	483.3	765.5
Other assets	0.8	1.0
	$484.2	$771.5
Short-term debt	$ 49.7	$249.2
Accrued liabilities	1.9	1.3
Long-term debt	196.9	200.0
Senior subordinated notes	32.0	36.0
Capital notes payable to Honeywell	50.0	140.0
Stockholder's equity	153.7	145.0
	$484.2	$771.5

11. Other Companies

Following is a summary of financial data pertaining to other nonconsolidated subsidiaries and companies owned 20 to 50 percent. Major companies included are Yamatake Honeywell Co., Ltd., Coeur d'Alene Development Inc. and Magnetic Peripherals Inc. Cii Honeywell Bull was included in 1981 and 1980. The amounts for equity in income and net assets are net of intercompany adjustments and eliminations.

	1982	1981	1980
Revenue	$1,323.9	$2,679.5	$2,490.5
Gross profit	$ 258.9	$ 709.9	$ 862.0
Income before extraordinary income	$ 25.2	$ 1.8	$ 119.6
Extraordinary income		0.1	18.4
Net income	$ 25.2	$ 1.9	$ 138.0
Equity in income—			
Before extraordinary income	$ 10.4	$ 0.4	$ 37.4
Extraordinary income		1.1	9.4
Net income	$ 10.4	$ 1.5	$ 46.8
Current assets	$ 525.6	$1,446.0	
Noncurrent assets	197.6	956.1	
	723.2	2,402.1	
Current liabilities	407.3	1,193.0	
Noncurrent liabilities	79.4	576.1	
	486.7	1,769.1	
Net assets	$ 236.5	$ 633.0	
Equity in net assets	$ 98.4	$ 274.3	

12. Other Property, Plant and Equipment

	1982	1981
Land	$ 40.3	$ 33.7
Buildings and improvements	424.4	379.9
Machinery and equipment	1,069.7	891.5
Construction in progress	101.7	89.9
	$1,636.1	$1,395.0

13. Other Accrued Liabilities

	1982	1981
Payroll and related costs	$232.9	$201.8
Retirement and pension plans	72.1	70.2
Other taxes	32.9	34.3
Interest	20.7	23.4
Sundry	329.8	291.7
	$688.4	$621.4

Notes to Financial Statements

14. Short-Term Debt

Honeywell has lines of credit that total $1,279.2, various amounts of which are available to different parts of the Company, including in some cases nonconsolidated finance and real estate subsidiaries. Of these lines, $113.0 serve as backup for a like amount of short-term borrowings.

Domestic confirmed and revolving credit lines of $671 with 43 banks are available. In addition, multi-currency revolving credit lines of $203 with 16 domestic and foreign banks are available. There were no borrowings on these lines at December 31, 1982. These lines have commitment fee and/or compensating balance requirements. During 1982 the Honeywell collected bank balances, including compensating balances for the credit lines and services, averaged $10.6 and the equivalent Honeywell recorded balances averaged less than $1.0. The difference from bank balances is attributable to the normal items in process of collection.

The remaining credit facilities have been arranged by foreign subsidiaries in accordance with customary lending practices in their respective countries of operation.

Short-term debt consists of the following:

	1982	1981
Notes payable	$ 67.3	$ 81.3
Current maturities of long-term debt	48.6	33.7
	$115.9	$115.0

15. Long-Term Debt

HONEYWELL INC.		
9⅜% due 1984	$ 50.0	$ 50.0
6% due 1986	6.2	6.2
9.06% due 1987	50.0	50.0
4.8% due 1983 to 1990	25.0	26.8
6.1% due 1986 to 1992	31.1	35.9
11⅛% due 1992	100.0	
6⅜% to 10% due 1983 to 1998	7.3	3.9
9⅜% due 1990 to 2009	150.0	150.0
14⅛% due 1992 to 2011	150.0	150.0
CONSOLIDATED SUBSIDIARIES		
5% convertible due 1983, U.S. dollars (a)	15.5	15.5
9½% to 23⅞% due 1983 to 1990, Italian lira	75.6	79.7
5% to 17½% due 1983 to 2006, various currencies	14.2	21.5
6% subordinated convertible due 1986, U.S. dollars (a)	50.0	50.0
	724.9	639.5
Less amount included in short-term debt	48.6	33.7
	$676.3	$605.8

(a) Convertible at principal amount into shares of Honeywell common stock at the option of the holder. The conversion privilege related to the debentures due 1983 expired in February 1983; the subordinated debentures due 1986 are convertible at any time at $120 per share. Honeywell has reserved 567,345 shares for possible conversion of the convertible debentures outstanding at December 31, 1982.

Although substantially all long-term debt may be redeemed prior to maturity at the option of Honeywell, $100.0 is not pre-payable until 1989 and $50.0 is not pre-payable until 1985. Two issues of $150.0 each are not pre-payable until 1989 or 1991 if the prepayment is in conjunction with refunding at a lower interest cost.

Annual sinking-fund and maturity requirements for the next five years on long-term debt outstanding at December 31, 1982 are as follows:

1983	$48.6
1984	75.0
1985	16.2
1986	70.4
1987	58.9

16. Capital Stock

	Common Stock	Additional Paid-In Capital	Treasury Stock
Balance January 1, 1980	$33.4	$594.4	$ —
Exercise of stock options— 429,868 newly issued shares	0.6	30.3	
Balance December 31, 1980	34.0	624.7	—
Exercise of stock options— 514,115 newly issued shares	0.8	36.9	
Balance December 31, 1981	34.8	661.6	—
Purchase of treasury stock— 1,519,600 shares			(108.9)
Exercise of stock options— 573,366 treasury shares issued		0.2	42.1
17,169 newly issued shares		0.6	
Acquisitions— 482,925 treasury shares issued		(3.3)	34.8
Balance December 31, 1982	$34.8	$659.1	$ (32.0)

Key Employee Stock Option Plans—Options to purchase common stock have been granted at 100 percent of the market price at time of granting, pursuant to plans approved by the stockholders. At December 31, 1982 there were 515,117 shares reserved for options granted and for granting additional options. The following is a summary of stock options:

	1982	1981	1980
Granted—			
Number of shares	154,830	114,550	2,075
Price per share	$68	$88-$105	$89
Exercised—			
Number of shares	50,717	19,250	62,616
Price per share	$38-$80	$38-$68	$33-$73
Outstanding, December 31—			
Number of shares	363,903	271,192	183,503
Price per share	$33-$105	$33-$152	$33-$152

Long Range Stock Incentive Plan—The plan authorizes the issuance of common stock to certain key employees, as compensation, based on actual performance measured against pre-established Honeywell earnings per share growth objectives. The Board of Directors may elect to pay up to one half of this compensation in cash. The plan has been approved by the stockholders. The cost of the plan was not significant in any year. At December 31, 1982 there were 500,000 shares reserved for the long-range stock incentive plan.

Employee Stock Purchase Plans—Options have been granted to eligible employees of Honeywell and certain subsidiaries to purchase common stock principally at the lower of 85 percent of the market price at the time of grant or at the time of exercise. At December 31, 1982, there were 1,391,029 shares reserved for employee stock purchase plans. The following is a summary of options exercised under these plans:

	1982	1981	1980
Number of shares	489,815	495,938	367,552
Average price per share	$68	$69	$65

Preference Stock—Twenty-five million preference shares with a par value of $1 have been authorized. None have been issued at December 31, 1982.

17. Retained Earnings

	1982	1981	1980
Balance January 1	$1,401.6	$1,215.3	$ 989.1
Net income	272.9	259.3	288.9
Dividends—			
1982—$3.50 per share			
1981—$3.20 per share			
1980—$2.80 per share	(78.4)	(73.0)	(62.7)
Balance December 31	$1,596.1	$1,401.6	$1,215.3

Certain long-term debt agreements contain restrictions as to the amount of retained earnings available for the payment of dividends by Honeywell. Under the most restrictive agreement, retained earnings of approximately $650 were available for payment of dividends at December 31, 1982. There are no significant restrictions as to the payment of dividends by Honeywell's consolidated subsidiaries.

The undistributed earnings of nonconsolidated subsidiaries amounted to $111.5 at December 31, 1982. Of this amount $17.9 is restricted as to the payment of dividends. The undistributed earnings of companies owned 20 to 50 percent amounted to $47.5 at December 31, 1982.

18. Retirement Plans

Honeywell and its domestic subsidiaries provide retirement plans for employees, which are financed by Honeywell contributions. Actuarially determined amounts are charged to expense and paid to the master trust maintained in conjunction with the plans. These trust funds are irrevocably devoted to servicing retirement benefits and are not available to the Company. The cost of these plans totaled $91.5 in 1982, $94.3 in 1981, and $79.9 in 1980. Cost includes the funding of prior service costs, which are amortized over periods not exceeding 30 years. In 1982 the amortization period for one plan was reduced from 20 to 10 years, which increased 1982 costs by $4.1.

A comparison of estimated benefits and net assets at June 30, the fiscal year end of the plans, is as follows:

	1982	1981
Actuarial present value of accumulated plan benefits—		
Vested	$775.3	$746.6
Nonvested	120.7	92.4
	$896.0	$839.0
Net assets available for benefits	$787.7	$741.8

Retirement costs were determined by our actuary in 1981 using the "Entry Age Normal" actuarial cost method. In 1982 the plans were changed to the "Unit Credit" actuarial cost method. The change is expected over an extended period to reduce fluctuations in retirement costs as a percentage of payroll. The change reduced 1982 retirement costs by $10.8. The assumed rate of return used in determining the actuarial present value of accumulated plan benefits was eight percent except for retirees for whom assets have been dedicated in 1982 to cover benefit payments over a 38-year period. The dedicated assets earn interest at 15.6 percent, which resulted in a reduction in 1982 retirement costs of $9.8.

On January 1, 1982 the retirement plans were amended to provide additional benefits, which increased annual costs by $2.6. The present value of vested benefits increased by $26.6, and the nonvested benefits decreased by $1.6.

All major foreign subsidiaries provide plans for employees consistent with local practices. The foreign plans are not required to report pursuant to ERISA and do not otherwise determine the actuarial value of accumulated benefits or net assets available for benefits as calculated and disclosed above.

The cost of all plans, domestic and foreign, totaled $108.2 in 1982, $111.9 in 1981 and $98.7 in 1980.

19. Foreign Subsidiaries

The following is a summary of financial data pertaining to foreign subsidiaries:

	1982	1981	1980
Net income	$ 88.4	$ 77.4	$ 112.5
Assets	$1,368.2	$1,453.2	
Liabilities	673.0	730.6	
Net assets	$ 695.2	$ 722.6	

Insofar as can be reasonably determined, there are no foreign exchange restrictions that materially affect the financial position and the operating results of Honeywell and its subsidiaries; however, certain foreign countries have various exchange control regulations that do not permit ready transfers of funds without appropriate approvals.

The cumulative unremitted foreign earnings for which no U.S. income taxes have been accrued were $535.8 at December 31, 1982. There is no intention to remit a significant amount of such earnings to the parent company, since continued reinvestment is required to assist in financing foreign operations. It is anticipated that, to the extent such earnings are remitted, it will not result in any material additional tax liability under current tax laws.

Notes to Financial Statements

20. Segment Information

Honeywell is engaged in four industry segments—Control Products, Control Systems, Aerospace and Defense, and Information Systems.

Control Products includes microelectronic and electro-mechanical components and products for residential, commercial, and industrial applications which are marketed on an individual product basis to wholesalers, distributors, and original equipment manufacturers. Control Systems includes sophisticated commercial building and industrial systems, both analog and digital computer-based, which are designed for data acquisition, monitoring, control, and management of customer processes and equipment. Aerospace and Defense includes the design, development and production of guidance systems and controls for military and commercial aircraft, space vehicles, missiles, naval vessels and military vehicles. Information Systems includes products and services related to electronic data processing systems for business, governmental and scientific applications.

Information concerning Honeywell's revenue, operating profit and identifiable assets by industry segment can be found on Page 7. This information for 1982, 1981 and 1980 is an integral part of these financial statements. Revenue includes external revenue only. Intersegment revenue is not significant. Corporate assets are principally cash, time deposits and marketable securities, and investments. Following is additional financial information relating to industry segments.

	1982	1981	1980
Capital expenditures			
Control Products	$ 86.2	$ 88.3	$ 75.2
Control Systems	73.5	56.4	63.2
Aerospace and Defense	76.8	47.5	38.6
Information Systems—			
Equipment for lease to others	245.2	308.3	282.1
Other property, plant and equipment	61.9	80.6	69.4
Corporate	53.0	58.5	27.8
	$ 596.6	$ 639.6	$ 556.3
Depreciation			
Control Products	$ 40.0	$ 32.3	$ 24.5
Control Systems	37.6	32.8	28.1
Aerospace and Defense	27.2	23.3	15.6
Information Systems—			
Equipment for lease to others	128.1	154.5	146.6
Other property, plant and equipment	51.1	42.3	30.9
Corporate	15.7	14.8	10.5
	$ 299.7	$ 300.0	$ 256.2
U.S. government contract revenue			
Control Products	$ 7.4	$ 8.3	$ 6.2
Control Systems	51.5	46.0	44.0
Aerospace and Defense	771.4	696.1	612.6
Information Systems	213.8	198.5	169.3
	$1,044.1	$ 948.9	$ 832.1

Honeywell engages in material operations in foreign countries, the majority of which are located in Europe. Other geographic areas of operations include Canada, Mexico, Australia, South America, and the Far East.

Following is financial information relating to geographic areas:

	1982	1981	1980
External revenue			
United States	$3,988.6	$3,838.5	$3,456.3
Europe	1,022.4	1,052.7	1,086.4
Other areas	479.4	460.0	382.0
	$5,490.4	$5,351.2	$4,924.7
Transfers between geographic areas			
United States	$ 241.9	$ 262.6	$ 266.9
Europe	16.6	25.5	27.4
Other areas	14.1	13.8	12.9
	$ 272.6	$ 301.9	$ 307.2
Total revenue			
United States	$4,230.5	$4,101.1	$3,723.2
Europe	1,039.0	1,078.2	1,113.8
Other areas	493.5	473.8	394.9
Eliminations	(272.6)	(301.9)	(307.2)
	$5,490.4	$5,351.2	$4,924.7
Operating profit			
United States	$ 252.8	$ 363.9	$ 342.8
Europe	128.8	75.6	145.1
Other areas	30.9	53.3	41.6
Eliminations	14.3	6.5	(12.4)
Operating profit	426.8	499.3	517.1
Gain on sale of interests in Cii-HB and GEISCO	90.8		
General corporate expense	(25.8)	(13.2)	(28.7)
Interest expense	(118.1)	(123.1)	(91.0)
Income before income taxes	$ 373.7	$ 363.0	$ 397.4
Identifiable assets			
United States	$2,690.6	$2,373.9	$2,160.4
Europe	791.2	878.6	800.9
Other areas	356.9	324.4	254.4
Corporate	769.8	893.8	701.5
Eliminations	(137.6)	(139.9)	(124.6)
	$4,470.9	$4,330.8	$3,892.6

Honeywell transfers products from one geographic area for resale in another. These transfers are not comparable to direct sales to unaffiliated customers. They are normally priced lower than external selling prices and are intended to provide both areas with an equitable share of the overall profit.

21. Contingencies

Honeywell has substantial U.S. government contracts and subcontracts, the prices of which are subject to redetermination. Management anticipates that adjustments, if any, would not have a material effect on net income.

At December 31, 1982, Honeywell has guaranteed $50.7 of its nonconsolidated companies' debt and is contingently liable for receivables discounted in the amount of $9.9.

Honeywell is a party to a large number of legal proceedings, some of which are for substantial amounts. It is the opinion of management and legal counsel that losses in connection with these matters will not have a material effect on net income.

22. Quarterly Data (Unaudited)

1982	1st Qtr.	2nd Qtr.	3rd Qtr.	4th Qtr.
Revenue	$1,261.0	$1,321.4	$1,335.8	$1,572.2
Cost of revenue	815.3	828.7	866.3	1,031.3
Income before extraordinary income	55.1	84.5	43.7	88.0
Per share	2.46	3.78	1.96	3.89
Net income	55.5	85.6	43.8	88.0
Per share	2.48	3.83	1.96	3.89
1981				
Revenue	$1,210.8	$1,304.3	$1,269.5	$1,566.6
Cost of revenue	760.0	837.9	818.1	1,006.2
Income before extraordinary income	50.9	70.7	32.1	102.6
Per share	2.25	3.11	1.43	4.46
Net income	52.3	71.4	32.4	103.2
Per share	2.31	3.15	1.43	4.49

Net income for the first quarter of 1982 included $36.0 ($1.60 per share) from the sale of Honeywell's interest in GEISCO. Net income for the second quarter of 1982 included $30.3 ($1.35 per share) from the sale of a 27.1 percent interest in Cii Honeywell Bull and $9.1 ($0.41 per share) from previously deferred earnings on sales to Cii Honeywell Bull.

Net income for the fourth quarter of 1982 and 1981 was reduced $15.8 and $20.0, respectively, for the cost of consolidating operations in the United States.

	Dividends Per Share	Common Stock Price (New York Stock Exch.) High	Low
1982—First Quarter	$.85	$ 77⅞	$ 62⅛
Second Quarter	.85	75¼	64¼
Third Quarter	.90	86¾	59½
Fourth Quarter	.90	105¾	77¼
1981—First Quarter	$.75	$114½	$ 96
Second Quarter	.75	106½	82
Third Quarter	.85	91¼	77¾
Fourth Quarter	.85	86¾	69

Stockholders of record on February 3, 1983 totaled 42,792.

23. Supplementary Financial Data Adjusted for the Effect of Changing Prices (Unaudited)

The following information shows the impact of inflation on Honeywell's operations.

In the column headed "Adjusted for Specific Price Changes (Current Cost)," depreciation and cost of revenue are restated to reflect the current cost of the related assets.

The effects of specific price changes are determined as follows:

(a) Cost of revenue and inventories are valued at latest standards adjusted to actual cost by application of variances and, where appropriate, by the use of current price quotations or indexes published by U.S. or foreign government agencies.

(b) Property values are estimated based on current market quotations or by adjusting historical costs by indexes published by U.S. or foreign government agencies. Equipment for lease to others is valued based on estimated costs of equipment of equivalent performance that is currently manufactured. Land and building values are based on current appraisals, assessments or engineering estimates. Depreciation is calculated on current property values, using the same method and rates of depreciation that are used to prepare Honeywell's primary financial statements.

The impact of inflation is calculated only on cost of revenue, depreciation, inventories and property. Restatement of these items reflects the most significant impact of inflation, because inventories and property are acquired over an extended period and are reported at historical cost in the financial statements. No adjustments are made to income tax expense for deferred income taxes that might arise because of differences between income as restated for changing prices and income as reported for tax purposes.

Adjustments to Current Cost information to reflect the effects of general inflation are based on the U.S. Consumer Price Index for all Urban Consumers.

Financial statements based on historical costs have served Honeywell well, and we believe that they continue to fairly present our operating results and financial position. However, we support experiments to account for the effects of inflation.

Notes to Financial Statements

Supplementary Statement of Income Before Extraordinary Income Adjusted for Changing Prices
For the Year Ended December 31, 1982

	As Reported (Historical Cost)	Adjusted for Specific Price Changes (Current Cost)
Revenue	$5,490.4	$5,490.4
Cost of revenue (excluding depreciation)	3,302.6	3,324.7
Depreciation	299.7	324.9
Other costs and expenses (excluding depreciation)	1,605.2	1,605.2
Gain on sale of interests in Cii-HB and GEISCO	(90.8)	(90.8)
Income taxes	112.8	112.8
Equity income	(10.4)	(10.4)
Income before extraordinary income	$ 271.3	$ 224.0
Income before extraordinary income per common share	$ 12.09	$ 9.98
Foreign currency translation		$ (67.0)
Inventories		$ 946.3
Equipment for lease to others (net of depreciation)		326.3
Other property (net of depreciation)		1,313.6
Gain from decline in purchasing power of net monetary items		$ 20.6
Increase in specific prices (current cost) of inventories, equipment for lease to others, and other property held during the year		$ 161.6
Increase in general price level		105.7
Excess of increase in specific prices over increase in general price level		$ 55.9

Five-Year Comparison of Selected Supplementary Financial Data Adjusted for Effects of Changing Prices
Years Ended December 31

	1982	1981	1980	1979	1978
Average Consumer Price Index	289.1	272.4	246.8	217.4	195.4
As Reported					
Revenue	$5,490.4	$5,351.2	$4,924.7	$4,209.5	$3,547.8
Income before extraordinary income	271.3	256.3	276.3	235.9	
Income before extraordinary income per common share	12.09	11.25	12.36	10.76	
Dividends per common share	3.50	3.20	2.80	2.40	2.05
Net assets	2,143.4	2,098.0	1,874.0	1,616.9	
Year-end market price per common share	85.38	69.88	111.75	83.25	69.50
In Average 1982 Dollars					
Revenue	$5,490.4	$5,679.3	$5,768.8	$5,597.8	$5,249.1
Income before extraordinary income—adjusted for specific price changes	224.0	265.4	251.8	293.0	
Income before extraordinary income per common share—adjusted for specific price changes	9.98	11.64	11.26	13.36	
Dividends per common share	3.50	3.40	3.28	3.19	3.03
Net assets—adjusted for specific price changes	2,374.1	2,345.8	2,359.1	2,267.2	
Year-end market price per common share	84.42	71.77	125.03	104.69	99.03
Gain from decline in purchasing power of net monetary items	20.6	56.9	78.1	71.1	
Excess of increase in general price level over decrease of increase in specific prices.	(55.9)	273.0	169.4	186.6	

Statement of Consolidated Income

Squibb Corporation and Subsidiaries
Years ended December 31. 1982. 1981 and 1980
(Amounts in thousands except per share figures)

	1982	1981	1980
Net Sales	$1,660,766	$1,523,911	$1,334,184
Costs and Expenses:			
Cost of sales	678,472	676,444	584,892
Marketing and administrative	647,908	597,001	514,023
Research and development	122,962	95,302	73,787
Other (net)	1,890	3,818	5,825
	1,451,232	1,372,565	1,178,527
Profit from Operations	209,534	151,346	155,657
General Corporate Income (Expenses):			
Interest income	60,832	31,980	34,383
Interest expense	(40,257)	(43,453)	(49,380)
Administrative expenses and other (net)	(10,624)	(15,174)	(12,367)
	9,951	(26,647)	(27,364)
Income before Costs of Restructuring	219,485	124,699	128,293
Costs of restructuring	—	62,859	—
Income before Taxes on Income	219,485	61,840	128,293
Provision for taxes on income	65,849	20,742	24,920
Income from Continuing Businesses	153,636	41,098	103,373
Income from businesses sold (net of taxes)	—	12,181	24,371
Gain (loss) on sale of businesses (net of taxes)	—	58,068	(318)
Income before Extraordinary Charge	153,636	111,347	127,426
Extraordinary charge	—	6,532	—
Net Income	$ 153,636	$ 104,815	$ 127,426
Per Share:			
Income from continuing businesses	$3.01	$ .83	$2.15
Income from businesses sold	—	.24	.51
Gain (loss) on sale of businesses	—	1.16	(.01)
Income before extraordinary charge	3.01	2.23	2.65
Extraordinary charge	—	.13	—
Net income	$3.01	$2.10	$2.65

See accompanying notes to financial statements.

Statement of Consolidated Retained Earnings

Squibb Corporation and Subsidiaries
Years ended December 31. 1982, 1981 and 1980
(Amounts in thousands)

	1982	1981	1980
Balance at beginning of year	$ 857,259	$809,702	$734,981
Companies acquired	9,700	3,134	2,852
Net income	153,636	104,815	127,426
	1,020,595	917,651	865,259
Cash dividends–$1.28 per share			
($1.21½ in 1981 and $1.15½ in 1980)	(65,199)	(60,392)	(55,557)
Balance at end of year	$ 955,396	$857,259	$809,702

See accompanying notes to financial statements.

Exhibit 2.3. Illustrated financial statements (Squibb Corporation). Reprinted by permission from the 1982 annual report of Squibb Corporation.

Consolidated Balance Sheet

Squibb Corporation and Subsidiaries
December 31, 1982, 1981 and 1980
(Dollar amounts in thousands)

	1982	1981	1980
Assets			
Current Assets:			
Cash	$ 26,813	$ 41,728	$ 9,700
Time deposits	106,669	116,570	28,525
Marketable investments, at cost	2,039	169	447
Receivables (net)	408,295	394,018	344,561
Notes receivable from sale of businesses	25,638	25,429	75,225
Inventories	371,413	390,917	388,968
Prepaid expenses	28,124	23,081	22,053
Deferred taxes on income	56,468	67,574	31,473
Total current assets	1,025,459	1,059,486	900,952
Net Assets of Businesses Sold	—	—	155,303
Investments and Long-Term Receivables	316,012	344,295	216,729
Property, Plant and Equipment (net)	511,821	479,720	479,591
Other Assets	76,420	66,859	64,476
	$1,929,712	$1,950,360	$1,817,051
Liabilities and Shareholders' Equity			
Current Liabilities:			
Current installments of long-term debt	$ 11,586	$ 3,364	$ 3,573
Notes payable	50,831	39,770	72,903
Accounts payable and accrued expenses	317,416	299,028	217,464
Taxes on income	61,839	119,435	62,280
Total current liabilities	441,672	461,597	356,220
Long-Term Debt	336,314	398,771	392,419
Deferred Taxes on Income	16,768	19,416	22,216
Other Liabilities	39,139	40,951	43,726
Shareholders' Equity:			
Common stock, par value $1.00 per share:			
Authorized 100,000,000 shares; issued 51,472,063 shares (49,993,592 in 1981 and 48,551,705 in 1980)	51,472	49,994	48,552
Additional paid-in capital	171,151	158,129	144,340
Retained earnings	955,396	857,259	809,702
Cumulative foreign currency adjustments	(82,126)	(35,717)	—
	1,095,893	1,029,665	1,002,594
Less cost of 12,071 shares of stock held in treasury (10,972 in 1981 and 24,246 in 1980)	74	40	124
Total shareholders' equity	1,095,819	1,029,625	1,002,470
	$1,929,712	$1,950,360	$1,817,051

See accompanying notes to financial statements.

Statement of Changes in Consolidated Financial Position

Squibb Corporation and Subsidiaries
Years ended December 31, 1982, 1981 and 1980
(Amounts in thousands)

	1982	1981	1980
Sources of Working Capital			
Income from continuing businesses	$153,636	$ 41,098	$103,373
Items not requiring (providing) working capital:			
Depreciation and amortization of fixed assets	31,270	28,175	24,003
Costs of restructuring	—	22,353	—
Other (net)	(2,402)	550	(1,871)
Working capital provided from continuing businesses	182,504	92,176	125,505
Decrease in long-term receivables from sale of businesses	27,542	12,163	8,080
Disposals of property, plant and equipment (net)	16,295	15,464	3,244
Issuance of treasury shares and shares under stock option and compensation plans (net)	14,389	1,523	869
Decrease in property, plant and equipment from foreign currency translation	13,120	13,230	—
Companies acquired	9,777	16,926	11,719
Decrease in investments by trustees under note agreements	1,599	8,286	7,338
Income from businesses sold	—	12,181	24,371
Extraordinary charge	—	(6,532)	—
Proceeds from sale of businesses (net of noncurrent notes in the principal amounts of $155,000 in 1981 and $24,900 in 1980)	—	64,871	91,622
Decrease in net assets of businesses sold	—	—	36,891
	265,226	230,288	309,639
Uses of Working Capital			
Cash dividends paid	65,199	60,392	55,557
Additions to property, plant and equipment:			
Capital expenditures	87,280	69,851	79,996
Fixed assets of businesses acquired (net)	5,506	4,441	3,443
Payment of 9.40% notes	50,000	—	—
Decrease in equity from foreign currency adjustments	46,409	35,717	—
Decrease (increase) in other long-term debt (net)	12,457	(6,352)	5,020
Increase in other assets (net)	10,665	8,527	13,218
Decrease in other liabilities (net)	1,812	4,555	5,799
	279,328	177,131	163,033
(Decrease) Increase in Working Capital	$(14,102)	$ 53,157	$146,606
Changes in Components of Working Capital–(Decrease) Increase			
Cash	$(14,915)	$ 32,028	$(19,622)
Time deposits	(9,901)	88,045	12,087
Marketable investments	1,870	(278)	(866)
Receivables (net)	14,277	49,457	32,532
Notes receivable from sale of businesses	209	(49,796)	75,225
Inventories	(19,504)	1,949	65,598
Prepaid expenses	5,043	1,028	210
Deferred taxes on income	(11,106)	36,101	10,654
Current installments of long-term debt	(8,222)	209	(2,021)
Notes payable	(11,061)	33,133	13,219
Accounts payable and accrued expenses	(18,388)	(81,564)	(25,316)
Taxes on income	57,596	(57,155)	(15,094)
(Decrease) Increase in Working Capital	$(14,102)	$ 53,157	$146,606

See accompanying notes to financial statements.

Notes to Financial Statements

Squibb Corporation and Subsidiaries

Summary of Significant Accounting Policies

Principles of Consolidation
The consolidated financial statements include the accounts of the Corporation and its majority owned subsidiaries. The end of the fiscal year of most foreign subsidiaries and branches differs from that of the Corporation but is within three months thereof. The Corporation follows the equity method of accounting for its minority investments (20%–50%) in other companies.

Inventories
Inventories are valued at the lower of cost (by methods which approximate current costs) or market.

Property, Plant and Equipment
The cost of significant improvements to property, plant and equipment is capitalized. Maintenance and repairs are expensed as incurred. The cost of buildings and equipment is depreciated primarily on the straight line method over the estimated useful life of the assets. Leasehold improvements are amortized over the shorter of their useful life or the term of the lease. Upon sale or retirement of items of property, the cost and related accumulated depreciation or amortization are eliminated from the accounts and any resulting gain or loss is credited or charged to income. Interest incurred on certain additions to property, plant and equipment is capitalized as part of the cost of such assets.

Cost in Excess of Net Assets of Businesses Acquired
The cost in excess of net assets of businesses acquired prior to November 1, 1970 is not amortized when, in the opinion of management, there is no diminution in the value of the acquired businesses. For businesses acquired after October 31, 1970, such excess cost is amortized over varying periods up to forty years.

Foreign Currency Translation
The Corporation adopted FASB Statement No. 52 effective January 1, 1981. Under the provisions of the Statement, substantially all assets and liabilities of the Corporation's international operations are translated at year end exchange rates and the resulting adjustments are accumulated in shareholders' equity. Income and expenses are translated at exchange rates prevailing during the year. Foreign currency transaction gains and losses are included in net income, except for those relating to intercompany transactions of a long-term investment nature which are accumulated in shareholders' equity.

Pension Plans
Substantially all employees of the Corporation's domestic operations are covered under noncontributory pension plans. Pension costs are funded as accrued, and unfunded past service costs are amortized over an initial term of forty years. Pension plans of the Corporation's international operations are influenced principally by social legislation of the countries in which these operations are located.

Taxes on Income
Certain of the Corporation's policies used for financial accounting purposes differ from those used for income tax purposes, thereby causing a deferral of taxes on income. The Corporation accounts for investment tax credits on the flow through method.

Net Income per Share
Calculations of per share amounts are based on the average number of shares outstanding during each year and assume the conversion of the outstanding 4¼% convertible debentures and the exercise of stock options.

Business Acquisitions
During 1982, 1981 and 1980, certain businesses were acquired on a pooling of interests basis in exchange for 908,698 shares, 943,823 shares and 2,717,604 shares of common stock, respectively. As the effect of restating data relating to these acquisitions would not materially affect previously issued financial statements, no restated or separate entity operating results have been presented. In addition, during 1981 and 1980, several other businesses were purchased for 435,500 shares and 81,834 shares of common stock, respectively, and their results of operations, not material in amount, have been included from their respective dates of acquisition.

Businesses Sold
In 1981, the Corporation sold the business of Life Savers, Inc., resulting in a gain of $58,068,000 (net of taxes on income of $24,575,000), or $1.16 per share. In 1980, pursuant to plans adopted in 1979, the Corporation sold Dobbs Houses, Inc., Table Talk, Inc. and certain related operations, resulting in a nominal loss of one cent per share, or $318,000 (net of income tax benefits of $1,712,000).

The results of the businesses sold have been segregated as a separate component of income in the statement of consolidated income.

Combined operating results relating to businesses sold were as follows:

	1981	1980
	(Amounts in thousands)	
Net sales	$322,503	$511,772
Income before taxes on income	21,099	41,652
Provision for taxes on income	8,918	17,281
Income from businesses sold	$ 12,181	$ 24,371

The net assets of Life Savers, Inc. have been segregated and stated at book value in the consolidated balance sheet at December 31, 1980.

Operations in Puerto Rico
Certain domestic subsidiaries operate in Puerto Rico and primarily manufacture and sell to other affiliates of the Corporation. The income from these subsidiaries is currently exempt from Federal income taxes and partially exempt from Puerto Rican income taxes.

In August, 1982, the United States Congress passed the Tax Equity and Fiscal Responsibility Act of 1982 which amends the provisions of the law, effective in 1983, concerning the tax credit available to domestic subsidiaries operating in Puerto Rico. Until regulations are issued by the Treasury Department, the Corporation will not be able to assess precisely how the new law will affect the Puerto Rican operations. It is anticipated, however, that the Corporation's effective tax rate will increase as a result of this new law.

During 1980, pursuant to the Puerto Rico Industrial Incentives Act of 1978, the Corporation entered into agreements with the Commonwealth of Puerto Rico whereby certain existing grants covering subsidiaries with full exemption from Puerto Rican income taxes were converted to partial tax exemption and the periods of such grants were generally extended an additional ten years, the earliest of which expires in 1997.

Under Puerto Rican tax law, remittances to the parent company of the income generated by these operations result in a "toll" tax, not to exceed 10%. When a determination is made to remit dividends, the Corporation provides for Puerto Rican toll taxes on the income to be remitted as such income is earned. In 1982, approximately $98,000,000 was remitted to the Corporation ($73,000,000 in 1981 and $98,000,000 in 1980). The Corporation has reinvested or plans to reinvest the undistributed earnings of these operations, on which toll taxes have not been provided. At December 31, 1982, approximately $93,000,000 of time deposits and marketable notes, bonds and other securities ($97,000,000 in 1981 and $105,000,000 in 1980) were owned by subsidiaries operating in Puerto Rico.

The tax savings arising from the Federal and Puerto Rican exemptions relating to these operations were approximately $40,000,000 in 1982 ($30,000,000 in 1981 and in 1980). The tax savings are net of appropriate toll taxes and Puerto Rican income taxes.

Foreign Currencies
One of the principal factors impacting the results of foreign operations are changes in currency exchange rates. The Corporation measures this as follows:

1982 versus 1981. The adverse effect of foreign currency fluctuations under FASB Statement No. 52 was as follows:

	1982	1981
	(Amounts in thousands)	
Income before taxes on income:		
Balance sheet and transactions		
(included in other expenses)	$ 9,207	$23,209
Sales and expenses effect	22,600	(a)
	$31,807	$23,209
Income from continuing businesses:		
Balance sheet and transactions	$ 7,560	$22,361
Sales and expenses effect	16,200	(a)
	$23,760	$22,361

(a) The "sales and expenses effect" has been approximated by translating the 1982 income statements of international operations at the average exchange rates in effect during 1981, and accordingly, 1981 shows no effect since it is the base year for this comparison.

1981 versus 1980. The adverse effect of foreign currency fluctuations was as follows:

	1981	1980
	(Amounts in thousands)	
Income before taxes on income:		
Balance sheet and transactions		
(included in other expenses) (b)	$23,209	$10,125
Sales and expenses effect	23,900	(c)
	$47,109	$10,125
Income from continuing businesses:		
Balance sheet and transactions (b)	$22,361	$ 7,926
Sales and expenses effect	14,500	(c)
	$36,861	$ 7,926

(b) The Corporation adopted FASB Statement No. 52 effective January 1, 1981. In 1981, the effect of adopting this Statement was to increase income before taxes on income by $26,100,000 and income from continuing businesses by $23,600,000.

(c) The "sales and expenses effect" has been approximated by translating the 1981 income statements of international operations at the average exchange rates in effect during 1980, and accordingly, 1980 shows no effect since it is the base year for this comparison.

An analysis of the separate component of shareholders' equity, "cumulative foreign currency adjustments," is as follows:

	1982	1981
	(Amounts in thousands)	
Balance at beginning of year	$(35,717)	$ (6,953)
Aggregate translation adjustments and gains and losses from intercompany balances of a long-term investment nature (net of taxes of $2,550 in 1982 and $2,416 in 1981)	(46,409)	(28,764)
Balance at end of year	$(82,126)	$(35,717)

Pension Costs
Pension costs of the Corporation's domestic operations aggregated $17,422,000 in 1982, $15,714,000 in 1981 and $14,350,000 in 1980 ($24,736,000 in 1982, $22,684,000 in 1981 and $21,677,000 in 1980 for worldwide operations).

Accumulated benefits and net assets of the Corporation's defined benefit plans for domestic operations, as of the most recent valuation date, were:

	January 1,		
	1982	1981	1980
	(Amounts in thousands)		
Actuarial present value of accumulated plan benefits:			
Vested	$150,900	$136,000	$120,000
Nonvested	5,300	5,400	6,000
	$156,200	$141,400	$126,000
Net assets available for benefits	$139,000	$128,300	$102,000

An assumed rate of return of 7% on investments was used in determining the actuarial present value of accumulated plan benefits.

The above data have not been determined for pension plans of international operations that are not required to report such information to governmental agencies. For these plans, however, the estimated vested benefits do not exceed fund assets in material amounts.

Costs of Restructuring

In 1981, the Corporation provided a special charge in the amount of $62,859,000 for costs of restructuring. Approximately $40,000,000 of the charge related to closing certain facilities in New Brunswick, New Jersey, and included losses on the disposition of property, plant and equipment and estimated costs of severance. The balance of the provision included costs associated with the discontinuance of a number of small businesses and product lines and estimated costs of relocating a number of corporate functions to Princeton, New Jersey.

Provision for Taxes on Income

The components of income before taxes on income were:

	1982	1981	1980
	(Amounts in thousands)		
Domestic operations	$142,012	$ 4,894	$ 57,570
International operations	77,473	56,946	70,723
	$219,485	$61,840	$128,293

The provision for taxes on income from continuing businesses consisted of the following:

	1982	1981	1980
	(Amounts in thousands)		
Current Federal	$ 1,058	$ 2,051	$(7,993)
Current foreign	42,270	39,857	29,117
Current state, local and Puerto Rican	18,316	12,102	8,817
Deferred Federal	8,214	(31,229)	(6,480)
Deferred foreign	(4,009)	(2,039)	1,459
	$65,849	$20,742	$24,920

In 1982, deferred Federal taxes resulted principally from the deduction for income tax purposes in the current year of restructuring costs deferred in prior years. Deferred Federal taxes, in 1981, resulted primarily from a benefit related to the costs of restructuring which were deferred for income tax purposes, and, in 1980, from a benefit related to the deferral for income tax purposes of certain research and development costs.

The major elements contributing to the difference between the Federal statutory tax rate and the effective tax rate were:

	1982	1981	1980
	(Percent of pretax income)		
Federal statutory tax rate	46.0	46.0	46.0
Increases (decreases) in taxes resulting from:			
Tax exemptions of operations in Puerto Rico	(18.0)	(47.7)	(23.3)
Anticipated dividends	—	14.9	—
International operations	(2.1)	2.9	(4.6)
Foreign currency fluctuations	1.2	15.9	1.9
State and local income taxes	3.1	4.1	1.6
Other (net)	(.2)	(2.6)	(2.2)
Effective tax rate	30.0	33.5	19.4

United States taxes on income (to the extent such taxes would exceed the taxes paid directly by the operating entities) have not been provided on the undistributed earnings of international operations since the Corporation has reinvested or plans to reinvest such earnings.

The Corporation's consolidated Federal income tax returns have been examined by the Internal Revenue Service through the year 1977.

Extraordinary Charge

The extraordinary charge in 1981 of $6,532,000, or $.13 per share, related to the Iranian government's takeover of the Corporation's operations in that country.

Net Income per Share

Calculations of per share amounts are based on the average number of shares outstanding during each year and assume the conversion of the outstanding 4¼% convertible debentures and the elimination of the charge to income for the related interest expense (net of taxes on income) on these debentures in the amounts of $539,000 in 1982, $590,000 in 1981 and $816,000 in 1980, and the exercise of stock options. Average shares used to compute the per share amounts were 51,257,000 in 1982, 50,233,000 in 1981 and 48,399,000 in 1980.

Receivables (net)

	1982	1981	1980
	(Amounts in thousands)		
Receivables	$429,250	$411,001	$357,739
Less allowance for doubtful items	20,955	16,983	13,178
	$408,295	$394,018	$344,561

Inventories

	1982	1981	1980
	(Amounts in thousands)		
Raw materials and supplies	$123,430	$142,071	$156,593
Work in process	60,175	77,350	71,102
Finished products	187,808	171,496	161,273
	$371,413	$390,917	$388,968

Investments and Long-Term Receivables

	1982	1981	1980
	(Amounts in thousands)		
Time deposits	$ 3,140	$ 6,800	$ 32,402
Marketable notes and bonds, at cost ($100,000, $89,000 and $93,000, at market)	127,734	125,542	119,334
Investments by trustees, at cost (approximates market)	11,412	13,011	21,297
Other investments, principally at cost	32,915	33,263	12,868
Long-term receivables	140,811	165,679	30,828
	$316,012	$344,295	$216,729

Long-term receivables include interest bearing notes in the principal amounts of $130,000,000 in 1982 and $155,000,000 in 1981 received in connection with the sale of Life Savers, Inc. These notes are due in annual installments of $25,000,000, with a final payment of $30,000,000 in 1988.

Investments by trustees represents the proceeds remaining from issuance of the Corporation's 6⅜% and 6½% notes, which can only be used to finance the construction of a pharmaceutical products manufacturing facility in Puerto Rico or to repay the obligations under these notes.

Undistributed earnings of 50% or less owned investments included in retained earnings amounted to $2,000,000 at December 31, 1982.

Property, Plant and Equipment (net)

	1982	1981	1980
	(Amounts in thousands)		
Land and land improvements	$ 32,581	$ 40,878	$ 39,486
Buildings	233,161	234,898	242,992
Leasehold improvements	19,395	16,525	17,116
Machinery and equipment	328,291	295,062	270,783
Construction in progress	90,009	73,439	100,130
	703,437	660,802	670,507
Less accumulated depreciation and amortization	191,616	181,082	190,916
	$511,821	$479,720	$479,591

The Corporation incurred interest costs of $48,005,000 in 1982, $52,164,000 in 1981 and $53,168,000 in 1980, of which $7,748,000, $8,711,000 and $3,788,000, respectively, were capitalized as part of the cost of certain additions to property, plant and equipment.

Other Assets

	1982	1981	1980
	(Amounts in thousands)		
Cost in excess of net assets of businesses acquired (net)	$52,535	$47,011	$42,636
Patents, trademarks and licenses (net)	5,295	2,925	3,430
Other	18,590	16,923	18,410
	$76,420	$66,859	$64,476

Notes Payable and Lines of Credit

At December 31, 1982, short-term notes payable included $14,196,000 due to holders of commercial paper ($32,237,000 at December 31, 1980), with the balance due primarily to banks. At December 31, 1981, short-term notes payable were due primarily to banks.

The Corporation has a revolving credit and term loan agreement which provides for a credit line of up to $150,000,000, either in domestic or Eurodollar borrowings, until October 31, 1984, at which time the outstanding balances will be converted into a term loan. A commitment fee of ⅜ of 1% per annum on the unused portion of the credit line is required. Outstanding borrowings bear interest at the prime rate or London interbank rate until October 31, 1984 and at ¼ of 1% over prime or ½ ⅝ of 1% over the London interbank rate thereafter. Amounts borrowed will be repayable in eight consecutive semiannual installments from April 30, 1985 to October 31, 1988. There were no borrowings outstanding under this agreement at December 31, 1982.

The Corporation has lines of credit with several banks which may be withdrawn any time at their option. The unused total amount of these lines was $20,000,000 at December 31, 1982. These lines support commercial paper borrowing arrangements. The interest rate

payable with respect to borrowings under these lines approximates the prime rate.

At December 31, 1982, compensating balances maintained in support of short-term borrowings and lines of credit were not material.

Accounts Payable and Accrued Expenses

	1982	1981	1980
	(Amounts in thousands)		
Accounts payable	$108,234	$ 90,652	$ 89,933
Accrued expenses:			
Commissions and payrolls	56,000	51,564	42,948
Costs of restructuring	15,858	29,456	—
Other	137,324	127,356	84,583
	209,182	208,376	127,531
	$317,416	$299,028	$217,464

Long-Term Debt

	1982	1981	1980
	(Amounts in thousands)		
8.14% notes—$10,000 due annually 1983 to 1992 and $15,000 due annually 1993 to 1997	$175,000	$175,000	$175,000
8% notes due 1985	100,000	100,000	100,000
9.40% notes due 1982	—	50,000	50,000
6⅜% and 6½% notes payable in installments of $2,000 to $4,000 from 1995 to 2004	30,000	30,000	30,000
4¼% Subordinated Guaranteed Convertible Debentures due 1987	21,251	23,581	25,531
Other, primarily 3% to 14¼% due to banks from 1983 to 2008	21,649	23,554	15,461
	347,900	402,135	395,992
Less current installments	11,586	3,364	3,573
	$336,314	$398,771	$392,419

The annual maturities of long-term debt are $11,586,000 in 1983, $16,764,000 in 1984, $111,520,000 in 1985, $12,010,000 in 1986 and $33,275,000 in 1987. Changing economic conditions permitted the Corporation to pay in September, 1982, the then outstanding $50,000,000 principal balance of its 9.40% notes, which had been classified as long-term debt at December 31, 1981.

The Corporation's note agreements impose certain restrictions on the payment of dividends, redemption or acquisition of capital stock and incurrence of debt and lease obligations. At December 31, 1982, approximately $405,000,000 of consolidated retained earnings was not subject to restriction. The Corporation is also required to maintain consolidated working capital of at least $275,000,000, less amounts invested as long-term time deposits and certificates of deposit.

The 4¼% debentures are convertible into common stock of the Corporation at $57 per share and are redeemable at the option of the Corporation at any time at par value. During 1982, the Corporation repurchased $2,330,000 principal amount of these debentures ($1,950,000 in 1981 and $10,144,000 in 1980). At December 31, 1982, there were 372,825 shares of common stock reserved for issuance on conversion of the outstanding debentures.

Leases

The Corporation was obligated at December 31, 1982 under long-term operating leases for various types of property and equipment, with minimum aggregate rentals totaling $150,588,000, as follows: $24,361,000 in 1983, $17,861,000 in 1984, $13,696,000 in 1985, $9,700,000 in 1986, $7,992,000 in 1987 and $76,978,000 in later years. Minimum aggregate rentals have not been reduced by minimum sublease rentals of $78,104,000 under noncancelable subleases.

Most of the Corporation's leases contain renewal options and clauses for escalations, payment of real estate taxes, maintenance, insurance and certain other operating expenses of the properties. Certain leases are expected to be renewed or replaced at expiration. Total rental expense for operating leases was:

	1982	1981	1980
	(Amounts in thousands)		
Minimum rentals	$31,926	$29,718	$22,484
Contingent rentals	994	735	685
Sublease rentals	(3,814)	(3,150)	(2,816)
	$29,106	$27,303	$20,353

The Corporation's obligations under capital leases are not material.

Capital Stock and Additional Paid-in Capital

	Shares of common stock		Additional paid-in capital
	Issued	Treasury	
			(Amounts in thousands)
Balance at January 1, 1980	45,641,978	25,153	$137,514
Companies acquired	2,799,438	—	6,068
Stock options	110,289	—	722
Compensation plans	—	(909)	36
Purchases	—	2	—
Balance at December 31, 1980	48,551,705	24,246	144,340
Companies acquired	1,379,323	—	12,413
Stock options	62,564	—	1,078
Compensation plans	—	(30,794)	298
Purchases	—	17,520	—
Balance at December 31, 1981	49,993,592	10,972	158,129
Companies acquired	908,698	—	(832)
Stock options	569,773	6,317	13,852
Compensation plans	—	(7,332)	2
Purchases	—	2,114	—
Balance at December 31, 1982	51,472,063	12,071	$171,151

At December 31, 1982, the Corporation had 4,000,000 authorized and unissued shares of preferred stock.

Stock Option and Performance Unit Plans

During 1982, the Board of Directors of the Corporation approved, subject to shareholder approval, the 1982 Option and Performance Unit Plan. Under the terms of the plan, 1,750,000 shares of the Corporation's common stock may be issued for options granted and for payment of performance units awarded. Options may be granted for a period of not more than ten years and generally become exercisable in either two or four equal annual installments commencing one year after grant. At December 31, 1982, options to purchase 1,571,300 shares of common stock were available for future grants under this plan.

Under the 1978 and 1974 Option and Performance Unit Plans and the 1968 Stock Option Plan, options were granted on a qualified or nonqualified basis for periods of up to ten years. No further options can be granted under these plans.

During 1982, pursuant to a merger agreement, outstanding options under a plan of an acquired company became options to purchase 19,521 shares of the Corporation's common stock at a price of $16.86 per share. Prior to 1981, pursuant to merger agreements, outstanding options under plans of acquired companies became options to purchase 384,083 shares of the Corporation's common stock at prices ranging from $2.50 to $13.95 per share. No further options can be granted under these plans.

In connection with the sale of a subsidiary in 1981, fully exercisable options were granted in 1982 to purchase an aggregate of 138,238 shares of the Corporation's common stock at prices ranging from $30.75 to $46.97 per share. Options to purchase 93,702 shares of common stock at prices ranging from $31.57 to $47.29 per share were also granted in 1980 in connection with the sale of a subsidiary. These options expire at various dates on or before December 30, 1984.

Option changes during the three years ended December 31, 1982 for all of the above plans were:

		Exercise price	
	Shares	From	To
Balance at January 1, 1980	1,817,321	$ 6.73	$50.32
Granted	451,002	24.69	47.29
Assumed (acquired company)	360,000	2.50	12.50
Exercised	(110,289)	2.50	32.00
Terminated	(267,796)	5.00	50.13
Balance at December 31, 1980	2,250,238	2.50	50.32
Granted	429,250	28.57	37.07
Exercised	(62,564)	2.50	35.22
Terminated	(369,412)	8.47	50.13
Balance at December 31, 1981	2,247,512	2.50	50.32
Granted	482,838	30.50	46.97
Assumed (acquired company)	19,521	16.86	—
Exercised	(569,773)	2.50	42.50
Terminated	(170,749)	12.50	50.32
Balance at December 31, 1982	2,009,349	2.50	46.97
Exercisable at December 31, 1982	1,097,233	$ 2.50	$46.97

Performance unit awards granted under the 1982, 1978 and 1974 plans are payable in varying amounts at the conclusion of the award cycle, which must be a minimum of three years, if certain cumulative growth objectives (which may include earnings per share or pretax income) of the Corporation or its subsidiaries are met. No further performance unit awards can be granted under the 1978 and 1974 plans.

Each year, a charge to income may be made to cover a pro rata portion of the anticipated payout due at the end of the award cycle based on cumulative growth objectives realized in each year and preceding years. In 1982, $642,000 was charged to income. In 1981, no charge or credit was made to income and, in 1980, $115,000 was credited to income.

Performance unit changes under the 1982, 1978 and 1974 plans during the three years ended December 31, 1982 were:

	Number of units	Unit base value From	To
Balance at January 1, 1980	166,283	$22.69	$37.50
Awarded	1,301	34.19	—
Terminated	(7,086)	22.69	37.50
Matured	(30,630)	25.63	29.57
Balance at December 31, 1980	129,868	22.69	37.50
Awarded	76,839	31.69	36.63
Terminated	(6,456)	27.25	37.50
Matured	(54,433)	22.69	34.19
Balance at December 31, 1981	145,818	27.25	37.50
Awarded	26,819	46.00	—
Terminated	(3,547)	31.69	37.50
Matured	(38,872)	27.25	30.50
Balance at December 31, 1982	130,218	$31.69	$46.00

At December 31, 1982, a total of 3,580,649 shares of unissued common stock was reserved for issuance under the stock option and performance unit plans, and treasury shares were reserved for options granted to purchase 12,500 shares of the Corporation's common stock (other than under such plans) at an exercise price of $28.94 per share.

Contingencies and Litigation

Several products of the Corporation are currently under review by the Food and Drug Administration. Although the ultimate outcome cannot be predicted with any certainty, these proceedings will not, in the opinion of the management of the Corporation, result in a material adverse effect on the consolidated financial position of the Corporation and its subsidiaries.

Various suits and claims are also pending against the Corporation and its subsidiaries, including product liability suits in which women have instituted actions against a number of pharmaceutical manufacturers, including a subsidiary of the Corporation, seeking to recover substantial damages for injuries suffered by them allegedly as a result of their mothers having taken diethylstilbestrol (a prescription drug) during pregnancy. Although the outcome of such suits and claims cannot be predicted with certainty, the disposition thereof will not, in the opinion of the management of the Corporation, result in a material adverse effect on the consolidated financial position of the Corporation and its subsidiaries.

Segment Information

With the completion of the restructuring program in 1981, the Corporation has redefined its industry segments, as follows: pharmaceutical products, specialty health products and medical systems, and personal care products. Accordingly, industry segment data for 1981 and 1980 have been reclassified.

The Corporation's major segment, pharmaceutical products, engages in the research and development, manufacture and sale of pharmaceuticals for human and veterinary use, and diagnostic agents which include contrast agents and radiopharmaceuticals.

The specialty health products and medical systems segment engages in the development, manufacture and sale of surgical and ophthalmic instruments, ostomy care products, sterilization-monitoring systems, diagnostic imaging systems and patient monitoring systems.

The Corporation's personal care products segment manufactures and sells a variety of fragrances and cosmetics. Fragrances are distributed principally under the names *Yves Saint Laurent*, *Yves Saint Laurent Opium*, *Gianni Versace*, *Senchal*, *Kouros*, *Enjoli* and *Jean Naté*. Also included in this segment is a wide range of cosmetics sold primarily under the *Yves Saint Laurent*, *Charles of the Ritz*, *Revenescence* and *Alexandra de Markoff* brand names, and *Bain de Soleil* suntan preparations.

Generally, interarea sales are reflected at the inventory cost of the selling location plus a margin. Geographic area adjustments/eliminations are comprised of interarea sales, the net change in interarea profit in beginning and ending inventories and interarea profit in ending inventories.

Total segment assets may be reconciled to consolidated assets, as follows:

	1982	1981	1980
		(Amounts in millions)	
Segment assets	$1,479.3	$1,436.2	$1,325.4
Net assets of businesses sold	—	—	155.3
General corporate assets (principally interest earning)	450.4	514.2	336.4
Consolidated assets	$1,929.7	$1,950.4	$1,817.1

Net assets related to international operations amounted to approximately 42% of shareholders' equity at December 31, 1982 (47% at December 31, 1981 and 1980). Undistributed earnings of international operations, for which United States taxes on income have not been provided, approximated $371,000,000 at December 31, 1982.

Segment Information (Amounts in millions)

Industry Segments

	Pharmaceutical products	Specialty health products and medical systems (a)	Personal care products	Adjustments/ eliminations	Total
1982					
Net sales	$ 978.3	$340.5	$342.0	$ —	$1,660.8
Profit from operations	122.4	52.2	34.9	—	209.5
Assets	1,006.2	286.3	186.8	—	1,479.3
Capital expenditures	64.5	13.0	9.7	.1	87.3
Depreciation and amortization	23.1	5.4	2.3	.5	31.3
1981 (b)					
Net sales	$ 934.1	$264.4	$325.4	$ —	$1,523.9
Profit from operations	89.7	33.4	28.2	—	151.3
Assets	1,025.6	225.8	184.8	—	1,436.2
Capital expenditures	50.6	12.9	6.3	.1	69.9
Depreciation and amortization	22.3	3.4	2.0	.5	28.2
1980 (b)					
Net sales	$ 869.1	$178.3	$286.8	$ —	$1,334.2
Profit from operations	100.0	28.3	27.4	—	155.7
Assets	1,007.6	142.9	174.9	—	1,325.4
Capital expenditures	55.0	19.7	4.5	.8	80.0
Depreciation and amortization	19.8	1.7	2.0	.5	24.0

Geographic Areas

| | | International | | | Adjustments/ | |
	Domestic	Europe	All other	Total	eliminations	Total
1982						
Net sales	$ 955.0	$429.2	$276.6	$705.8	$ —	$1,660.8
Interarea sales to affiliates	121.5	85.4	5.7	91.1	(212.6)	—
	1,076.5	514.6	282.3	796.9	(212.6)	1,660.8
Profit from operations	149.2	62.8	(.1)	62.7	(2.4)	209.5
Assets	933.0	383.8	207.7	591.5	(45.2)	1,479.3
1981						
Net sales	$ 797.5	$429.4	$297.0	$726.4	$ —	$1,523.9
Interarea sales to affiliates	119.2	100.3	6.1	106.4	(225.6)	—
	916.7	529.7	303.1	832.8	(225.6)	1,523.9
Profit from operations	80.7	34.4	18.4	72.8	(2.2)	151.3
Assets	884.0	361.6	233.4	595.0	(42.8)	1,436.2
1980						
Net sales	$ 661.5	$412.6	$260.1	$672.7	$ —	$1,334.2
Interarea sales to affiliates	105.3	89.2	4.8	94.0	(199.3)	—
	766.8	501.8	264.9	766.7	(199.3)	1,334.2
Profit from operations	92.3	60.1	12.0	72.1	(8.7)	155.7
Assets	758.2	390.5	217.3	607.8	(40.6)	1,325.4

(a) Acquisitions during 1982 and 1981 had a significant favorable impact on the sales and profit growth of this segment.
(b) Certain 1981 and 1980 data have been reclassified to conform with the current year's presentation

Supplementary Data on Changing Prices (Unaudited)

Background. FASB Statement No. 33, as amended, requires disclosure and explanation of the effects of changing prices on the Corporation's operations. The accompanying supplementary data estimate the changes in specific prices ("current cost") on the Corporation's inventories, property, plant and equipment, and related cost of sales and depreciation and amortization.

Methodology. The estimated current costs of inventory and related cost of sales are based primarily on the application of standard costs and relevant indexes, taking into consideration inventory turnover. The estimated current costs of property, plant and equipment and related depreciation and amortization are based principally on external price indexes which are related to the assets of each operation. The estimated effects of general inflation for international and domestic operations are based on the United States Consumer Price Index for All Urban Consumers (CPI-U).

The methodologies followed in computing the accompanying supplementary data are experimental and require the use of numerous generalized assumptions and estimates, many of which are not applicable to the business of the Corporation. Accordingly, the data should not be considered a reliable measurement of the effect of changing prices on the Corporation's operations. Management also believes that the current cost amounts do not represent the actual future costs of replacement, because of possible future changes in cost levels, technological improvements, and various efficiencies.

Analysis. Although the recessionary economic conditions during 1982 have reduced the rate of inflation both in the United States and other major countries, inflation continues to have a serious and adverse impact on the business of the Corporation and on its reported results. However, the Corporation uses various means to lessen the impact of inflation on its operations. To the extent permitted by competitive and regulatory conditions, the Corporation increases prices to help offset rising costs; moreover, introductions of new products with good gross margins and high growth potential, increased productivity, cost control programs, and improved manufacturing techniques also alleviate inflationary pressures.

Although net sales, as reported in the statement of consolidated income, increased 9% in 1982, competitive and regulatory pressures on the Corporation resulted in selective price increases which did not keep pace with the rise in general price levels, particularly for established product lines. Despite the limitations on price increases, the effects of unit volume growth, particularly from new products, resulted in net sales growth on an inflation adjusted basis during the year. Inflation adjusted income from continuing businesses was lower in 1982 than the comparable amount reported in nominal dollars. This decline is primarily attributable to increases in inflation adjusted costs and expenses.

Another factor that inflation affects is the purchasing power of monetary assets and liabilities. During 1982, the Corporation has been in a net monetary asset position, primarily as a result of notes received in connection with the sale of Life Savers, Inc. at the end of 1981, and thus experienced a $2,000,000 decline in the purchasing power of net monetary assets. Higher interest rates during periods of inflation are intended, in part, to compensate for lost purchasing power. During 1982, the Corporation realized net interest income of $20,575,000.

Statement of Income from Continuing Businesses Adjusted for Effects of Changing Prices (Unaudited)
Year ended December 31, 1982
(Amounts in millions of average 1982 dollars)

Net sales	$1,661.0
Costs and expenses (excluding depreciation and amortization)	1,437.0
Depreciation and amortization	48.0(1)
Profit from operations	176.0
General corporate income	10.0
Provision for taxes on income	66.0(2)
Income from continuing businesses	$ 120.0
Decline in purchasing power of net monetary assets held during the year	$ 2.0(3)
Effect of increase in specific prices of inventories and property, plant and equipment held during the year	$ 57.0
Increase in general price level	43.0(3)
Excess of increase in specific prices over increase in general price level	$ 14.0
Aggregate translation adjustments and gains and losses from intercompany balances of a long-term investment nature	$ (111.0)

(1) Depreciation and amortization expense is calculated using the same methods and rates of depreciation and amortization as those used in the statement of consolidated income. Depreciation and amortization of $31.3 million in the statement of consolidated income includes $19.5 million charged to cost of sales and $11.8 million charged to marketing and administrative expenses.
(2) In accordance with FASB Statement No. 33, as amended, the provision for taxes on income has not been adjusted to reflect any timing differences, allocations or adjustments that may result from applying the current cost methodology.
(3) Based on the U.S. CPI-U.
(4) At December 31, 1982, current cost of inventories was $375.0 million and current cost of property, plant and equipment, net of accumulated depreciation and amortization, was $792.0 million.

Five-Year Comparison of Selected Supplementary
Financial Data Adjusted for Effects of Changing Prices (Unaudited)
(Amounts in millions of average 1982 dollars)

	1982	1981	1980	1979	1978*
Net sales	$1,661.0	$1,617.0	$1,563.0	$1,476.0	$1,343.0
Income from continuing businesses	120.0	2.0	77.0	77.0	
Income per share from continuing businesses	$2.35	$ .05	$1.61	$1.70	
Excess of increase in specific prices over increase in general price level	14.0	(76.0)	(27.0)	(28.0)	
Net assets at year end	1,364.0	1,344.0	1,500.0	1,505.0	
Other information:					
Increase (decrease) in purchasing power of net monetary balances	(2.0)	13.0	25.0	31.0	
Cash dividends per share	$1.28	$1.29	$1.35	$1.46	$1.53
Market price per share at year end	$ 44	$ 34	$ 33	$ 47	$ 40
Average Consumer Price Index (CPI-U) (1967 = 100)	289.1	272.4	246.8	217.4	195.4

*Certain information for 1978 has been omitted pursuant to the provisions of FASB Statement No. 33, as amended.

Quarterly Financial Data (Unaudited)
(Amounts in millions except per share figures)

	First	Second	Third	Fourth	Total
1982					
Net sales	$374.2	$392.4	$437.5	$456.7	$1,660.8
Gross profit	224.3	233.6	260.3	264.1	982.3
Net income	31.4	35.6	50.1	36.5	153.6
Per share:					
Net income	.62	.71	.97	.71	3.01
1981					
Net sales	$339.0	$365.1	$410.0	$409.8	$1,523.9
Gross profit	191.5	208.7	230.6	216.7	847.5
Income (loss) from continuing businesses	17.5	26.0	37.3	(39.7)	41.1
Income before extraordinary charge	18.6	28.0	42.1	22.6	111.3
Net income	18.6	28.0	42.1	16.1	104.8
Per share:					
Income (loss) from continuing businesses	.36	.52	.74	(.79)	.83
Income before extraordinary charge	.38	.56	.84	.45	2.23
Net income	.38	.56	.84	.32	2.10
1980					
Net sales	$272.1	$310.0	$373.8	$378.3	$1,334.2
Gross profit	155.7	176.7	208.7	208.2	749.3
Income from continuing businesses	11.4	17.6	38.6	35.8	103.4
Net income	16.7	24.0	44.4	42.3	127.4
Per share:					
Income from continuing businesses	.25	.37	.80	.13	2.15
Net income	.36	.50	.92	.87	2.65

The 1981 fourth quarter results include the costs of restructuring, the gain on the sale of Life Savers and the extraordinary charge related to Iran.

Chapter Three

Special Supplementary Financial Information

INTRODUCTION

In addition to the basic financial statements, annual reports of public companies present supplementary financial information in order to give a more detailed picture of operating performance. This includes:

Financial data on segments of those business enterprises that are involved in diversified product lines or services.
Selected financial data that relate to quarterly results of a fiscal year.
Financial data adjusted for the effects of inflation.

Segment information, which is subject to an audit by the CPA, is always presented as part of the audited financial statements. Selected quarterly financial data and financial information adjusted for the effects of inflation are not subject to audit. Some companies present this information within a note to the financial statements that is labeled "unaudited," while other companies present the data in parts of their annual reports outside of the financial statements. This chapter covers the design, nature, scope, and impact of this special supplementary financial information in order to give investors an appreciation of its importance with respect to the overall financial health of public companies. Illustrations of this type of information, reproduced from the notes to financial statements of certain well-known public companies, are provided within the illustrated financial statements at the end of Chapter Two.

SEGMENT INFORMATION

Relationship to Consolidated Financial Statements

Q: What does segment information represent with respect to the consolidated financial statements?

A: Segment information is a rearrangement of financial information that is included in a corporation's consolidated financial statements. The inclusion of segment information in consolidated financial statements is analogous to the financial information included in the statement of changes in financial position, which basically rearranges information reported on the balance sheet and income statement.

Purpose

Q: What is the purpose of presenting segment information within the financial statements?

A: Segment information is designed to provide investors with a better understanding of a business enterprise as a whole, since various industry segments, geographic areas, and markets may have different rates of profitability, degrees and types of risks, and opportunities for growth. Also, there may be differences in the rates of return on investment in the various industry segments or geographic areas. Segment information therefore serves as a progress report on the components (i.e., business segments) of a diversified corporation. For example, segment information will indicate the extent of revenues and profit or loss derived from domestic (i.e., U.S.) and foreign operations. As a result, investors can then assess each business segment's profitability.

Method of Presentation

Q: Why do some companies include segment information in the notes to the financial statements, while other companies present such information in other parts of the annual report?

A: It is a matter of preference. Information about the reportable segments of a diversified company may be included in the company's financial statements in any of the following ways:

Within the body of the financial statements, with appropriate explanatory disclosures in the notes to the financial statements.

Entirely in the notes to the financial statements.
In a separate schedule within the annual report that is regarded
as an integral part of the audited financial statements.

Accounting Principles

Q: Are the accounting principles used to prepare segment information the same as those used to prepare consolidated financial information?

A: The accounting principles underlying segment information are the same as those on which the consolidated financial statements are based. Segment information is a disaggregation of the consolidated financial statements. However, most intersegment transactions are not eliminated in the segment data as they are normally eliminated in consolidation.

Determining Business Segments

Q: How does a diversified company go about determining its business segments?

A: In order for a diversified company to determine whether or not it has business segments that should be reported within its financial statements, the company will (1) identify the individual products and services from which it derives revenues, (2) group those products and services by industry lines into industry segements, and (3) select those industry segments that are significant for the company as a whole. Some companies have profit centers for internal planning and control purposes; these often serve as a logical starting point for determining industry segments. However, if a company's profit centers cross industry lines, the company will break up its existing profit centers into smaller groups of related products and services. The customary groupings of products and services used by trade or industry associations with which the company is associated may also provide guidance in classifying the business activities of the company. Prior disclosures of line of business information included in annual reports of similar companies may also be useful to a diversified company in determining industry segments.

Q: Diversified companies often provide numerous products and services to the public. How do such companies go about deciding whether or not their products or services are related, and therefore be grouped into a single industry segment, or unrelated, and should therefore be grouped into two or more industry segments?

A: The management of a diversified company generally considers the following factors:

> *The nature of the product. Since related products or services have similar uses, they are usually expected to have similar rates of profitability, degrees of risk, and opportunites for growth.*
>
> *The nature of the production process. An implication may be made that products or services are related if they share production or sales facilities, equipment, labor, or basic raw materials.*
>
> *Markets and marketing methods. A relationship among products or services may be implied if geographic marketing areas, types of customers, or marketing methods are similar. For example, a relationship among products or services may be indicated by the use of a common or interchangeable sales force and by sensitivity of the market to changes in price and economic conditions.*

Some diversified companies may be able to group their products or services into various industry segments by considering different combinations of these factors. For example, a food company that manufactures both spice and dairy products may identify its industry segments on the basis of differences in the production processes. As an alternative, the company may determine that the most useful information is provided by segmentation along market lines, such as restaurant sales and supermarket sales. In these situations, the decision is usually made by company management on the basis of selection of those industry segments that will provide investors with the most meaningful information evaluating the degrees and types of risks, rates of profitability, and opportunities for growth of the business enterprise as a whole.

Q: Are there any parameters or materiality standards for a diversified company to follow in order to determine whether or not one or more of its business lines is a segment that needs to be reported within the financial statements, such as dollar amounts, sales volume, and percentages?

A: A business segment is considered to be reportable for financial statement purposes if it meets one or more of the following quantitative tests for any of the fiscal years being presented:

1. Its revenue, which also includes transfers between business segments, is 10% or more of the combined revenue (i.e., sales to unaffiliated customers and intersegment transfers) of all of the company's industry segments.
2. Its operating profit or loss is 10% or more of the greater of (a) combined operating profit of all industry segments that did not incur an operating loss, or (b) combined operating loss of all industry segments that did incur an operating loss.
3. Its identifiable assets are 10% or more of the combined identifiable assets of all industry segments.

The significance of a segment may also be evaluated by company management in terms of past and expected future levels of operations. For example, if a segment has been significant in the past and is expected to be significant in the future, a company will generally report that segment even if it fails to meet the quantitative tests.

Interim Financial Reports

Q: Is segment information required within interim or quarterly financial reports?

A: Segment information is required within interim reports only in those cases where a complete set of interim financial statements is presented (i.e., balance sheet, income statement, and changes in financial position). Also, those interim financial statements must be expressly described as presenting financial position, results of operations, and changes in financial position in conformity with generally accepted accounting principles. For example, segment information would be required in a complete set of interim period financial statements included within SEC registration statements, or when issued in compliance with loan agreements.

Multinational Companies

Q: How does a multinational company that is also diversified in its product lines and services distinguish between domestic and foreign operations for purposes of segment reporting?

A: Foreign operations relate to those revenue producing operations that are (a) located outside of the company's home country, and (b) generating revenue either from sales to unaffiliated customers or from intraenterprise sales or transfers between geographic areas. The distinction between domestic and foreign operations may be difficult to make in certain situations, and allows management to exercise judgment in identifying foreign operations based on the facts and circumstances of the particular enterprise. Revenues generated by domestic operations include both sales to customers within the company's home country and sales to customers in foreign countries (i.e., export sales). A problem may arise when a company manufactures certain products in its home country and ships them abroad for assembly or final processing. In this situation, if the marketing effort is directed from a foreign base, then their classification as foreign operations would be appropriate. On the other hand, if finished or semifinished units are shipped only after specific foreign orders have been obtained by domestic offices, then the revenue is considered to be export sales or revenues generated by domestic operations.

Q: Is a multinational and diversified company required to present segment information on an individual country-by-country basis?

A: No. Management of a diversified company generally groups its foreign operations into geographic areas consisting of individual countries or groups of countries with similar business environments. Because of the variety of ways in which foreign operations are conducted, it is impossible to define appropriate geographic areas for all companies. However, the following general guidelines are often considered by company management in grouping two or more foreign countries into geographic areas:

> *Proximity of operations in various countries.*
> *Similarities in the business and political environment in various countries (e.g., highly controlled versus free markets; stable versus unstable).*
> *Nature, scale and degree of interrelationship of operations in various countries.*
> *Economic affinity of the various countries.*

If a country has significant foreign operations, it is required to present information separately for each significant foreign geographic area (and in the aggregate for all other geographic areas) and for its domestic operations with respect to revenue, profitability, and assets. A geographic area is significant if either its revenue from sales to unaffiliated customers or its identifiable assets are 10% or more of the related consolidated amounts. If no single foreign geographic area meets these tests, the tests are applicable to foreign operations in the aggregate. Separate disclosure of export sales in consolidated financial statements is required if export sales to unaffiliated customers are 10% or more of total revenue.

SELECTED QUARTERLY FINANCIAL DATA

Purpose

Q: What is the purpose of selected quarterly financial data within the annual report?

A: Such information is designed to provide investors with an understanding of the pattern of corporate activities during the year and the trend of business operations over segments of time, such as the significance of seasonal impacts on sales and earnings and any unusual or infrequently occurring items for a particular interim period or quarter. Quarterly financial data within annual reports can be especially helpful to those investors who have not had the opportunity to review interim financial reports issued quarterly by a corporation.

Applicability of Disclosure

Q: Is the disclosure of selected quarterly financial data within annual reports optional for corporations, or is such disclosure a requirement?

A: It is required by the SEC and is designed to be a protective measure for investors. The SEC believes that the disclosure of selected quarterly financial data within annual reports provides important information for investors in companies whose activities are closely followed by analysts and investors.

Q: Which companies are required to include quarterly data in the notes to their annual financial statements?

A: The requirement that quarterly financial data be disclosed in the notes to the annual financial statements applies only to large companies whose securities are actively traded. A large company is defined as one that had an income of $250,000 or more after taxes (but before extraordinary items and the cumulative effect of an accounting change) for each of the last three fiscal years. If a company had an income of less than $250,000, it is still considered large if it had total assets of $200 million or more as of the end of the last fiscal year. A company's securities are deemed to be actively traded if they are listed on a national securities exchange and also meet certain requirements for continued inclusion on the list of Over-the-Counter (OTC) margin stock.

Extent of Disclosure

Q: What minimum quarterly data must be included in the notes to the annual financial statements of a company?

A: The notes to the annual financial statements of a company generally disclose the following on a quarterly basis:

> *Net sales.*
> *Gross profit.*
> *Income before extraordinary items and cumulative effect of an accounting change.*
> *Net income.*
> *Per-share data.*

Unaudited Information

Q: Must the quarterly data included in the annual report to shareholders be audited?

A: No. The note disclosing quarterly financial data is always labeled "unaudited." However, the independent auditor is required to perform certain limited review procedures with respect to this unaudited quarterly information. Accordingly, the limited review procedures will be necessary whenever audited financial statements include unaudited quarterly information.

Limited Review by a CPA

Q: What is the difference between an audit and a limited review performed by an independent auditor?

A: The purpose of the annual audit is to enable the independent auditor or CPA to express an opinion on the financial statements taken as a whole. On the other hand, the purpose of a limited or quarterly review is to increase the care and attention devoted by corporate management to quarterly financial data. Such care will increase the likelihood that management will discover needed financial statement adjustments on a timely basis.

Method of Presentation

Q: Why are selected quarterly financial data presented within a note to the financial statements by some corporations and in other parts of the annual report by others?

A: It is a matter of preference, although most corporations include the data in a note to the financial statements. It is important to bear in mind that the selected quarterly financial data are unaudited, along with inflation-adjusted data, whereas other financial data in the financial statements and related notes are audited.

REPORTING THE EFFECTS OF INFLATION

Applicability of Disclosure

Q: Are all publicly listed companies required to disclose financial information adjusted for the effects of inflation?

A: All companies are encouraged to provide such information. However, the requirement to provide financial information adjusted for the effects of inflation specifically applies to public companies that have, at the beginning of the fiscal year for which financial statements ar being presented, one of the following:

1. Inventories and property, plant, and equipment that exceed $125 million before deductions are made for depreciation.
2. Total assets that exceed $1 billion after deducting accumulated depreciation.

Property, plant, and equipment include land and other natural resources as well as capitalized leasehold interests.

Purpose

Q: What is the purpose of providing financial information adjusted for the effects of inflation within annual reports?

A: Conventional financial reporting is based on historical cost, which is considered to be reliable and conceptually sound. However, historical cost as a basis for financial reporting has not been able to adequately reveal the effects of inflation on business enterprises. For example, historical cost often compares revenues in terms of dollars received during a current period with certain costs incurred in the distant past. The purchasing power of a 1983 dollar is much less than the purchasing power of a 1963 dollar. As a result, 1983 dollars are no more comparable to 1963 dollars than are Italian lire or German marks to U.S. dollars. In order to provide investors and other users of financial statements with some idea as to the impact of inflation on historical cost-based financial statements, the FASB issued its Statement No. 33, "Financial Reporting and Changing Prices," which requires companies of a certain size to supplement their conventional financial statements with information concerning income from continuing operations and other financial information as determined by the following:

1. Historical cost/constant dollar basis, which deals with general inflation (i.e, changes in the purchasing power of the dollar).

2. Current cost basis, which addresses the effect of specific price changes on a company's resources.

Deliberations on standards for changing prices generated a great deal of controversy among preparers, auditors, and users of financial statements over how the FASB should proceed with inflation accounting. Since the FASB realized that a consensus could not be reached on how to report the effects of inflation on business enterprises, the Board concluded the companies should give supplemental information under two fundamentally different measurement approaches: the historical cost/constant dollar basis and the current cost basis. Applying the techniques of either of these two approaches to conventional, historical cost financial statements results in a restatement of certain financial information that can be compared with the basic, conventional statements to measure the effects of inflation on a business enterprise, especially on net income. Financial statement disclosure of these effects to investors and other interested readers of financial reports is what reporting the effects of inflation is all about.

General Inflation and Specific Price Changes

Q: How do the terms *general inflation* and *specific price chages* as contained in FASB Statement No. 33 differ from each other?

A: The terms *general inflation* and *specific price changes* are used by the FASB in the following context:

> *General inflation* means a rise in the general level of prices or a decline in the general purchasing power of the monetary unit.

Inflation in this context is measured by a broad-based, general index like the Consumer Price Index.

Specific price changes *refer to the specific price increases or decreases of individual goods and services, which are measured by appropriate methods selected by management.*

While specific price changes of individual goods and services may be due in part to general inflation, they also can be caused by other factors such as supply and demand, governmental regulation, etc. Since a broad-based, general index is a composite of many specific price changes, the individual specific price changes do not necessarily move in the same direction as the general index. For example, during past years the price of calculators decreased substantially while the Consumer Price Index increased. Conversely, the price of oil increased at a much faster rate than the general price level. Also, specific price changes can occur even while the general price level remains stable when there is no inflation.

Importance to Investors

Q: How does financial information adjusted for the effects of inflation aid investors?

A: Such information aids investors in the following ways:

It provides useful and timely information for the assessment of future cash flows because it measures historical costs in terms of current prices when prices are changing.

It provides an assessment of company performance, since the worth of a company can be increased as a result of prudent timing of purchases during a time when prices are rising.

It provides an assessment of a company's operating capability or the ability of a company to supply a fixed quantity of goods and services. For example, a company may buy an item of inventory for $100 and sell it for $150. The transaction would contribute $50 to income determined on an historical cost basis.

However, the enterprise may need to replace the inventory at a cost of $115. In this case, only $35 raised from the sale ($150 less $115) are available for distribution without impairing operating capability. A larger distribution, for paying taxes or dividends, could result in an erosion of the capital required to maintain operating capability. Information on the current prices of resources that are used to generate revenues can help investors assess the extent and manner in which operating capability has been maintained by a company.

It provides an asssessment as to whether or not a company has maintained the purchasing power of its capital, since larger amounts of money are required to maintain a fixed amount of purchasing power when general price levels increase. For example, the investment of $1,000 at 20% will yield $200 per year. If the general price level increases by 25%, $125 will be needed to maintain the purchasing power of the yield. If the rate of return remains at 20%, the investment will have to be increased to $1,250 to maintain purchasing power.

Q: What does inflation-adjusted financial information tell an investor with regard to capital intensive industries?

A: Inflation-adjusted figures tell an investor that it costs more today to replace plant, machinery, and equipment of companies that are capital intensive than it did to acquire those items. This is analogous to the plight of a homeowner who sells one home and tries to buy a comparable home. Inflation-adjusted figures also indicate that as a result of technological improvements, the cost of replacing a plant generally increases at a slower rate than the rate of general inflation.

Historical Cost Versus Inflation-Adjusted Information

Q: How does the conventional basis of historical cost differ from the historical cost/constant dollar basis and the current cost basis?

A: The difference among the three bases can be illustrated by the following example. Assume that a depreciable asset is purchased for $100,000. Under historical cost accounting, the asset would remain on the books of the company at $100,000, less accumulated depreciation. If it is to be fully depreciated over 20 years on the straight-line basis, each year's income would be charged with a depreciation expense of $5,000. Under historical cost/constant dollar accounting, the asset would be restated each year to reflect changes in the purchasing power of the dollar, as measured by the Consumer Price Index for All Urban Consumers (CPI-U). If the Index were currently 80% higher than when the asset was acquired, the carrying amount of the asset would be restated at $180,000 with a corresponding adjustment of accumulated depreciation. The current year's depreciation charge of $9,000 (i.e., $180,000 ÷ 20 years) would reflect the fact that the asset's original cost of $100,000 is now equal in purchasing power to $180,000 in current day dollars. Under current cost accounting, the asset would also be restated each year, but the restated amount would be the asset's estimated cost or the estimated cost of an equivalent asset in the current market, less depreciation based on its current cost. If the asset would currently cost $160,000 new and it were one-quarter depreciated, it would be restated at a net current cost of $120,000. The current year's depreciation charge of approximately $8,000 (i.e., $120,000 ÷ 15 years) would reflect the utilization of the asset at current prices.

Q: Are the figures provided by the historical cost/constant dollar basis and the current cost basis designed to replace historical cost?

A: No. The primary financial statements continue to be based on historical cost or the number of dollars exchanged in actual transactions at various times in the past. The historical cost/constant dollar basis retains historical cost measurements but expresses those measurements in dollars that have the same purchasing power. The current cost basis supplements historical cost measurements with estimates of the costs that would be incurred if assets already owned had to be acquired. Such information, restated by these two methods, is designed to supplement rather than replace financial statements based on historical cost.

Constant Dollar Versus Current Cost

Q: Which method of adjusting or restating financial information for the effects of inflation is more meaningful to investors, constant dollar or current cost?

A: Both methods are meaningful in that each serves a specific purpose. Constant dollar accounting is a method of reporting financial items in dollars that have the same purchasing power. It attempts to portray how general inflation has affected the exchange value of the dollar on those financial statement items most affected by inflation, namely, inventories and property, plant, and equipment, and monetary assets and liabilities. On the other hand, current cost accounting is a method of measuring assets and related expenses at their current cost on the balance sheet date or the date they are sold or used. It focuses on specific price changes for individual assets rather than on price changes caused by general inflation. The philosophy of current cost accounting declares that the dollars expended at some point in the past have no relevance to the preparation of present-day financial statements during an inflationary period. According to this view, the only relevant numbers are the dollars that would be expended if an asset were to be acquired on the balance sheet date, and any other method of valuation is not economically realistic during an inflationary period. Like constant dollar accounting, current cost accounting applies only to inventories, property, plant, and equipment, and related costs and expenses.

Q: What is the basic difference in the measurement bases used for constant dollar accounting and current cost accounting?

A: The constant dollar approach takes the amount of dollars reflected at historical costs as contained in the financial or accounting records of a business enterprise and applies a general price index

(CPI-U) to these historical dollar balances to restate them in terms of dollars of uniform purchasing power as of the date of the balance sheet. Current cost measurements are made for the assets presently owned and used by a company (i.e., reproduction cost) and not for replacement assets. Current cost measurements require the management of companies to select appropriate methods of determining the current costs of the items to be measured, which may include any of the following: internally or externally generated price indexes for the class of goods or services to be measured, references to current invoice prices, vendors' price lists or other quotations or estimates, or standard manufacturing costs that reflect current costs.

Extent of Disclosure

Q: Why is disclosure within annual reports regarding the effects of inflation limited to certain figures within the basic financial statements?

A: The required disclosures relate only to those balance sheet and income statement items that are most affected by inflation, such as inventories; fixed assets; sales revenues; cost of goods sold; depreciation, depletion, and amortization expense; and net income. As a result, FASB Statement No. 33 requires companies to disclose certain information for the current fiscal year as measured by the historical cost/constant dollar basis and the current cost basis. Information required for the current year includes:

> *Income from continuing operations on an historical cost/constant dollar basis and on a current cost basis.*
>
> *The purchasing power gain or loss on net monetary items on a constant dollar basis.*
>
> *The current cost amounts of inventory and property, plant, and equipment at the end of the current fiscal year.*
>
> *Increases or decreases for the current fiscal year in the current cost amounts of inventory and property, plant, and equipment, and net of inflation.*

Also, the following selected financial data must be disclosed for the most recent five years:

Net sales and other operating revenues.

Income from continuing operations on a constant dollar basis and on a current cost basis.

Income per common share from continuing operations on a constant dollar basis and on a current cost basis.

Net assets at fiscal year end on a constant dollar basis and on a current cost basis.

Increases or decreases in the current cost amounts of inventory and property, plant, and equipment, net of inflation.

Purchasing power gain or loss on net monetary items.

Cash dividends declared per common share.

Market price per common share at the end of the fiscal year.

The average or end-of-year level of the Consumer Price Index.

Consumer Price Index

Q: In adjusting historical cost dollars to dollars of the same general purchasing power or constant dollars, companies indicate that they use the CPI-U as the basis for the adjustment. What is the nature and significance of this index?

A: The CPI-U is published by the Bureau of Labor Statistics of the U.S. Department of Labor on a monthly basis in a publication entitled *Monthly Labor Review.* The CPI-U is used for all constant dollar calculations and includes, in addition to regular wage earners such as clerical, managerial, and technical workers, the self-employed, short-term workers, the unemployed, retirees, and others not in the labor force. This index covers approximately 80% of the population of the United States. The Index does not include persons in the military service, institutions, or those living outside of urban areas, such as farm families.

Net Monetary Items

Q: Information on financial data adjusted for the effects of inflation often refers to an item called "gain or loss on net monetary items." What are net monetary items?

A: Net monetary items represent the difference between a company's monetary assets and monetary liabilities which results in a gain or loss in the purchasing power of the dollar. This difference is also referred to as a purchasing power gain or loss. A monetary asset represents either money or a claim to money that is fixed in dollar amount, or an amount that can be determined without a reference to future prices of specific goods or services. Examples of monetary assets include: cash on hand and demand bank deposits, time deposits, bonds other than convertible debentures, accounts and notes receivable, allowance for doubtful accounts, loans to company employees, long-term receivables, refundable deposits, advances to unconsolidated subsidiaries, and cash surrender value of life insurance. A monetary liability represents an obligation to pay a sum of money in a fixed dollar amount or an amount that can be determined without reference to future prices of specific goods or services. Examples of monetary liabilities include: accounts and notes payable, accrued expenses payable (e.g., wages and salaries), cash dividends payable to stockholders, advances from customers, bonds payable and other long-term debts, and deferred income tax credits.

Unaudited Information

Q: Why is the financial information adjusted for the effects of inflation labeled "unaudited" instead of being subject to audit like other financial statement data?

A: FASB Statement No. 33, which requires the disclosure of certain financial information adjusted for the effects of inflation, was issued as an experiment. The FASB intends to study the extent to

which the supplementary financial information is used, the types
of people that find it useful, and the purposes for which such
information is used. The requirements of the statement may be
amended or withdrawn by the Board approximately five years
after its date of issuance in September 1979. Because of the
experimental nature of the statement's requirements for financial
reporting, companies have been given wide latitude in developing and communicating the information to be presented within
annual reports. As a result, companies have used assumptions and
techniques that are not standardized as are other measurement
principles, such as generally accepted accounting principles. For
example, in arriving at current cost, a company is free to use
internally or externally generated price indexes for the class of
goods or services to be measured. References to current invoice
prices, vendors' price lists or other quotations or estimates, or
standard manufacturing costs that reflect current costs can all be
used. Therefore, the effects of changing prices on financial information may differ from one company to another, as well as from
year to year. In general, financial information adjusted for the
effects of inflation is supplementary information to the basic financial statements that applies only to companies of a specific size.
Also, because of its supplementary nature and because such financial information is presented on an experimental basis, with measurements that are subjective among companies, financial data
adjusted for the effects of inflation are not audited by CPAs.

Understanding Inflation-Adjusted Data

Q: The information contained within annual reports on accounting
and financial reporting for the effects of inflation is often long and
detailed. How can investors understand such information without
getting lost in its technicalities?

A: Concentrate on the narrative information, which is generally
designed to help readers understand the purpose, limitations, and

impact of inflation-adjusted data, as well as differences in the methods used (i.e., the difference between constant dollar and current cost).

Q: Since the information required by FASB Statement No. 33 is experimental in nature, does it have any flaws?

A: Although many companies disclose financial information adjusted for the effects of inflation as required by FASB Statement No. 33, many of those companies believe that such information has certain flaws and is therefore not meaningful to investors. Such companies will indicate this point of view within the narrative portion of their note on this information. Both constant dollar and current cost methods have been criticized. For example, constant dollar accounting uses the CPI-U in order to report financial statement items in dollars having the same general purchasing power. The CPI-U measures the change in the cost of a market basket of goods and services for consumers and not for businesses. As a result, some companies believe that it is not an accurate reflection of the effects of inflation on business. Current cost accounting is a method wherein assets are reported at their reproduction cost. It assumes that assets will be replaced with identical assets (e.g., electromechanical switching equipment in a telephone company will be replaced with similar equipment and not with modern electronic switching equipment). Since this is not what actually happens, it also is not an accurate reflection of the effects of inflation on business. In reality, replacement of fixed assets generally occurs over a period of years. Also, the current cost method does not take into account possible higher future selling prices or cost savings that new and technologically advanced equipment may provide when existing assets are replaced. Another flaw in FASB Statement No. 33 pointed out by some companies is that none of the methods used to determine inflation-adjusted income take into consideration the operating efficiency that will result from new replacement assets; nor do the methods consider the new revenue generating services that will be possible with new assets. As a result, some companies believe that neither a complete, nor an accurate picture of inflation's effects on business is being presented.

The presentation of financial information has been a subject of contention among accountants, financial analysts, and financial executives for quite some time, and will continue to remain controversial during its experimental stage. Such information should be viewed with respect to the company that is presenting the data. If a particular company believes that the financial information adjusted for the effects of inflation has certain flaws or limitations, those facts are generally covered in the narrative portion of the related note or supplementary data.

Chapter Four

Audit
Reports

INTRODUCTION

An audit report on the financial statements of a publicly listed corporation is similar to the well-known "Good Housekeeping" seal of approval on consumer products. It is the means by which a CPA acknowledges a company's financial statements based on an examination of those statements. The audit report most often presented within the annual reports of publicly listed corporations includes an unqualified opinion on the financial statements. The unqualified opinion is often referred to as the *clean* opinion that CPAs include within a standard audit report, provided the following conditions have prevailed:

1. The audit or examination has been conducted in accordance with generally accepted auditing standards.
2. The financial statements are fairly presented in conformity with generally accepted accounting principles; this includes adequate disclosure.
3. The accounting principles used by the company have been consistently applied from year to year.
4. There are no unusual uncertainties with respect to the financial statements, such as the future outcome of a lawsuit, contract negotiations with the government, or federal tax matters.

An example of a standard audit report on a company's comparative financial statements follows:

The Board of Directors
Name of Company

We have examined the balance sheets of (name of company) as of December 31, 19X3 and 19X2, and the related statements of income, retained earnings, and changes in financial position for each of the three years in the period ended December 31, 19X3. Our examinations were made in accordance with generally accepted auditing standards, and, accordingly, included such tests of the accounting records and such other auditing procedures as we considered necessary in the circumstances.

In our opinion, the financial statements referred to above present fairly the financial position of (name of company) as of December 31, 19X3 and 19X2, and the results of its operations and the changes in its financial position for each of the three years in the period ended December 31, 19X3, in conformity with generally accepted accounting principles applied on a consistent basis.

(date of report)   (signature of accountant
                                              or public accounting firm)

The purpose of this chapter is to cover the purpose and significance of audit reports and those circumstances that may warrant modifying the standard form generally used by CPAs. Illustrations of audit reports covering the financial statements included within the 1982 annual reports of certain well-known public companies are provided at the end of this chapter.

OVERVIEW OF AUDIT REPORTS

Purpose

Q: What is the purpose of an audit report?

A: An audit report is designed to convey, to a reader of financial statements:

1.   The nature of the work undertaken by an auditor or certified public accountant, that is, an audit or examination of a company's financial statements according to certain professional standards.
2.   What the auditor uncovered during the examination as expressed by an opinion on the overall financial statements.

Nature of an Audit

Q: What is an audit?

A: An audit is a sophisticated process undertaken by a public accounting firm comprised of CPAs who test the credibility of a company's financial statements. An audit initially involves a study and evaluation of a company's internal accounting controls. Based on a review of internal accounting controls, the auditor decides on the nature, timing, and extent of auditing procedures to be performed during the audit. In other words, the auditor does not test every transaction. Depending on the adequacy of a company's internal accounting controls, the auditor applies the concept of selective testing of transactions as they pertain to cash, accounts receivable, accounts payable, and other accounts. If an auditor were to apply auditing procedures to every transaction and related account, the cost in money and time for an audit would be staggering to a company. Audits are required on an annual basis by public companies whose stocks are listed on a recognized stock exchange. It is considered to be the highest level of service that a CPA can provide to a client company.

Benefit to Investors

Q: What benefit does an audit report provide to an investor?

A: An audit report enables a reader of a company's financial statements (e.g., an investor) to determine the extent to which reliance can be placed on those financial statements. Depending on the type of opinion expressed by the CPA, an audit report provides reasonable assurance that financial statements reflect a company's financial position and results of operations according to an established framework of generally accepted accounting principles. In this way, an investor can obtain some degree of confidence that a company's financial statements are reliable for making an investment decision, because those statements have been audited (i.e., examined) by a CPA who was independent of the company.

Independence of CPA

Q: What does it mean when a CPA is independent of the company under audit?

A: In the practice of public accounting, a certified public accountant is governed by a code of professional ethics that provides guidance concerning independence with respect to his or her clients. These rules require CPAs to be independent in fact and in appearance. Independence in fact implies objectivity on the part of a CPA when performing an audit. For example, the quality of the CPA's audit work should not be influenced by personal advantage. Independence in appearance implies that the CPA is free from any potential conflicts of interest, which might lead parties outside the company business to question the CPA's independence in fact. For instance, if the CPA is involved in business transactions with a client, is related through family bloodlines to an officer of a company under audit, or owns stock in the client company, such relationships might raise questions as to the CPA's objectivity when conducting the audit. In other words, independence in fact would be questioned. When a CPA is independent both in fact and appearance, investors are able to derive some measure of confidence concerning the credibility of a company's financial statements. If a CPA is not independent both in fact and in appearance with respect to a company, that CPA is precluded, by professional standards of the American Institute of Certified Public Accountants, from expressing an opinion on the financial statements taken as a whole.

Certified Public Accountants

Q: What are certified public accountants?

A: Certified public accountants are individuals who have demonstrated their competence as licensed professional accountants by meeting the statutory requirements of the state in which they practice public accounting. In order to become a CPA, an accountant must fulfill certain educational and work-experience requirements that relate to the practice of public accounting. Work-experience requirements vary from state to state. Educational and work-experience requirements generally include:

> *A degree from an accredited college or university with a certain number of hours in accounting and related business courses, as well as in liberal arts subjects.*
>
> *Completion of the CPA examination, which emphasizes theoretical and practical applications of financial and management accounting, federal income taxation, auditing, and commercial law.*
>
> *Employment as a professional accountant with a public accounting firm for a certain period of time.*

CPAs are engaged by companies to perform audits, tax work, management advisory services, and other forms of financial and tax-related consultation services.

Q: Does an audit report imply that the CPA is responsible for the financial statements?

A: The management of a company is responsible for the contents of the financial statements, *not* the CPA or auditor. Management is the originator of the information presented in the financial statements, while the CPA may be considered the evaluator of the information presented. In this way, the roles of management and the auditor are distinct. If these roles were not distinct, and the CPA were held responsible for the representations made in the financial statements, any evaluations concerning the financial data in those statements made by the CPA would not be considered by third-party users of the financial statements to be independent evaluations. As a result, a certain amount of credibility concerning the financial statement information might be impaired. Management is held responsible for the representations made in the respective company's financial statements for the following reasons:

Management is continuously involved with the operations of the company.

Management has first-hand knowledge of all transactions that take place throughout the company.

Management's experience with the business places it in a prime postion to be the originator of any judgments concerning operating policies, procedures, and final decisions concerning company operations.

Any service provided by CPAs, the end result of which is often documented by some form of report, is similar to that of an objective reporter. In this way, the CPA or auditor acts as an independent intermediary between management and third-party users of the financial statements. Another way to view a CPA is as an independent contractor who is hired from outside a company to perform a specific service, In this case an examination of a company's financial statements.

Q: What objectives does a CPA try to achieve during an audit of a company's financial statements?

A: During an audit, a CPA endeavors to determine the following:

1. Whether or not all transactions affecting the company's accounts are recorded, and whether or not all recorded items are the result of actual transactions.
2. Whether or not all assets are owned by the company, all liabilities are owed to creditors, and all outstanding shares of capital stock are owned by shareowners.
3. Whether or not all amounts are recorded accurately, and if they reflect any subsequent changes in value.
4. Whether or not all recorded amounts are correct and are listed in the proper fiscal period.

5. Whether or not detailed amounts are correctly summarized when arriving at aggregate amounts in the financial statements.
6. Whether or not all relevant information is included within the financial statements.

Q: What support does a public accounting firm have for its audit report on a particular company?

A: During the course of an audit, the independent auditors or CPAs will prepare and maintain working papers, the form and content of which are designed to meet the requirements of an audit for a particular company. These working papers represent records maintained by the auditors on the procedures and tests applied to verify accounts and transactions, the information obtained from the company's management, and the conclusions reached with regard to the audit. Working papers generally include audit programs that serve as guidelines as to specific steps or tests an auditor undertakes in examining specific accounts, memoranda, letters, abstracts of company documents, and various forms of schedules. In general, working papers consist of various forms of documentation undertaken by an auditor during an examination of a company's financial statements which support the audit report.

Q: Are the auditor's working papers relating to the audit of a company available to investors as is the audit report found within the company's annual report?

A: Working papers are the sole property of the auditors who prepare them. They are not available to investors and are generally not available to the management of the client company that has undergone an audit. In some cases audit working papers may serve as a useful reference source for a client company if the auditor gives his or her express permission. However, they are never used as a substitute for the company's accounting records.

Date of Audit Report

Q: The date at the lower left-hand conrner of an audit report is usually a month or two later than the date of the financial statements. Why do those dates differ?

A: The date at the lower left-hand corner of an audit report represents the date that the auditor completed his examination of the company's financial statements or the date that the auditor's field work was completed. That date may be from one to three months after the date of the financial statements.

Detecting Troubled Companies

Q: How can investors detect a troubled situation in a company by reading the audit report?

A: A troubled situation in a company can be noted within an audit report by the following indicators:

> *Unusual wording or an unusually long report.*
>
> *Reference to material uncertainties with respect to the financial statements, such as pending litigation or asset realizations noted with an auditor's opinion that partially reads "subject to, etc."*
>
> *The report is dated long after the close of the company's fiscal year.*

In those cases where a "subject to" phrase appears, the investor should read carefully the report as well as the footnote to which it refers, since that note should describe the nature and impact of the event giving rise to the "subject to" opinion.

SCOPE PARAGRAPH

Purpose

Q: What is the implication of the first paragraph of an audit report?

A: The first paragraph of an audit report, referred to as the scope paragraph, is designed to describe the nature or scope of an auditor's work, namely, an examination of those financial statements of a particular company that are specifically identified within the scope paragraph, such as the balance sheet and related statements of income, retained earnings, and changes in financial position.

Auditing Standards

Q: What are generally accepted auditing standards?

A: Generally accepted auditing standards represent professional criteria or a "road map" for auditors to follow in the performance of audits. Auditing standards that are generally accepted by the public accounting profession include:

General standards that govern the professional qualities an auditor needs to possess, such as adequate technical training, independence in mental attitude, and diligent care when conducting audits.

Field work standards that govern the nature, extent, quality of work performed by auditors, and judgments exercised by auditors during an examination of financial statements.

Reporting standards that govern the parameters of reporting on the results of audits, such as form and content of audit reports, and the degree of an auditor's responsibility.

Q: Who develops auditing standards?

A: Auditing standards are developed by the Auditing Standards Board of the American Institute of Certified Public Accountants, a national professional organization of CPAs. The Board includes professional CPAs from public accounting firms of various sizes who discuss, evaluate, and eventually formulate auditing standards in a manner similar to the work of the Financial Accounting Standards Board when it develops generally accepted accounting principles.

Auditing Procedures

Q: What are auditing procedures?

A: Auditing procedures, which are performed by an independent auditor or CPA based on a study and evaluation of a company's internal accounting controls, are often referred to as substantive tests or tests of details of accounting transactions and balances of accounts. In general, auditing procedures include, but are not limited to, the following: verification of account balances, tracing transactions to various supporting documents, confirmation of balances with outside parties, physical observations and inspections of inventories, examination of sales invoices, verification of accounts payable, and checking dividend payments to stockholders. Auditing procedures are also designed to help the CPA search for any existing errors or irregularities that might have an effect on the financial statements. However, auditing procedures do not guarantee that errors or irregularities will be uncovered during an audit. In general, auditing procedures encompass the actual work a CPA undertakes during an examination of financial statements; those procedures are generally tailored to the particular characteristics of the company.

Q: Does the CPA test all of the accounts and transactions that are summarized in the financial statements?

A: An audit includes tests of samples of a company's accounting records and transactions. Since it is impractical for a CPA to check all the information in the company's accounting records, the company's internal accounting controls assure the CPA that information obtained from the accounting records is reliable. This in turn enables the CPA to reduce the extent of information that needs to be verified, and therefore reduces the extent of auditing procedures to be performed by the CPA.

Internal Accounting Controls

Q: What are the internal accounting controls of a company, and how do they relate to the work of an auditor?

A: Internal accounting controls consist of all methods and procedures concerned with the safe protection of a company's assets and the reliability of financial records. These include:

Authorization and approval of transactions.
Separation of duties related to the maintenance of accounting records and reports from those duties related to the custody of assets and company operations.
Physical control of company assets.
Prevention of unauthorized access to accounting records and assets.

The extent and sophistication of internal accounting controls will vary with the size and operations of a particular company. A review of a company's internal accounting controls by a CPA is often referred to as tests of compliance. Such tests are designed to provide the auditor with some assurance that compliance with a company's internal accounting control procedures is being maintained. The nature, extent, and timing of tests of transactions and auditing procedures undertaken by a CPA during an audit will depend on the adequacy or efficiency of a company's internal accounting controls. The study and evaluation of a company's internal accounting controls and the auditing procedures performed by the auditor form the basis for the CPA's independent opinion of the company's financial statements taken as a whole.

Going Concern Problem

Q: What are some of the indicators that would lead a CPA to conclude that the company under audit has a going-concern problem?

A: Going-concern problems generally involve financing problems, whereby the company has difficulty meeting its obligations, and/ or operating problems, whereby the company has been unable to operate successfully. Indicators of a financing problem may include one or more of the following:

> *Current liabilities exceed current assets, which makes it difficult for a company to meet its current obligations to bankers and other creditors.*
>
> *There is a deficit in retained earnings, which brings to question the company's solvency position.*
>
> *The company has been unable to meet its debt payment schedules.*
>
> *The company has violated one or more of the debt covenants of its loan agreements, such as failure to maintain a minimum working capital balance.*
>
> *The company has been unable to obtain additional funds from various capital sources.*

Indicators of an operating problem may include one or more of the following:

> *The company has shown operating losses for more than one past period.*

Revenue has been insufficient for maintaining operations on a day-to-day basis.

There have been cutbacks in operations, such as reduction in personnel.

The ability to operate as a business has been curtailed as a result of legal proceedings or the refusal of suppliers of operating materials to transact business with that company.

Company management has been unable to control operations in an efficient manner as indicated by several uncorrected problems that continually repeat themselves.

Unaudited Financial Information

Q: Does the CPA follow any procedures to verify the selected quarterly financial data labeled "unaudited" in the annual report?

A: Although the selected quarterly financial data is not audited, and therefore not covered by the audit report, the CPA does review such information by making inquiries of management and following analytical review procedures. Inquiries are generally made about the company's accounting system, any significant changes in internal accounting control, changes in accounting practices, and whether or not the interim financial information has been prepared in conformity with generally accepted accounting principles. Analytical review procedures generally include a comparison of the interim financial information with comparable information for the immediately preceding interim period and for corresponding previous periods, and with anticipated results; and a study of the relationships of elements of financial information that would be expected to conform to a predictable pattern based on the company's experience (e.g., the ratios of sales to operating profit and debt to equity).

Q: Even though financial information adjusted for the effects of inflation is labeled "unaudited" in the annual report, does a CPA follow any verification procedures with respect to such information?

A: The CPA applies certain limited procedures to such supplementary financial information. These are generally in the form of inquiries of company management, and are directed toward the judgments made concerning the measurement and presentation of the financial information in accordance with guidelines prescribed by the FASB. The CPA also compares the financial information for consistency with (1) company management responses to the CPA's inquiries, (2) audited financial statements, and (3) other knowledge that might have been obtained during the audit.

OPINION PARAGRAPH

Purpose

Q: What is the implication of the second paragraph of an audit report?

A: The second paragraph of an audit report, referred to as the opinion paragraph, represents the CPA's "stamp of approval" and indicates that the financial statements represent what they were intended to represent. This opinion relates to the financial statements taken as a whole and is often referred to as the *attest function*. In this way, the CPA or auditor expresses an expert and professional judgment (i.e., opinion), and is reasonably certain that the financial statements do not contain any material misstatements and that no essential information has been omitted by company management.

Q: Is the opinion of the CPA a form of guarantee as to the credibility of a company's financial statements?

A: It is most important for readers of reports on audited financial statements to understand that the opinion in the report is the CPA's *opinion*. Nothing more! It is *not* a form of guarantee that the financial statements are perfect representations of a company's financial health. The opinion is based on the CPA's professional judgment. It is similar to an evaluation given by a jeweler on the worth of a diamond or that of a real estate appraiser on the value of a piece of property. The use of professional judgment on any matter, including financial statements, does not necessarily guarantee that all flaws will be detected. Although an audit opinion is not to be regarded as a guarantee that there are no misrecorded transactions, incorrect accounting judgments, omitted disclosures, or actual fraud, the chances that significant errors and irregularities actually exist are minimized as a result of an audit.

Significance of "Present Fairly"

Q: What are the meaning and significance of the phrase *present fairly* when the CPA states that the financial statements of the company present fairly the financial position of the company as of a certain date and that the results of its operations and changes in financial position conform to generally accepted accounting principles?

A: The phrase *present fairly* indicates to a reader that the company's financial statements are reasonably accurate. *Present fairly* in conformity with generally accepted accounting principles (GAAP) also implies appropriate (1) application of GAAP as financial accounting information was accumulated and processed, (2) disclosure of changes in GAAP from the preceding year, and (3) description in the financial statements of information from accounting records.

Generally Accepted Accounting Principles

Q: Under what circumstances does the CPA conclude that the financial statements actually conform to generally accepted accounting principles?

A: A CPA concludes that a company's financial statements conform to

generally accepted accounting principles when the following conditions prevail:

> *The accounting principles that are used by the management of
> the audited company are generally accepted by the public
> accounting profession.*
>
> *The accounting principles used by the management of the
> audited company were appropriate for the company's circum-
> stances.*
>
> *The financial statements contain all the necessary disclosures so
> that they will not mislead a reader.*
>
> *The financial statements present the substance of events and
> transactions that have taken place during the operating fiscal
> year. Such events and transactions must be reflected within the
> financial statements with a reasonable degree of precision.*

Q: What does the opinion paregraph imply when it states that generally accepted accounting principles were applied on a consistent
basis?

A: In some cases, generally accepted accounting principles include
alternative accounting practices that allow companies to use different methods of accounting for a particular event or transaction.
An example is the use of either the FIFO or LIFO method of
accounting for inventory. The phrase "on a consistent basis"
means that the company used the same accounting methods in the
current year that it used in the previous year. In this way the
reader of the audit report can be reasonably certain that the
financial statements are comparable from one year to the next.

Responsibility of CPA Implied by the Opinion

Q: What is the extent of a CPA's responsibility as to the credibility of
the financial statements when an opinion is expressed on those
statements?

A: CPAs may assume varying degrees of responsibility in their audit reports, based on the types of opinion they express. There are four basic types: an unqualified opinion, a qualified opinion, an adverse opinion, and a disclaimer of opinion. As the degree of a qualification increases, the CPA assumes less responsibility for the credibility of the audited financial statements. In other words, CPAs assume more responsibility for an unqualified opinion, which is the standard opinion or "clean opinion" reflected in the majority of annual reports, than for a qualified opinion. An unqualified opinion informs a reader that he or she can rely on the company's financial statements. On the other hand, a qualified opinion cautions a reader to rely less on the company's financial statements, while an adverse opinion cautions a reader to place little or no reliance on the financial statements. Therefore, the risk assumed by a CPA decreases as the degree of responsibility with respect to the credibility of the company's financial statements decreases. The specific risk incurred by the CPA is that of failing to inform a reader of the audit report of any deficiences in the presentation of the company's financial information. In general, an investor's reliance on a company's financial statements depends on the type of opinion issued by a CPA.

Q: What is the independent auditor's responsibility for detecting fraud?

A: When an independent auditor undertakes an audit engagement for a company, a responsibility is also undertaken to plan the audit or examination of financial statements in such a way as to search for errors or irregularities that would have a material effect on the financial statements. This search for errors or irregularities that may result in fraud is ordinarily accomplished by the independent auditor when performing those auditing procedures that, in the auditor's judgment, are appropriate to serve as a basis for an expression of an opinion on the financial statements. The standard audit report, with its unqualified opinion, is an implication of the independent auditor's belief that the financial statements taken as a whole are not materially misstated as a result of errors or irregularities. In those cases where an independent auditor detects errors or irregularities, the auditor has the responsibility to discuss the matter with the appropriate management of the company. If management does not investigate the discrepancies, the independent auditor then has the responsibility to note them in the audit report.

Q: In some cases, there has been publicity in the financial press concerning lawsuits against firms of certified public accountants. Should investors place reliance on the financial statements that were audited by a CPA firm that is involved in a lawsuit?

A: In most instances, reliance can be placed on the financial statements. Although there have been lawsuits against firms of certified public accountants, the number of such lawsuits is small compared to the thousands of audits of publicly listed corporations performed each year. Of course, many of these lawsuits have damaged the credibility of audited financial statements. Certain of these lawsuits have resulted from an error by a CPA firm in some major aspect in the performance of an audit. In such cases, the CPA firm has been held liable, and the error may have been attributable to the erroneous judgment of one or two professional CPAs, and therefore not necessarily to the entire CPA firm. However, most of the legal suits against CPA firms have occurred because of a lack of understanding by the courts as to the extent of a CPA's responsibilities as required by their rules of professional conduct.

MODIFICATIONS TO AUDIT REPORTS

Reasons for Modified Audit Reports

Q: Are there any circumstances that would cause a CPA to modify or change a standard audit report on a company's financial statements?

A: A CPA would modify a standard audit report under the following circumstances:

> *Part of the audit was performed by another CPA or independent auditor.*
>
> *The CPA emphasizes a specific matter regarding the financial statements, even though an unqualified opinion is expressed, such as an important event that may have occurred after the company's balance sheet date.*
>
> *The financial statements are presented in conformity with generally accepted accounting principles "except for" or "subject to" a certain situation or set of circumstances.*
>
> *The financial statements are not presented in conformity with generally accepted accounting principles.*
>
> *The CPA is unable to form an opinion on the financial statements.*

In the first two circumstances, the CPA's opinion would remain unqualified, while in the other circumstances the CPA would issue a qualified opinion, an adverse opinion, or a disclaimer of opinion.

Qualified Opinion

Q: What is a qualified opinion?

A: A qualified opinion is a modification of an auditor's clean opinion or standard report. In such cases, the opinion will indicate that the company's financial statements as a whole are presented in conformity with generally accepted accounting principles "subject to" or "except for" a certain situation or set of circumstances. There are basically four types of situations in which an accountant will render a qualified opinion on a company's financial statements. In

each situation, the opinion paragraph of the audit report is modi-
fied. Qualified opinions are described as follows:

1. The auditor has been unable to conduct certain auditing
    procedures, or the scope of the audit examination has been
    limited because of restrictions imposed by the client or
    circumstances. For example, the auditor may not have
    been able to observe the taking of the company's physical
    inventory and was also not satisfied as to inventory quan-
    tities by other audit procedures, other than physical
    inventory observation, because of the nature of the com-
    pany's accounting records. In such a case, an explanatory
    paragraph is added to the audit report between the scope
    and opinion paragraphs that describes the nature of the
    qualified opinion. An example follows:

The Board of Directors
Name of Company

We have examined the balance sheets of (name of company) as of
December 31, 19X3 and 19X2, and the related statements of
income, retained earnings and changes in financial position for
each of the three years in the period ended December 31, 19X3.
Our examinations were made in accordance with generally accepted auditing standards and, accordingly, included such tests of the
accounting records and such other auditing procedures as we
considered necessary in the circumstances, except as explained in
the following paragraph.

We did not observe the taking of physical inventories as of December 31, 19X3 and 19X2 in the amounts of $400,000 and $300,000,
respectively, in accordance with the terms of our engagement. We
were unable to satisfy ourselves as to the inventory quantities by
means of other auditing procedures because of the nature of the
company's accounting records.

In our opinion, except for the effects of such adjustments, if any, as
might have been determined to be necessary had we been able to
observe the taking of physical inventories, the financial statements

referred to above present fairly the financial position of (name of company) as of December 31, 19X3 and 19X2, and the results of its operations and the changes in its financial position for each of the three years in the period ended December 31, 19X3, in conformity with generally accepted accounting principles applied on a consistent basis.

(date of report)   (signature of CPA
                                              or public accounting firm)

2.   The financial statements do not fairly present the financial position or the results of operations of a company because of a lack of conformity with generally accepted accounting principles or because of inadequate disclosure. A middle paragraph is added between the scope and opinion paragraphs of the audit report to describe the reason for the qualified opinion (e.g., a specific disclosure item missing from the financial statements). An example follows:

The Board of Directors
Name of Company

We have examined the balance sheets of (name of company) as of December 31, 19X3 and 19X2, and the related statements of income, retained earnings and changes in financial position for each of the three years in the period ended December 31, 19X3. Our examinations were made in accordance with generally accepted auditing standards, and, accordingly, included such tests of the accounting records and such other auditing procedures as we considered necessary in the circumstances.

On January 5, 19X3, the company issued capital stock in the amount of $50,000 for the purpose of expanding operations.

In our opinion, except for the lack of information as stated in the preceding paragraph, the financial statements referred to above present fairly the financial position of (name of company) as of December 31, 19X3 and 19X2, and the results of its operations and the changes in its financial position for each of the three years in

the period ended December, 19X3, in conformity with generally
accepted accounting principles applied on a consistent basis.

(date of report)   (signature of CPA
                                              or public accounting firm)

3.   An unusual uncertainity exists with respect to future develop-
      ments in the company, and the effects on the financial statements
      of such developments cannot be reasonably estimated or
      resolved. In this case, the reader would refer to the middle
      paragraph of the audit report and also to the note to the financial
      statements for a description of the nature of the qualification. An
      example follows:

          The Board of Directors
          Name of Company

          We have examined the balance sheets of (name of company) as of
          December 31, 19X3 and 19X2, and the related statements of
          income, retained earnings and changes in financial position for
          each of the three years in the period ended December 31, 19X3.
          Our examinations were made in accordance with generally accept-
          ed auditing standards, and, accordingly, included such tests of the
          accounting records and such other auditing procedures as we
          considered necessary in the circumstances.

          As described in Note 6 to the financial statements, the company is
          involved in a number of antitrust suits, which it is contesting.
          Since the outcome of these legal suits cannot presently be deter-
          mined, the company has not made any provision for a liability in
          the financial statements.

          In our opinion, subject to the effects on the financial statements of
          such adjustments, if any, as might have been required had the
          litigation described in the preceding paragraph been resolved and
          related amounts been known, the financial statements referred to
          above present fairly the financial position of (name of company) as
          of December 31, 19X3 and 19X2, and the results of its operations
          and the changes in its financial position for each of the three years

in the period ended December 31, 19X3, in conformity with generally accepted accounting principles applied on a consistent basis.

(date of report)   (signature of CPA
                                                  or public accounting firm)

4.   A lack of consistency in the application of generally accepted accounting principles in the current year in relation to the preceding year. This type of qualification does not require an explanatory middle paragraph in the audit report. The nature of the qualification is explained in a note to the financial statements. Also, the qualification due to consistency is not as onerous as the first three types described. The reason for the qualification stems from the fact that the accounting change (e.g., from the straight line depreciation method to an accelerated method) has a material effect on the financial statements in the year the change in accounting was made or in the current year. The auditor is merely bringing this fact to the attention of the reader so that the reader will understand the reason for differences in depreciation expense and net income between the current and prior year. An example follows:

The Board of Directors
Name of Company

We have examined the balance sheets of (name of company) as of December 31, 19X3 and 19X2, and the related statements of income, retained earnings and changes in financial position for each of the three years in the period ended December 31, 19X3. Our examinations were made in accordance with generally accepted auditing standards and, accordingly, included such tests of the accounting records and such other auditing procedures as we considered necessary in the circumstances.

In our opinion, the financial statements referred to above present fairly the financial position of (name of company) as of December 31, 19X3 and 19X2, and the results of its operations and the changes in its financial position for each of the three years in the period ended December 31, 19X3, in conformity with generally accepted accounting principles applied on a consistent basis, except for the change, with which we concur, in the depreciation method for equipment as described in Note 8 to the financial statements.

(date of report)   (signature of CPA
                                                        or public accounting firm)

Q: What is the basic difference between an "except for" qualified opinion and a "subject to" qualified opinion?

A: An "except for" qualified opinion indicates that the independent auditor is satisfied as to the overall credibility of the financial statements except for a particular item, such as the following:

The financial statements contain a departure from GAAP.
There is a difference in GAAP between the current and prior year.
The auditor is unable to carry out one or more audit procedures because of a limitation placed on the scope of the audit.

A decision as to whether or not an "except for" qualification is appropriate depends on the materiality of the matter. Materiality is also a factor an auditor considers with respect to a "subject to" opinion, which is appropriate in those cases when the outcome of a matter affecting the financial statements cannot be estimated, such as a major legal suit or tax assessment. Therefore, when a material uncertainty prevails, the outcome of which cannot be determined, the independent auditor qualifies the audit opinion "subject to" resolution of the uncertainty.

Adverse Opinion

Q: What is an adverse opinion?

A: An adverse opinion is rendered by a CPA whenever the company's financial statements, taken as a whole, do not present fairly the financial position or results of operations in conformity with generally accepted accounting principles. This type of opinion is rarely seen in financial reports since most companies, upon the advice of their independent auditors, will correct any items that are improperly treated on their financial statements.

Disclaimer of Opinion

Q: What is a disclaimer of opinion?

A: The disclaimer of opinion means that the accountant is unable to give an opinion on the financial statements. In other words, the accountant "disclaims" an opinion on the financial statements taken as a whole. The two most common reasons for a disclaimer of opinion are:

1. A limitation is imposed in the scope of the audit, usually by the client, which appears to be too material with respect to the effect on the financial statements to warrant an unqualified opinion. An example of this type of audit report follows:

The Board of Directors
ABC Company

We have examined the balance sheets of ABC Company as of December 31, 19X2 and 19X1, and the related statements of income, ratained earnings and changes in financial position for the years then ended. Our examinations were made in accordance with generally accepted auditing standards and, accordingly, included such tests of the accounting records and such other auditing procedures as we considered necessary in the circumstances, except as explained in the following paragraph.

We did not observe the taking of physical inventories as of December 31, 19X2 and 19X1 in the amounts of $800,000 and $600,000, respectively, in accordance with the terms of our engagement. We were unable to satisfy ourselves as to the inventory quantities by means of other auditing procedures because of the nature of the company's accounting records.

Since we did not observe the taking of physical inventories and since we were unable to apply any alternative auditing procedures as to inventory quantities, as noted in the preceding paragraph, the scope of our work was not sufficient to enable us to express, and we do not express an opinion on the financial statements referred to above.

(date of report)   (signature of CPA
                                          or public accounting firm)

2.   The existence of unusual uncertainties which appear to be too material with respect to the effect on financial statements to warrant an unqualified opinion. An example might be the outcome of a material contingency or the possibility that the company's existence as a going concern is doubtful. An example of this type of audit report follows:

The Board of Directors
ABC Company

We have examined the balance sheets of ABC Company as of December 31, 19X2 and 19X1, and the related statements of income, retained earnings and changes in financial position for the years then ended. Our examinations were made in accordance with generally accepted auditing standards and, accordingly, included such tests of the accounting records and such other auditing procedures as we considered necessary in the circumstances.

The company has experienced a number of operating losses during the past five years, which resulted in an equity deficiency of $900,000 and $800,000 at December 31, 19X2 and 19X1, respectively. Its continuing as an operating business depends on future operations being profitable and also upon obtaining such additional financing as may be necessary to continue operations. Termination of the company may result in significant adjustments to stated assets, and such adjustments cannot presently be determined.

Because of the effects of such adjustments, if any, as might have been required if the outcome of the uncertainty referred to in the preceding paragraph had been known, we do not express an opinion on the financial statements referred to in the first paragraph of this report.

(date of report)   (signature of CPA
                                            or public accounting firm)

A disclaimer of opinion is rare with respect to publicly traded corporations. As a rule, most companies will rectify the problems that might lead the CPA to give a disclaimer of opinion on the financial statements in order to prevent that form of opinion from being displayed in the annual report.

Auditors' Report

To the Shareholders and Board of Directors
of Champion International Corporation:

We have examined the consolidated balance sheet of Champion International Corporation (a New York corporation) and subsidiaries as of December 31, 1982 and 1981, and the related statements of consolidated income, retained earnings and changes in financial position for each of the three years in the period ended December 31, 1982. Our examinations were made in accordance with generally accepted auditing standards and, accordingly, included such tests of the accounting records and such other auditing procedures as we considered necessary in the circumstances.

In our opinion, the financial statements referred to above present fairly the financial position of Champion International Corporation and subsidiaries as of December 31, 1982 and 1981, and the results of their operations and the changes in their financial position for each of the three years in the period ended December 31, 1982, in conformity with generally accepted accounting principles applied on a consistent basis.

New York, N.Y.,
January 14, 1983.   *Arthur Andersen & Co.*

Exhibit 4.1. Illustrated audit reports with an unqualified opinion. Reprinted by permission from the 1982 annual reports of Champion International Corporation, Honeywell, Inc., and Squibb Corporation.

Independent Auditors'
Opinion

To the Stockholders of Honeywell Inc.:

We have examined the balance sheet of Honeywell Inc. and consolidated subsidiaries as of December 31, 1982 and 1981 and the related income statement and changes in financial position for each of the three years in the period ended December 31, 1982. Our examinations were made in accordance with generally accepted auditing standards and, accordingly, included such tests of the accounting records and such other auditing procedures as we considered necessary in the circumstances.

In our opinion, such financial statements present fairly the financial position of Honeywell Inc. and consolidated subsidiaries at December 31, 1982 and 1981 and the results of their operations and the changes in their financial position for each of the three years in the period ended December 31, 1982, in conformity with generally accepted accounting principles consistently applied during the period, except for the change, with which we concur, in 1982 in translating foreign currencies as described in Note 2 to the financial statements.

Deloitte Haskins & Sells

Deloitte Haskins & Sells
Minneapolis, Minnesota
February 17, 1983

Accountants' Report

To the Board of Directors and Shareholders
of Squibb Corporation:

We have examined the consolidated balance sheet of Squibb
Corporation and subsidiaries as of December 31, 1982, 1981 and
1980 and the related consolidated statements of income, retained
earnings and changes in financial position for the years then ended.
Our examinations were made in accordance with generally accepted
auditing standards and, accordingly, included such tests of the accounting records and such other auditing procedures as we considered necessary in the circumstances.

In our opinion, the aforementioned consolidated financial statements present fairly the financial position of Squibb Corporation and
subsidiaries at December 31, 1982, 1981 and 1980 and the results of
their operations and the changes in their financial position for the
years then ended, in conformity with generally accepted accounting
principles consistently applied during the period, except for the
change, with which we concur, in the method of accounting for
foreign currency translation as described in the notes to the consolidated financial statements.

Peat, Marwick, Mitchell + Co.

New York, New York
February 25, 1983

Independent Auditors' Opinion

Kimberly-Clark Corporation,
Its Directors and Stockholders:

We have examined the consolidated balance sheets of Kimberly-Clark Corporation and Subsidiaries as of December 31, 1982 and 1981 and the related statements of consolidated income and retained earnings and of changes in consolidated financial position for the years ended December 31, 1982, 1981, and 1980. Our examinations were made in accordance with generally accepted auditing standards and, accordingly, included such tests of the accounting records and such other auditing procedures as we considered necessary in the circumstances. We did not examine the financial statements of certain equity companies. The Corporation had equity in the net income of such companies of $19.6 million, $42.5 million, and $31.5 million in 1982, 1981, and 1980, respectively. These statements were examined by other independent auditors whose reports thereon have been furnished us and our opinion expressed below, insofar as it relates to amounts included for these companies, is based solely upon the reports of other auditors.

In our opinion, based upon our examinations and in part upon the reports of other auditors, the accompanying consolidated financial statements of Kimberly-Clark Corporation and Subsidiaries (pages 12 through 24) present fairly the financial position of the companies at December 31, 1982 and 1981 and the results of their operations and the changes in their financial position for the years ended December 31, 1982, 1981, and 1980, in conformity with generally accepted accounting principles applied on a consistent basis.

Deloitte Haskins & Sells

Certified Public Accountants
Chicago, Illinois   February 1, 1983

Exhibit 4.2.   Illustrated audit report referring to the use of other auditors. Reprinted by permission from the 1982 annual report of Kimberly-Clark Corporation.

The Board of Directors and Shareholders
Posi-Seal International, Inc.

We have examined the accompanying consolidated balance sheets of Posi-Seal
International, Inc. at February 28, 1982 and 1981 and the related consolidated statements
of income and retained earnings, capital in excess of par value and changes in financial
position for each of the three years in the period ended February 28, 1982. Our examinations were made in accordance with generally accepted auditing standards and, accordingly, included such tests of the accounting records and such other auditing procedures as we
considered necessary in the circumstances.

As discussed in Note 8, the Company is a defendant in certain lawsuits. The ultimate
outcome of the lawsuits cannot be determined, and no provision for any liability that may
result has been made in the consolidated financial statements.

In our opinion, subject to the effects of such adjustments, if any, as might have been
required had the outcome of the uncertainties referred to in the preceding paragraph been
known, the statements mentioned above present fairly the consolidated financial position of
Posi-Seal International, Inc. at February 28, 1982 and 1981 and the consolidated results of
operations and changes in financial position for each of the three years in the period ended
February 28, 1982, in conformity with generally accepted accounting principles applied on
a consistent basis during the period.

Arthur Young & Company

April 14, 1982

NOTE 8
Contingencies

In 1975, Richard F. Chipperfield, a former officer and director of the Company, instituted an
action against the Company, certain present and former officers and directors of the Company
and an individual unaffiliated with the Company. One Stanton Saunders, also a former officer
and director of the Company, later joined Chipperfield as a plaintiff in the action. The action
was tried in November and December of 1980 before the United States District Court, for the
District of Rhode Island. The derivative and class action claims asserted by the plaintiffs were
both withdrawn with prejudice prior to trial and with court approval. At trial, plaintiffs' only
claim against the Company (a claim by Chipperfield for unpaid wages) was dismissed by the
Court. The Court also dismissed all of plaintiffs' claims against two of the defendants. The jury
found all of the remaining defendants not liable to Saunders on all of his claims and found one
present officer and director not liable to Chipperfield. Certain other present and former officers and directors were found liable to Chipperfield and have moved to set aside the verdict.
The defendants have also asked the court to clarify the verdict. The defendants contend that
the verdict was for $1.1 million while Chipperfield contends that the verdict was for $3.3
million. If the Court refuses to set aside the verdict, the Company has been advised that it is
likely that one or more of the parties will appeal.

Under certain circumstances, the Company is obligated by its by-laws and Delaware law to
indemnify its present and former officers, directors and employees against their costs and expenses of defending suits brought against them in such capacity. Under other circumstances,
the Company has the discretion under its by-laws and Delaware law to indemnify such persons, including the discretion to indemnify them for all or part of a judgment for which such
persons may be liable. Because this case is still proceeding, the Company does not know
what, if any, obligation it may have to indemnify the defendants.

On May 7, 1979, an action was brought against the Company and another defendant alleg-
ing faulty design and manufacture of valves by the Company and claiming total damages of
approximately $3,600,000. The action is now proceeding in the State Court of Rhode Island,
and the parties are presently engaged in the discovery process. The Company cannot now
estimate the extent of damages, if any, that may be assessed under this action. Accordingly,
the Company has made no provision for this matter in its consolidated financial statements.

Exhibit 4.3. Illustrated audit report with an opinion qualified "subject to" an uncertainty regarding litigation. Reprinted by permission from the 1982 annual report of Posi-
Seal International, Inc.

Shareholders and Board of Directors
Chrysler Corporation
Detroit, Michigan

We have examined the accompanying consolidated balance sheet of Chrysler Corporation and consolidated subsidiaries at December 31, 1982 and 1981, and the related consolidated statements of operations and changes in financial position for each of the three years in the period ended December 31, 1982. Our examinations were made in accordance with generally accepted auditing standards and, accordingly, included such tests of the accounting records and such other auditing procedures as we considered necessary in the circumstances.

In our report dated February 24, 1982, our opinion on the 1980 and 1981 financial statements was qualified as being subject to the effects of such adjustments, if any, which might have been required had the outcome of the uncertainties regarding Chrysler's going concern status and its investment in Peugeot S.A. been known. As explained in Note 2 Chrysler continues to face uncertainties in the future, some of which are beyond its control. However, in 1982 Chrysler generated significant cash from working capital management and the sale of Chrysler Defense Inc., and demonstrated its ability to produce positive cash flow from its automotive operations

and to realize its assets and satisfy its liabilities in the normal course of business. In addition, as described in Note 7, Chrysler negotiated a new loan agreement with Peugeot S.A. which assures Chrysler control of its investment in Peugeot S.A. Accordingly, our opinion on the 1980 and 1981 financial statements, as presented herein, is no longer qualified.

In our opinion, the accompanying financial statements present fairly the financial position of Chrysler Corporation and consolidated subsidiaries at December 31, 1982 and 1981 and the results of their operations and changes in their financial position for each of the three years in the period ended December 31, 1982 in conformity with generally accepted accounting principles applied on a consistent basis, except for the change, with which we concur, in depreciation methods in 1981.

TOUCHE ROSS & CO.
Certified Public Accountants

Detroit, Michigan
February 24, 1983

Exhibit 4.4. Illustrated audit report with an unqualified opinion that was qualified in previous years "subject to" the company continuing as a going concern enterprise. Reprinted by permission from the 1982 annual report of Chrysler Corporation.

Note 2.
1982 Developments and Future Risks and Uncertainties

Chrysler's 1982 net earnings of $170.1 million includes a gain on sale of Chrysler Defense. Inc., of $239.0 million. The loss from continuing operations of $68.9 million is a $486.2 million improvement over the 1981 loss of $555.1 million. The operating loss in 1982 includes the effect, estimated at $125 million, of a production interruption resulting from a five week strike by employees in Chrysler's Canadian plants, as well as losses of approximately $55 million resulting from Chrysler's Mexican operations, reflecting the adverse effects of the financial and economic crisis in Mexico.

Despite the improvement over 1981, the 1982 operating loss was below the profit projected in Chrysler's Operating Plan submitted to the Chrysler Corporation Loan Guarantee Board ("the Guarantee Board") in December, 1981. The effect of depressed industry sales, which were more than 20% below the levels anticipated in the Operating Plan, was partially mitigated by an improvement in the mix of vehicles sold, increased operating efficiencies, further cost reductions, and lower net interest expense.

In accordance with the Chrysler Corporation Loan Guarantee Act ("the Act"), the Guarantee Board is required to make periodic determinations as to Chrysler's present and future viability and under certain circumstances if such determinations cannot be made the Guarantee Board has the power to accelerate the maturity of outstanding guaranteed loans. Chrysler has filed with the Guarantee Board Operating and Financing Plans dated December 7, 1982 ("the Plans"). Chrysler anticipates that the Plans will be approved as filed after the normal review process has been completed. The Plans project an improvement in the results from continuing operations in 1983 over 1982, based on assumptions as to a modest improvement in U.S. industry retail sales of cars and trucks and an improvement in Chrysler's share of the market. Capital expenditures for 1983 have been projected to be above the 1982 levels and the Plans indicate an ability to finance these expenditures.

Chrysler's improved results from continuing operations, coupled with the sale of Chrysler Defense. Inc., and stringent working capital management, have resulted in significantly higher cash levels at December 31, 1982. Chrysler's access to bank credit and traditional credit markets is limited and, therefore, this level of liquidity represents a significant resource to deal with future financing needs should Chrysler be unable to achieve its operating objectives in 1983.

Chrysler's long term viability is predicated upon its ability to achieve sustained levels of significant operating profits, which in turn requires that Chrysler succeed in launching and marketing new products. If Chrysler cannot finance its planned spending programs and, as a result, reduces the scope of its new products, Chrysler could be at a competitive disadvantage and its operating results could be adversely affected. Chrysler's success will depend on a number of factors, including the state of the economy and consumer confidence, interest rates and the availability of consumer financing, the degree of competition from generally larger foreign and domestic manufacturers, cooperation of its labor force, fuel price levels, consumer preferences, the effects of government regulation and the strength of Chrysler's marketing network.

Exhibit 4.4   *(Continued)*

REPORT OF CERTIFIED PUBLIC ACCOUNTANTS

The Board of Directors
and Stockholders of Holly Corporation

We have examined the consolidated balance sheets
of Holly Corporation at July 31, 1982 and 1981, and
the related consolidated statements of income and
changes in financial position for each of the three
years in the period ended July 31, 1982. Our examinations were made in accordance with generally
accepted auditing standards and, accordingly, included such tests of the accounting records and
such other auditing procedures as we considered
necessary in the circumstances.

In our opinion, the consolidated financial statements referred to above present fairly the consolidated financial position of Holly Corporation at July
31, 1982 and 1981, and the consolidated results of
operations and changes in financial position for
each of the three years in the period ended July 31,
1982, in conformity with generally accepted accounting principles applied on a consistent basis
during the period except for the change required by
Financial Accounting Standards Board Statement
No. 34, with which we concur, in the method of
accounting for interest costs as described in Note 1
to the consolidated financial statements.

Arthur Young & Company

Dallas, Texas
September 24, 1982

1. SUMMARY OF SIGNIFICANT ACCOUNTING
    POLICIES

Accounting change
Effective August 1, 1980, the Company adopted
Financial Accounting Standards Board Statement
No. 34 which requires the capitalization of interest
costs associated with the acquisition of certain
assets. During 1982 and 1981, interest costs
amounting to $734,000 and $2,104,000 were capitalized which had the effect of increasing net
income by $374,000 ($.04 per share) and
$1,079,000 ($.13 per share), respectively.

Exhibit 4.5. Illustrated audit report with an opinion qualified for consistency due to
an accounting change in interest costs. Reprinted by permission from the 1982 annual
report of Holly Corporation.

Accountants' Report

Board of Directors and Shareholders
Frederick & Herrud, Inc.
Southfield, Michigan

We have examined the consolidated balance sheets of
Frederick & Herrud, Inc. and subsidiaries as at May 28,
1982 and May 29, 1981, and the related consolidated statements of income (loss), shareholders' equity and changes
in financial position for each of the three years in the period
ended May 28, 1982. Our examinations were made in
accordance with generally accepted auditing standards
and, accordingly, included such tests of the accounting
records and such other auditing procedures as we considered necessary in the circumstances.

In our opinion, the consolidated financial statements
referred to above present fairly the financial position of
Frederick & Herrud, Inc. and subsidiaries as at May 28,
1982 and May 29, 1981, and the results of their operations
and changes in their financial position for each of the
three years in the period ended May 28, 1982, in conformity with generally accepted accounting principles applied
on a consistent basis, except for the change, with which
we concur, in the method of valuing inventories as described in Note 3 to the financial statements.

August 5, 1982   **Laventhol & Horwath**
Southfield, Michigan   Certified Public Accountants

Exhibit   4.6.   Illustrated audit report with an opinion qualified for consistency due to
an accounting change in inventory valuation. Reprinted by permission from the 1982
annual report of Frederick & Herrud, Inc.

3. Inventories:

	1982	1981
Supplies	$ 5,124,898	$ 3,383,648
Raw materials	5,501,302	3,471,861
Work-in-process.	2,080,805	2,176,499
Finished goods	7,196,037	9,063,580
	$19,903,042	$18,095,588

As of May 31, 1980, the Company adopted the last-in, first-out (LIFO) method of valuing inventories from principally the first-in, first-out (FIFO) method used in prior years. The change in method was made because management believes LIFO more clearly reflects income by reducing the effect of short-term price fluctuations and generally matches current annual cost against current revenues in the statements of income (loss).

There is no cumulative effect on prior years because the May 30, 1980 inventory value is the beginning inventory value under the LIFO method. The change to LIFO had the effect of decreasing the net income, after giving effect to income taxes, by $2,605,000 ($.73 per share) and $2,410,000 ($.68 per share) at May 28, 1982 and May 29, 1981, respectively. This decrease resulted in a net loss for the year ended May 29, 1981. Inventories would have been $9,287,000 and $4,463,000 higher at May 28, 1982 and May 29, 1981, respectively, if the FIFO method had been used for inventory valuation.

Chapter Five

Capsule and Narrative Financial Information

INTRODUCTION

Although the most important sections of annual reports are the basic financial statements, special supplementary information, and audit reports described in the previous chapters of this book, other areas of the annual report are also worthy of the attention of investors. Annual reports also include capsule type information described as financial highlights, financial review, and selected financial data. Other information that is geared toward an explanation of management performance is provided in a narrative form, such as the president's letter, the management's discussion and analysis of financial condition and results of operations, and the management report. The purpose of this chapter is to describe these noteworthy areas of financial reporting so that investors and nonfinancial managers might recognize their value and importance. Illustrations of financial highlights, selected financial data, management's discussion and analysis of financial condition and results of operations, and management reports from the 1982 annual reports of certain well-known public companies are also provided in this chapter.

CAPSULE FINANCIAL INFORMATION

Purpose

Q: Why do publicly listed companies provide such capsule type financial information within annual reports as financial highlights, financial review, and selected financial data, when this information is also included within the audited financial statements?

A: The purpose is to highlight to shareowners and investors the financial information that best indicates company performance. Capsule type information is designed for investors and shareholders who do not wish to spend the time reading the entire set of basic financial statements.

Selected Financial Data

Q: It appears that all companies provide within their annual reports selected financial data for a five-year period, but they do not always provide a financial review. What is the reason for this?

A: The inclusion of selected financial data within annual reports is required of all publicly listed corporations in accordance with rules and regulations of the SEC. On the other hand, the inclusion of financial highlights and/or a financial review is generally optional on the part of public corporations. The SEC requirement for selected financial data is designed to provide, in a convenient and readable format, selected data for at least five years, which highlights significant trends in the company's financial condition and results of operations. The following items are required; however, companies may include additional items:

> *Net sales or operating revenues.*
> *Income or loss from continuing operations.*
> *Income or loss from continuing operations per common share.*
> *Total assets.*
> *Long-term obligations and redeemable preferred stock, including long-term debt, capital leases and redeemable preferred stock.*
> *Cash dividends per common share.*

Analysis by Investors

Q: Which type of capsule financial information should investors direct their attention to: financial highlights, financial review, or selected financial data?

A: Since the information in all three areas is abbreviated, investors should look at all three areas, even though there may be some repetition from one area to another. In some cases, the financial review may serve as a company's notes to the financial statements, and is therefore subject to audit. The financial review has the added advantage of providing narrative explanations with regard to the capsule financial information.

Responsibility of CPA

Q: Since capsule type financial information is not subject to audit, how can an investor be certain that such information is consistent with the audited financial statements?

A: The CPA's responsibility with respect to financial information in an annual report does not extend beyond the information covered in the audit report, and therefore the CPA does not have an obligation to perform any procedures to corroborate capsule type financial information. However, the CPA generally reads such information and considers whether or not the data or the manner in which the information is presented is materially inconsistent with that appearing in the audited financial statements. If there is a material inconsistency, the CPA will determine whether the financial statements, the audit report, or the capsule information requires revision.

PRESIDENT'S LETTER

Purpose

Q: What is the overall purpose of the president's letter in an annual report?

A: The president's letter is designed as an informal communication device to inform company shareowners as to the following: financial results for the year and their impact on the company; major developments, such as mergers and acquistions; the nature and extent of resource allocations, reorganizations, and management changes, if any; social reform programs; and the progress and future direction of the company.

Social Issues

Q: In some annual reports, the president's letter addresses social issues. How important is such information to an investor?

A: Social issues are important to an investor only in those cases when the issue (e.g., inflation, taxation) directly affects the company's present or future operating position. Financial analysts generally assign minimal value to information on social issues. Investors should do likewise. There is nothing wrong with a company undertaking programs of social reform, such as special efforts to safeguard the environment, provided the company is able to contribute the necessary resources without jeopardizing the vested interest of shareowners. However, most financial analysts believe that corporate managers often use reporting on a company's social reform programs as a vehicle to enhance the company's public image. Although social reform has its place in society, the primary purpose of any company that operates in a capitalistic and competitive environment, such as the United States, is to earn a profit and therefore make money. This should be the prime concern of all corporate investors.

Consistency with Financial Statements

Q: How might an investor be assured that the information provided within the president's letter is consistent with the information contained within the financial statements?

A: Although information contained within the president's letter is not audited as is information in financial statements, such information is basically consistent with financial statement data. For example, the divestment of a major line of business or a plant closing should also be described in the notes to the financial statements. Most major items affecting a company that are described in the president's letter will generally be noted somewhere in the audited financial statements, usually in the footnotes.

Interpretation by Investors

Q: The president's letter in most annual reports contains impresseive language. How might an investor differentiate between the proverbial "bull" and the "down to earth" truth?

A: There are no hard and fast rules to follow, but investors should "read between the lines" and take a hard look at the language of the company president. Keep in mind that when a company has a banner year, the president usually tells you straight out, without any frills. When the year has been below standard, the language may be contrived. For example, whenever you see the phrase "year of transition," low earnings can be expected. If the transition period is moving away from infancy, the phrase "continued growth" or something similar will be the common term used. Be cautious of statements such as "Our products are doing well" or "We are going to do our best." These phrases appear positive and effective without getting down to specifics. How well is "well"? What is the corporate objective associated with the term "best"? These are questions that should arise in the minds of investors; the answers should be provided in other parts of the annual report.

MANAGEMENT'S DISCUSSION AND ANALYSIS OF FINANCIAL CONDITION AND RESULTS OF OPERATIONS

Purpose

Q: What is the purpose of the management's discussion and analysis of financial condition and results of operations?

A: The management's discussion is analogous to a report provided in
a newspaper that answers the questions who, what, where, when,
and why. The purpose is to explain the financial results for the
year in the context of the company's present position, past results,
and forward plans. What significant events took place? How did
they work out? Why did they happen? What do the results mean
for the future? What are the problems of the business? The
explanations should enable the investor to appraise more real-
istically the financial statements and the quality of earnings, to
evaluate the amounts and certainity of a company's cash flows
from operations and from outside sources, and to project future
earning power. For example, although the income statement
reveals whether or not revenues are increasing, the management's discussion will indicate whether or not a change in revenues is caused by rising prices or an increase in the number of
units sold.

Applicability of Presentation

Q: Is the inclusion within the annual report of management's discussion and analysis of financial condition and results of operations a
requirement, or is it optional on the part of publicly listed companies?

A: It is required by the SEC and is designed to include the three-year
period covered by a company's income statement and statement
of changes in financial postion. This requirement is similar to the
SEC requirement that calls for inclusion of selected financial data
for at least a five-year period.

Benefit to Investors

Q: How does the management's discussion and analysis of financial
condition and results of operations benefit investors?

A: The discussion supplements the financial statements by providing
information that cannot be readily ascertained from the financial

statements with regard to liquidity, capital resources, and results of operations. For example, favorable as well as unfavorable trends that affect sales or income from continuing operations are brought to the limelight in the discussion. The discussion also requires a narrative comment about the effects of inflation on a company's sales and income from continuing operations, even if the company is not subject to the financial statement disclosure requirements of FASB Statement No. 33, "Financial Reporting and Changing Prices." The discussion is the subjective aspect of annual reports; it gives management the opportunity to show its personality and establish the credibility of the company. For this reason, investors should pay special attention to this section of the annual report. It tells something about management performance, and should provide some sense of the direction in which the business is going, which may not be readily determined from the financial statements.

Content

Q: What specific financial information should be covered by the management's discussion and analysis of financial condition and results of operations?

A: The discussion basically covers three financial aspects of a company's business: liquidity, capital resources, and results of operations.

> *Liquidity refers to a company's ability to generate adequate amounts of cash for its cash disbursements. Companies are required to identify trends or unusual demands, commitments, events, or uncertainties resulting in, or which management reasonably expects to result in, a significant increase or decrease in liquidity. For example, the discussion should identify unused sources of liquid assets and should explain the courses of action taken or planned to remedy an identified liquidity deficiency. It should also indicate how a company's working capital is allocated among cash, receivables, and inventory; and the length of time it takes to convert assets into cash. These are*

important factors in evaluating the strength of a company's cash flow.

Capital resources *refers to a company's major commitments for capital expenditures and the sources of funds for meeting these commitments. Favorable or unfavorable trends should be described. For example, the discussion should cover changes between equity, debt, and off-balance-sheet financing arrangements, including their relative costs. The coverage of capital resources and liquidity are often combined if the disclosures are interrelated.*

Results of operations *refers to any unusual or infrequent events or transactions or any significant economic changes that materially affect the amount of reported income from continuing operations, and in each case, the extent to which income is actually affected. It is required that significant components of revenue or expense be described in order to enable investors and shareholders to understand better the company's results of operations. This includes revenues derived from business segments. The discussion should disclose unusual or infrequent events that significantly affect reported results. Also, trends or uncertainties that management expects will have a significant impact on future results of operations should be described. This discussion should include events (e.g., a labor contract containing significant wage increases) and other uncertainties that may affect the accuracy of the reported financial information as an indicator of future operating results. Disclosure of the extent to which sales increases are attributable to price increases, volume increases, and the introduction of new products or services is also required.*

Besides information on liquidity, capital resources, and results of operations, the discussion should also provide (1) a narrative explanation of the impact of inflation on revenues and income and (2) forward-looking information.

Q: What kind of forward-looking information might an investor look for in the management's discussion and analysis of financial conditions and results of operations?

A: Forward-looking information disclosed in the discussion might include a five-year forecast of revenues, sales, and cash flow, and future expenditures; major capital expenditures and their possible impact on debt; possible closings of plants or factories; and pending labor contract negotiations which may adversely affect future operating results. Forward-looking information is encouraged by the SEC but is not required of publicly listed companies. It does not include presently known data that will affect future operating results, such as increases in costs of labor or materials that are already known by the company.

Q: How much should investors rely on forward-looking information?

A: Very little. An investment decision should hinge on known facts, namely the financial results of the past year. Any futuristic type of financial information is subject to erratic changes that may result from future upturns or reverses in the economic and/or political climate. Thus forward-looking information is based on assumptions that may prove to be invalid in the future. Therefore, investors should consider forward-looking information for what it is, namely additional information based on assumptions for the future.

MANAGEMENT REPORTS

Comparision to Management's Discussion

Q: How does the management report differ from the management's discussion and analysis of financial condition and results of operations?

A: The management's discussion and analysis of financial condition and results of operations concentrates on a company's financial picture or management's performance in terms of liquidity, capital resources, and results of operations. On the other hand, the management report describes management's responsibility for its company's financial statements, the means by which that responsibility is fulfilled, and the roles of others—such as the independent auditors and the company's audit committee—with respect to the company's financial statements. In other words, the management's discussion and analysis of financial condition and results of operations describes the results of management's performance, and the management report describes how that performance was carried out.

Q: Does the SEC require that management reports be provided within annual reports as it requires the management's discussion and analysis of financial condition and results of operations?

A: The SEC encourages but does not require that management reports be included within annual reports. However, because of their importance as a means of informing users of financial statements as to management's responsibility with regard to those statements, the majority of publicly listed companies provide management reports in their annual reports.

Content

Q: What should investors look for in management reports?

A: Management reports generally contain the following information:

A statement of management's responsibility with regard to the company's financial statements, namely how they were prepared and on what basis (e.g., estimates based on judgment, integrity, and objectivity).

An indication that the financial statements have been prepared in conformity with generally accepted accounting principles.

The means by which management fulfills its responsibility, namely, the maintenance of a system of internal accounting control.

Whether or not internal auditors are used by the company.

The responsibility of the independent auditors (i.e., CPAs).

Reference to a company's audit committee.

Whether or not the management report is signed by the company's president and/or chief financial officer.

Reliability of Information

Q: Is the information contained within a management report as reliable as a company's audited financial statements?

A: Although management reports are not audited as financial statements are, the reports are similar to financial statements in that a potential liability does prevail for misstatements, falsifications, or fraud. A public corporation, its officers, and its directors might be liable for false statements made in the management report, management's discussion, or the financial statements. Therefore, the management report can be considered a reliable piece of information about a company. Also, the fact that a management report is usually signed by a company's president and/or chief financial officer adds some strength to the reliability of its content.

Internal Accounting Control

Q: What are the overall objectives of a company's internal accounting control as referred to within management reports?

A: The objectives of internal accounting control are as follows:

Transactions are executed in accordance with the authorization of company management.
Transactions are recorded in such a way as to allow the preparation of financial statements that conform to generally accepted accounting principles. In that way accountability for company assets is maintained.
Access to assets is permitted in accordance with the authorization of management.

Recorded assets are compared with existing assets, and appropriate action is taken if there are any differences.

Most management reports allude to these objectives in whole or in part.

Internal Auditors

Q: How do a corporation's internal auditors differ from independent auditors?

A: Internal auditors are employees of the corporation they serve. They perform a number of services for corporate management, such as evaluating internal accounting control and reviewing operating policies. Internal auditors represent a level of control within a corporation that determines whether or not the internal accounting control system is operating in an efficient manner. Independent auditors are hired from outside the corporation to examine the corporate financial statements as a service to the board of directors and shareholders. During the course of their examination, independent auditors often evaluate the work of the corporation's internal audit staff. This is a factor in determining the nature, timing and extent of the independent auditor's auditing procedures when they examine the corporation's financial statements.

Q: Are internal auditors subject to professional standards similar to those of independent auditors, who are subject to standards issued by the American Institute of Certified Public Accountants?

A: Even though internal auditors are employees of the publicly listed corporation that they serve, they are subject to professional standards and rules of conduct established by the Institute of Internal Auditors, a professional organization that is, in many respects, similar to the American Institute of Certified Public Accountants.

Audit Committees

Q: What is an audit committee as referred to in management reports?

A: An audit committee is generally a committee formed by a company's board of directors that is comprised primarily of nonofficer directors of a company. Their basic responsibilities include:

> *Selection of the independent auditors for the company.*
> *Review of the overall plan of the independent audit.*
> *Review of the financial statements and results of the independent audit.*
> *Overseeing the adequacy of a company's internal accounting control system.*
> *Review of the effectiveness of a company's internal audit function.*

In general, a corporate audit committee is responsible for monitoring the company's audit function, both independent and internal.

Q: Are corporations required to have audit committees?

A: Yes. As a condition for listing and continuing to list common stock on the New York Stock Exchange, corporations are required to establish and maintain audit committees comprised of directors who are independent of senior company management and executives, and who are free from any type of relationship that might be considered a conflict of interest (e.g., large holdings of company stock). The majority of audit committee members must be company directors who were not formerly officers of the company.

Q: How does an audit committee benefit a company's shareholders?

A: The audit committee provides a visible representation to shareholders to ensure that both company management and independent auditors face up to certain problems that they might otherwise tolerate or overlook, such as inadequacy in a company's internal accounting control system. In this way, an audit committee serves as a forum for airing the views of both company management and independent auditors. It also serves as a vehicle of communication for those responsible for various corporate affairs as to any matters that are not explicitly stated in the company's financial statements or independent auditor's report.

Q: What does an audit committee consider or look for in the selection of an independent auditor?

A: The most important factor an audit committee considers in the selection of independent auditors is the quality of the auditor's professional service and the reputation of the firm with which the auditor is associated. This includes the public accounting firm's standards of performance, that is, whether the firm conforms to generally accepted auditing standards; the firm's reputation as indicated by the recommendations of other clients; and whether or not the firm observes a professional development program so that its professional personnel possess the knowledge and expertise that is necessary to fulfill their assigned responsibilities during an audit engagement. Other considerations include:

> *Staff rotation policy on audit engagements after a reasonable number of years in order to provide a fresh perspective to the audit.*
>
> *Whether or not open discussions can be achieved with the public accounting firm's representatives.*
>
> *The extent to which the firm can provide the company with persons who possess specialized skills, such as tax work, SEC practice, accounting and auditing research, and management advisory services.*
>
> *Professional standing of key firm personnel in the public accounting profession, such as membership in the American Institute of Certified Public Accountants (AICPA) which also*

includes selected AICPA committees geared to improve professional practice, and in CPA state societies.

The firm's relationship with the SEC, that is, whether or not the firm is currently under investigation or has had restrictions imposed upon its practice in the past.

Whether or not the firm is involved in any litigation as a result of its accounting and audit practice.

Financial Highlights (in thousands, except per share)

Champion International Corporation and Subsidiaries

Years Ended December 31	1982	1981
Earnings		
Net Sales	$3,737,378	$4,004,027
Income Before Income Taxes	37,199	155,480
Income Taxes	(2,451)	35,834
Income From Continuing Operations	39,650	119,646
Discontinued Operations	–	(18,277)
Net Income	39,650	101,369
Per Common Share		
Primary Earnings:		
Continuing Operations	.45	1.91
Discontinued Operations	–	(.33)
Net Income	.45	1.58
Fully Diluted Earnings:		
Continuing Operations	.45	1.88
Discontinued Operations	–	(.32)
Net Income	.45	1.56
Cash Dividends Declared	.67	1.48
Cash Dividends Paid	.94	1.48
Shareholders' Equity	28.85	29.17
Financial Position		
Working Capital	402,798	409,216
Total Assets	3,471,994	3,443,226
Long-Term Debt and Other Liabilities	1,089,322	963,011
Total Shareholders' Equity	1,737,097	1,753,444
Additional Information		
Capital Expenditures:		
Capital Projects	189,198	235,431
Fee Lands, Reforestation, and Related Roads	28,095	38,024
Contract Timber and Related Roads	9,017	45,591
Capitalized Interest	30,107	15,102
Depreciation and Cost of Timber Harvested	167,161	168,598
U.S. Timber Acreage Owned or Controlled	3,329	3,381
Number of Employees	38.8	40.0
Number of Common Shareholders of Record at Year-End	28.5	30.3
Common Shares Outstanding at Year-End	54,952	54,893
Return on Average Shareholders' Equity –		
Continuing Operations	2.3%	6.8%

Exhibit 5.1. Illustrated financial highlights (Champion International Corporation). Reprinted by permission from the 1982 annual report of Champion International Corporation.

Financial Highlights

(Dollars in Millions Except Per Share Amounts)	1982	% Change	1981	% Change	1980
Revenue	$5,490.4	2.6	$5,351.2	8.7	$4,924.7
Income before income taxes	373.7	2.9	363.0	(8.7)	397.4
Income before extraordinary income	*271.3	5.9	256.3	(7.2)	276.3
Per common share	*12.09	7.5	11.25	(9.0)	12.36
Net income	*272.9	5.2	259.3	(10.2)	288.9
Per common share	*12.16	6.9	11.38	(11.9)	12.92
Dividends per common share	3.50		3.20		2.80
Stockholders' equity per common share	94.31		90.53		82.70
Return on average stockholders' equity	13.2%		13.2%		16.9%

*Includes $66.3 ($2.95 per share) from the gain on sale of interests in Cii Honeywell Bull and GE Information Services Co.

Exhibit 5.2. Illustrated financial highlights (Honeywell, Inc.). Reprinted by permission from the 1982 annual report of Honeywell, Inc.

Financial Highlights

Squibb Corporation and Subsidiaries
(Dollar amounts in thousands except per share figures)

	1982	1981	Change
Net Sales	$1,660,766	$1,523,911	9%
Profit from Operations	209,534	151,346	38%
Income before Costs of Restructuring	219,485	124,699	76%
Income before Taxes on Income	219,485	61,840	>100%
Income from Continuing Businesses	153,636	41,098	>100%
Gain on Sale and Income from Businesses Sold	—	70,249	—
Net Income	153,636	104,815	47%
Per Share:			
Income from Continuing Businesses	3.01	.83	>100%
Gain on Sale and Income from Businesses Sold	—	1.40	—
Net Income	3.01	2.10	43%
Cash Dividends	1.28	1.21½	5%
Research and Development	122,962	95,302	29%
Capital Expenditures	87,280	69,851	25%
Total Assets	1,929,712	1,950,360	(1)%
Shareholders' Equity	1,095,819	1,029,625	6%
Number of Shareholders	49,000	57,000	
Average Number of Shares and Share Equivalents	51,257,000	50,233,000	
Number of Employees	23,700	23,300	

Exhibit 5.3.   Illustrated financial highlights (Squibb Corporation). Reprinted by permission from the 1982 annual report of Squibb Corporation.

Ten-Year Selected Financial Data (in millions, except per share and ratio data)

Champion International Corporation and Subsidiaries

	1982	1981	1980	1979	1978	1977	1976	1975	1974	1973
Earnings:										
Continuing operations:										
Net sales	$3,737	4,004	3,753	3,751	3,475	3,127	3,079	2,530	2,658	2,333
Depreciation and cost of timber harvested	167	169	148	132	115	111	103	92	84	75
Gross profit	477	605	635	744	687	604	593	469	565	502
Income from operations	62	189	251	382	356	286	271	176	265	230
Interest and debt expense	75	81	58	41	45	54	59	61	55	34
Other (income) expense — net	(50)	(47)	(31)	(12)	(2)	(16)	(2)	(3)	(3)	6
Income before income taxes	37	155	224	353	313	248	214	118	213	190
Income taxes	(3)	36	42	106	109	86	89	34	79	84
Income from continuing operations	40	119	182	247	204	162	125	84	134	106
Income (Loss) from discontinued operations	—	(18)	(18)	—	(35)	(23)	11	3	(1)	6
Extraordinary item	—	—	(17)	—	—	—	—	—	—	(1)
Net income	40	101	147	247	169	139	136	87	133	112
Per Common Share:										
Primary earnings:										
Continuing operations	$ .45	1.91	3.28	4.70	4.05	3.21	2.60	1.79	2.97	2.32
Discontinued operations	—	(.33)	(.34)	—	—	(.48)	.24	.08	(.01)	.14
Extraordinary item	—	—	(.31)	—	(.73)	—	—	—	—	—
Net income	.45	1.58	2.63	4.70	3.32	2.73	2.84	1.87	2.96	2.46
Fully diluted earnings:										
Continuing operations	.45	1.88	3.19	4.42	3.65	2.90	2.31	1.63	2.58	2.06
Discontinued operations	—	(.32)	(.32)	—	—	(.41)	.20	.07	(.01)	.11
Extraordinary item	—	—	(.30)	—	(.63)	—	—	—	—	—
Net income	.45	1.56	2.57	4.42	3.02	2.49	2.51	1.70	2.57	2.17
Cash dividends declared	.67	1.48	1.44	1.32	1.17	1.05	1.00	1.00	.98	.88
Cash dividends paid	.94	1.48	1.42	1.28	1.135	1.025	1.00	1.00	.96	.86
Shareholders' equity	28.85	29.17	29.33	28.55	26.38	25.49	24.11	22.38	21.49	19.41
Financial Position:										
Current assets	$ 842	877	927	819	916	799	944	771	794	766
Property, plant, and equipment — net	1,902	1,854	1,759	1,612	1,333	1,111	1,114	1,070	982	767
Timber and timberlands — net	485	405	412	366	342	311	302	295	298	282
Other assets	243	247	242	243	265	244	204	183	186	161
Total assets	$3,472	3,443	3,340	3,040	2,856	2,465	2,564	2,319	2,260	1,976
Current liabilities	$ 439	468	478	429	445	355	471	403	398	346
Long-term debt and other liabilities	1,089	963	849	853	878	723	769	791	785	658
Deferred income taxes	173	219	248	184	131	94	118	98	88	76
Minority interest in subsidiaries	34	40	42	39	43	36	44	47	47	40
Shareholders' equity	1,737	1,753	1,755	1,535	1,359	1,257	1,162	980	942	856
Total liabilities and shareholders' equity	$3,472	3,443	3,340	3,040	2,856	2,465	2,564	2,319	2,260	1,976
Other Statistics:										
Expenditures for property, plant, and equipment	$ 214	245	273	387	337	209	141	177	282	169
Timber and timberlands expenditures	$ 42	89	82	65	57	35	28	17	31	17
U.S. timber acreage owned or controlled	3.3	3.4	3.4	3.4	3.4	3.4	3.4	3.8	3.0	2.9
Cumulative convertible preference shares outstanding at year-end	4	4	5	2	5	48	46	41	41	41
Common shares outstanding at year-end	55	55	55	53	50	48	10	10	10	8
Dividends declared on preferred and preference shares	15	6	6	4	8	10	10	39	36	32
Dividends declared on common shares	37	81	78	69	57	50	43	39	20	22
Current ratio	1.9	1.9	1.9	1.9	2.1	2.3	2.0	1.9	2.0	2.2
Ratio of debt to equity	.58:1	.53:1	.46:1	.53:1	.61:1	.54:1	.64:1	.77:1	.80:1	.74:1
Return on average shareholders' equity — continuing operations	2.3%	6.8%	11.1%	17.1%	15.6%	13.4%	11.7%	8.7%	14.9%	12.8%

Exhibit 5.4. Illustrated selected financial data (Champion International Corporation). Reprinted by permission from the 1982 annual report of Champion International Corporation.

Selected Financial Data

(Dollars and Shares in Millions Except Per Share Amounts)	1982	1981	1980	1979	1978
Results of Operations					
Sales	$4,593.9	$4,472.1	$4,118.8	$3,504.6	$2,845.7
Computer rental and service revenue	896.5	879.1	805.9	704.9	702.1
	5,490.4	5,351.2	4,924.7	4,209.5	3,547.8
Cost of sales	3,053.6	2,917.0	2,712.3	2,233.9	1,791.0
Cost of computer rental and service revenue	488.0	505.2	464.0	432.7	453.5
Research and development	396.9	368.8	295.4	234.6	187.2
Selling, general and administrative	1,217.1	1,146.0	1,015.5	901.7	795.8
Interest	51.9	51.2	40.1	22.3	21.8
	5,207.5	4,988.2	4,527.3	3,825.2	3,249.3
Gain on sale of interests in Cii-HB and GEISCO	90.8				
Income before income taxes	373.7	363.0	397.4	384.3	298.5
Income taxes	112.8	107.1	158.5	171.9	138.2
Equity income	10.4	0.4	37.4	23.5	18.5
Income before extraordinary income	271.3	256.3	276.3	235.9	178.8
Extraordinary income	1.6	3.0	12.6	20.5	19.9
Net income	$ 272.9	$ 259.3	$ 288.9	$ 256.4	$ 198.7
Earnings per Common Share					
Income before extraordinary income	$ 12.09	$ 11.25	$ 12.36	$ 10.76	$ 8.36
Extraordinary income	.07	13	.56	.94	.93
Net income	$ 12.16	$ 11.38	$ 12.92	$ 11.70	$ 9.29
Dividends per Common Share	$ 3.50	$ 3.20	$ 2.80	$ 2.40	$ 2.05
Financial Position					
Working capital—					
Current assets	$2,433.9	$2,151.7	$2,069.3	$1,751.6	$1,428.3
Current liabilities	1,266.5	1,199.5	1,150.5	990.8	861.9
	$1,167.4	$ 952.2	$ 918.8	$ 760.8	$ 566.4
Capitalization—					
Short-term debt	$ 115.9	$ 115.0	$ 106.3	$ 81.6	$ 118.8
Long-term debt	676.3	605.8	470.3	439.7	300.3
Total debt	792.2	720.8	576.6	521.3	419.1
Stockholders' equity	2,143.4	2,098.0	1,874.0	1,616.9	1,365.4
	$2,935.6	$2,818.8	$2,450.6	$2,138.2	$1,784.5

Exhibit 5.5. Illustrated selected financial data (Honeywell, Inc.). Reprinted by permission from the 1982 annual report of Honeywell, Inc.

	1982	1981	1980	1979	1978
Revenue					
Control Products.	$ 925.3	$ 944.6	$ 943.1	$ 800.6	$ 645.9
Control Systems	1,622.1	1,529.4	1,351.2	1,125.1	952.1
Aerospace and Defense.	1,258.3	1,103.5	996.3	831.2	656.2
Information Systems	1,684.7	1,773.7	1,634.1	1,452.6	1,293.6
	$5,490.4	$5,351.2	$4,924.7	$4,209.5	$3,547.8
Operating Profit					
Control Products.	$ 72.4	$ 88.8	$ 121.1	$ 150.0	$ 128.2
Control Systems	187.2	175.0	150.4	127.2	108.7
Aerospace and Defense.	87.4	77.2	62.1	44.6	42.6
Information Systems	79.8	158.3	183.5	148.8	104.0
Operating profit.	426.8	499.3	517.1	470.6	383.5
Gain on sale of interests in Cii-HB and GEISCO	90.8				
General corporate expense	(25.8)	(13.2)	(28.7)	(21.5)	(31.6)
Interest expense	(118.1)	(123.1)	(91.0)	(64.8)	(53.4)
Income before income taxes	$ 373.7	$ 363.0	$ 397.4	$ 384.3	$ 298.5
Assets					
Control Products.	$ 726.9	$ 687.8	$ 668.4	$ 513.9	$ 401.0
Control Systems	930.7	899.7	815.0	709.4	582.1
Aerospace and Defense.	674.4	478.1	367.1	333.0	236.0
Information Systems	1,369.1	1,371.4	1,340.6	1,204.7	1,096.1
Corporate.	769.8	893.8	701.5	578.6	510.9
	$4,470.9	$4,330.8	$3,892.6	$3,339.6	$2,826.1
Additional Information					
Average number of common shares outstanding	22.4	22.8	22.4	21.9	21.4
Return on average stockholders' equity.	13.2%	13.2%	16.9%	17.2%	15.5%
Stockholders' equity per common share. . . . . $	94.31	$ 90.53	$ 82.70	$ 72.73	$ 63.68
Percent of debt to total capitalization.	27%	26%	24%	24%	23%
Research and Development—					
Honeywell funded . . . . $	396.9	$ 368.8	$ 295.4	$ 234.6	$ 187.2
Customer funded	353.9	328.2	295.6	188.9	136.5
Capital expenditures—					
Equipment for lease to others	245.2	308.3	282.1	277.6	260.7
Other property, plant and equipment	351.4	331.3	274.2	182.1	137.6
Depreciation—					
Equipment for lease to others	128.1	154.5	146.6	156.2	173.8
Other property, plant and equipment	171.6	145.5	109.6	88.5	74.3
Employees at year end	94,062	96,923	97,202	94,620	86,328

Five-Year Financial History

Squibb Corporation and Subsidiaries
(Dollar amounts in thousands except per share figures)

	1982	1981	1980	1979	1978
Results of Operations					
Net sales:					
Pharmaceutical products....................................	$ 978,296	$ 934,140	$ 869,078	$ 783,897	$ 680,404
Specialty health products and medical systems...............	340,455	264,373	178,330	84,978	43,716
Personal care products...................................	342,015	325,398	286,776	241,248	183,189
Total net sales	1,660,766	1,523,911	1,334,184	1,110,123	907,309
Percent change...	*9%*	*14%*	*20%*	*22%*	*11%*
Profit from operations:					
Pharmaceutical products....................................	122,388	89,729	99,955	106,398	93,827
Specialty health products and medical systems...............	52,207	33,361	28,331	13,441	9,133
Personal care products...................................	34,939	28,256	27,371	20,731	18,983
Total profit from operations	209,534	151,346	155,657	140,570	121,943
Percent of net sales...................................	*13%*	*10%*	*12%*	*13%*	*13%*
General corporate income (expenses)					
(includes interest income and expense)	9,951	(26,647)	(27,364)	(35,649)	(18,763)
Costs of restructuring	—	(62,859)	—	—	—
Income before taxes on income.............................	219,485	61,840	128,293	104,921	103,180
Income from continuing businesses...........................	153,636	41,098	103,373	89,478	83,623
Percent of net sales.....................................	*9%*	*3%*	*8%*	*8%*	*9%*
Income from businesses sold	—	12,181	24,371	34,244	33,632
Gain (loss) on sale of businesses.............................	—	58,068	(318)	—	—
Extraordinary charge	—	(6,532)	—	—	—
Net income...	$ 153,636	$ 104,815	$ 127,426	$ 123,722	$ 117,255
Per share:					
Income from continuing businesses	$3.01	$ .83	$2.15	$1.97	$1.86
Income from businesses sold................................	—	.24	.51	.74	.74
Gain (loss) on sale of businesses	—	1.16	(.01)	—	—
Extraordinary charge	—	(.13)	—	—	—
Net income	$3.01	$2.10	$2.65	$2.71	$2.60
Cash dividends	$1.28	$1.21½	$1.15½	$1.09½	$1.03½
Financial Position					
Working capital	$ 583,787	$ 597,889	$ 544,732	$ 398,126	$ 369,102
Property, plant and equipment (net)...........................	511,821	479,720	479,591	423,399	378,509
Total assets...	1,929,712	1,950,360	1,817,051	1,716,850	1,492,680
Long-term debt..	336,314	398,771	392,419	397,439	326,074
Shareholders' equity	1,095,819	1,029,625	1,002,470	918,013	836,115
Return on average shareholders' equity	14%	10%	13%	14%	15%
Book value per share	21.29	20.60	20.66	20.12	18.73
Supplementary Data					
Capital expenditures.......................................	$ 87,280	$ 69,851	$ 79,996	$ 66,655	$ 61,633
Depreciation and amortization of fixed assets	31,270	28,175	24,003	20,619	17,699
Marketing expenses	446,741	398,394	339,361	272,807	216,410
Advertising expenditures	104,947	94,721	81,086	64,565	45,482
Research and development...................................	122,962	95,302	73,787	65,447	58,942
Interest income...	60,832	31,980	34,383	25,829	24,124
Interest expense	40,257	43,453	49,380	48,408	35,686
Cash dividends	65,199	60,392	55,557	49,406	46,204
Number of shareholders.....................................	49,000	57,000	61,000	61,000	59,000
Average number of shares and share equivalents................	51,257,000	50,233,000	48,399,000	46,000,000	45,498,000
Number of employees	23,700	23,300	22,400	21,200	20,300

Effective for 1981, the Corporation changed its method of accounting for foreign
currency translation by adopting FASB Statement No. 52.

Exhibit　5.6. Illustrated selected financial data (Squibb Corporation). Reprinted by permission from the 1982 annual report of Squibb Corporation.

MANAGEMENT'S DISCUSSION AND ANALYSIS OF FINANCIAL CONDITION AND RESULTS OF OPERATIONS

LIQUIDITY AND CAPITAL RESOURCES

Financial resources of $215 million during 1982 were adequate to meet the regular operating needs of the Company. The Company has ready access to funds to meet expected needs and anticipates no significant liquidity restraints in pursuing its growth strategies.

Year-end working capital amounted to $550 million at December 31, 1982 as compared to $600 million at December 31, 1981. The decline of $50 million is primarily reflected by the reduction of accounts receivable and·inventory as the Company experienced an 11% drop in sales volume from year to year.

Total additions of property, plant and equipment, including acquisitions, during 1982 amounted to $125 million as compared to $106 million in 1981. Total disposals of property, plant and equipment, including divestitures, during 1982 amounted to $19 million as compared to $44 million in 1981. Capacity for the majority of product lines is currently adequate for substantially increased production levels. Capital expenditures for 1983 are not expected to increase over 1982 and will be concentrated on improving manufacturing efficiencies and reducing costs.

Dana retired $25 million principal amount of the 8⅞% debentures in exchange for 668,883 shares of common stock. The total debt (short and long-term) to total capitalization ratio at December 31, 1982 was 29% as compared to 30% at December 31, 1981.

Dana issues commercial paper as a cost-effective way of financing its short-term financing needs. This commercial paper is supported by $201 million in open lines of credit maintained with a number of U.S. and international banks. At the end of 1982 there was $62 million of this paper outstanding at an average interest rate of 8.5%. In addition to short-term financing programs, Dana will utilize the long-term debt market for appropriate financing requirements when rates and conditions seem favorable.

RESULTS OF OPERATIONS

1982 vs. 1981

Total 1982 sales were down 11% from 1981. The most significant impact was in the industrial segment where sales declined $186 million or 27%. Off-highway and agricultural markets in the U.S. were substantially down in 1982 and North American heavy truck production was the lowest in over 20 years.

During the fourth quarter of 1982, Dana recorded a loss of $4 million as operating income was more than offset by special charges to income. These adjustments included a retroactive Brazilian tax law change, inventory write-offs, and plant closing expenses. The reduction in excess inventory and facilities, while reducing 1982 earnings, should lower costs and improve performance in 1983.

Low production volumes sharply penalized earnings throughout the year, and net income in 1982 was $52 million, down 55% from the $116 million earned in 1981. Income from U.S. operations was $53 million, down 47% from the $100 million earned in 1981. Consolidated international operations reflected a loss of $1 million in 1982 as compared to a $15 million profit in 1981.

Total consolidated income was also impacted by a charge of $12 million to record effects of the Mexican Peso devaluation. This accounted for most of the increase in foreign currency loss from $19 million last year to $31 million this year.

Various items outside of operations contributed to income during 1982. The exchange of common stock for debentures resulted in a gain of $9 million. Certain actuarial assumptions for accruing pension expenses were changed resulting in a net increase to income of $4 million.

Lower short-term borrowing levels, reduced long-term debt, and generally lower interest rates all helped to lower interest expense to $51 million in 1982 as compared to $66 million in 1981.

Two significant acquisitions were completed during 1982. Racine Hydraulics was acquired from Rexnord in November 1982 for $49 million, expanding Dana's base of hydraulic products for the mobile off-highway and industrial markets. In December 1982 assets of International Harvester's heavy truck axle and transmisson business were acquired for $45 million. These assets will be merged into Dana's current facilities to strengthen its overall position in these important markets.

1981 vs. 1980

Net sales increased $187 million or 7% and net income $19.9 million or 21% in 1981 versus 1980. While these results compare favorably with the prior year, the continuing recession in the United States and Europe and the inflationary economy combined to hold real growth in the Vehicular segment about flat with 1980. The Industrial segment, through completion of additional acquisitions and market penetration, gained approximately 13%.

The income improvement, although enhanced by a net gain on sale of assets (see page F-6), was primarily the result of strict cost controls and the benefits derived from reductions in capacity from plant closings in 1980.

Equity in earnings of affiliates and other income for 1981 increased $20.6 million (55%) over 1980 with approximately $16.4 million of the increase attributable to the gain on sale of assets referred to previously.

Foreign currency transaction adjustments were about $6.7 million above 1980, with Brazil's high inflation the primary cause.

Cost of sales as a percent of net sales declined (an improvement in gross margin) to 82%, from 83.4% in 1980, as a result of strict cost controls and plant closings. If the LIFO method for valuing domestic inventories had not been adopted in 1981, the cost of sales would have declined to about 81% of net sales.

Selling, general and administrative expenses increased about $26 million or 11%. Approximately $11.3 million or 43% of the increase resulted from the consolidation of companies recently acquired.

Interest expense increased $16.2 million or 33% in 1981, primarily due to sharply higher interest rates on short-term borrowings. The Company's successful efforts to reduce the total dollar amount of debt outstanding worked to offset to a significant degree the full impact of rate volatility.

A discussion of the effects of inflation on operations is presented on pages F-16 and F-17.

Exhibit   5.7.   Illustrated management's discussion and analyses of financial condition and results of operations (Dana Corporation). Reprinted by permission from the 1982 annual report of Dana Corporation.

MANAGEMENT'S ANALYSIS OF FINANCIAL CONDITION AND RESULTS OF OPERATIONS

Liquidity

The Company's financial condition remains quite strong. In 1982, AMETEK generated funds from operations of $65.3 million compared to $48.9 million in 1981. The substantial increase reflects the cash flow benefits of purchasing tax benefits of other entities and settling a long-term take-or-pay contract with a customer. Working capital at the end of 1982 amounted to $115.7 million, a 6% increase from 1981 year-end. The ratio of current assets to current liabilities at December 31, 1982 was 2.9 to 1 and at the end of each of the past five years has averaged 2.9 to 1. Temporary cash balances in excess of normal operating requirements are invested primarily in U. S. Government securities and the previously mentioned tax benefits. Cash and such securities at year-end 1982 totaled $50 million compared to $42.6 million at December 31, 1981.

The Company's long-term debt represents 23.3% of total capitalization, and the scheduled debt repayments in each of the next five years represent less than 9% of funds generated from operations. The average interest rate for long-term debt in 1982 was 8.3%. The Company's liquidity requirements are supplemented by a revolving credit and term loan agreement with a group of banks which provides for up to $60 million, none of which was used at year-end. The agreement was amended in 1982 to provide the Company with greater flexibility to select the most favorable interest rate from alternatives included in the agreement.

The Company had $7 million of short-term notes payable outstanding at December 31, 1982 which were repaid early in January, 1983.

Capital Resources

Additions to property, plant and equipment totaled $17.2 million in 1982, up 4% from 1981. With the exception of the new instruments plant in Largo, Florida that was completed early in 1982, capital expenditures in 1982 were primarily for equipment to improve productivity. In addition, during the fourth quarter of 1982 the relocation and consolidation of certain plants and equipment was initiated to maximize utilization of the Company's manufacturing resources. It is anticipated that all of 1983's capital expenditures will be financed by funds generated from the Company's operations.

Results of Operations

1982 OPERATIONS COMPARED WITH 1981

Sales in 1982 of $423.7 million fell below the record 1981 level by $24.4 million or by 5.5%. Business segment operating profit in 1982 of $63.5 million decreased by $1.2 million or by 1.9% and net income for 1982 increased by $.8 million or by 2.9%. The declines in sales and operating profit in 1982 were primarily a result of the continued economic recession as product shipments fell for several of the Company's businesses. Nevertheless, net income for 1982 increased to the highest level in the Company's history as a result of timely implemented cost cutting programs, productivity improvements, the lack of continued inflationary cost pressures, higher investment income and a lower effective income tax rate.

Electro-mechanical group sales increased $5.9 million or by 4.1% as a result of continued strong demand for aerospace products, undersea work vehicles and marine electronic systems and sales of a new business acquired in August, 1982, which were partially offset by reduced shipments of electric motors. Demand for motors in Europe was particularly soft as a result of weak European economic conditions and the strong U. S. dollar. Operating profit increased $.6 million or by 2.2% because of the improved volume, changes in product mix and the favorable effects of cost cutting efforts.

Process Equipment group sales decreased $6.1 million or by 7.8% because of lower product demand and lower prices for high-pressure pipe flanges and fittings, centrifuges and heat exchangers caused by the weakened economy. Operating profit declined $1.6 million or by 17.1% due to the lower sales and the costs of consolidating and relocating certain plant assets.

Sales of the Precision Instruments group decreased by $12.3 million or by 10.2% because of lower product demand attributable to the continued recession. Operating profit declined by $2.4 million or by 12.9% as a result of increased costs of developing new products for 1983 production, the lower sales volume and even greater reduction of production levels as the Company moved to reduce its inventories.

Sales of the Industrial Materials group decreased by $12 million or by 11.4% because of lower aluminum prices and reduced demand for products by the weakened housing and construction industries. Operating profit increased by $2.3 million or by 20.2% because of the combined effects of raw material cost savings, cost cutting efforts, productivity improvements and benefits realized from settling a long-term take-or-pay contract with a customer, which were partially offset by the costs associated with consolidation and relocation of certain plant assets for more effective utilization.

Corporate, administrative, research and net interest expenses declined slightly compared to 1981. Cost increases experienced in 1982 were offset by higher net investment income, primarily interest income from investments in U. S. Government securities and tax benefits purchased from other entities.

Depreciation expense increased by $2.8 million or 28.2% over 1981 as a result of increased capital investment at shorter than average depreciable lives. Pension expenses were higher in 1982 by $.8 million or by 13% because of increased benefit levels, increased plan compensation for active employees and two new plans.

Exhibit 5.8. Illustrated management's discussion and analysis of financial condition and results of operation (Ametek, Inc.). Reprinted by permission from the 1982 annual report of Ametek, Inc.

Research and development expenses were $10.3 million, up 5% from 1981. The effective income tax rate for 1982 was 46.3%, down from 48.7% in 1981, because of the favorable effects of increased investment income taxable at less than statutory rates and increased research tax credits.

A discussion regarding the impact of inflation on the results of operations and financial position of the Company is presented on pages 36 to 38 of this Annual Report.

1981 OPERATIONS COMPARED WITH 1980

Sales in 1981 of $448.1 million exceeded the record level set in 1980 by 12%. Business segment operating profit in 1981 increased by 16.8% and net income increased by 22.3%.

Sales of the Electro-mechanical group increased by 4.6% reflecting strong demand for aerospace products and marine electronic systems designed for the offshore oil industry. Related operating profit increased by $1.8 million or 7.9% because of the volume growth and improved margins.

Process Equipment group sales increased by 10.5% as a result of strong demand for winery equipment and heat exchangers. Related operating profit increased by $2.4 million or 32.8% because of the volume growth in 1981 and the negative effect of contract rework costs incurred in 1980.

Increased demand and market penetration for products of the Precision Instruments group resulted in a sales increase of 11.4%. Related operating profit increased by $1.4 million or 8.1% due to the volume growth and a favorable change in product mix.

Industrial Materials group sales increased by 26%, reflecting increased volume of a business acquired in the fourth quarter of 1980, strong demand for plastic compounds, and improved volume for most of the other products in this group. Related operating profit increased by 48.8% because of the improved sales volume, improved margins and favorable product mix.

Corporate, administrative, research and net interest expenses declined slightly compared to 1980. Cost increases experienced in 1981 were offset by higher interest income.

Depreciation expense increased by $1.5 million or 17.7% over 1980 as a result of the Company's capital expansion program. Pension expenses were higher by $.9 million because of increased benefit levels, two new plans and inclusion for a full year of plans covering employees of a business acquired late in 1980.

Research and development expenses were $9.8 million, up 21% from 1980. The effective income tax rate for 1981 and 1980 was 48.7%.

Net income increased in 1981 compared to the prior year for the reasons described above.

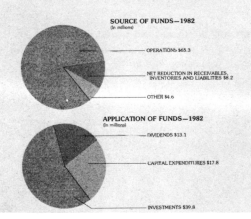

SOURCE OF FUNDS—1982
(In millions)

OPERATIONS $65.3

NET REDUCTION IN RECEIVABLES, INVENTORIES AND LIABILITIES $8.2

OTHER $4.6

APPLICATION OF FUNDS—1982
(In millions)

DIVIDENDS $13.1

CAPITAL EXPENDITURES $17.8

INVESTMENTS $39.8

Management's Review

Results of Operations

1982 versus 1981 — Operating revenues of $332.2 million in 1982 were 5% ahead of the $317.5 million reported last year. The Electronics Distribution and Fire-Fighting Products Groups both recorded revenue gains. The Maintenance Products Group, feeling the effects of the slowdown in industrial activity in general and, in particular, the construction market, reported a 9% reduction in operating revenues.

Other income of $8.0 million increased $4.0 million over 1981, largely due to an increase in interest income.

Cost of sales as a percent of operating revenues increased slightly, but was in line with the Company's historical rate.

Selling, administrative and general expenses rose 8% in fiscal 1982 due to higher payroll and related costs, along with increases in systems development costs aimed at supporting growth programs.

The effective federal income tax rate of 42.2% in 1982 compares with a 43.8% rate in 1981.

The foregoing factors resulted in a net earnings per share increase of $.10, or 6% over the previous year.

1981 versus 1980 — Operating revenues in 1981 were $317.5 million. This compares with 1980 revenues of $317.7 million which included $7.2 million from the sale of certain natural gas-producing properties. The Electronics Distribution and Fire-Fighting Products Groups both reported revenue gains. The Maintenance Products Group, in which the gas property sale was recorded in 1980, reported a 7% reduction in operating revenues,

Other income of $4.0 million increased $2.6 million over 1980 largely due to an increase in interest income to $3.9 million in 1981 from $.9 million in 1980.

Cost of sales as a percent of operating revenues was slightly lower in 1981 when compared with 1980 results, excluding the gas property sale

Selling, administrative and general expenses rose 3% to $84.5 million in fiscal 1981 due to higher payroll and benefit costs, partially offset by the favorable effect of cost improvement programs.

The effective federal income tax rate of 43.8% in 1981 was slightly higher than the 43.5% rate of 1980.

The foregoing factors resulted in a net earnings per share increase of $.06, or 4% over the previous year.

Liquidity

Current assets of $149.7 million were 72% of total assets. Working capital of $114.9 million increased $14.2 million as detailed in the Consolidated Statement of Changes in Financial Position. The ratio of current assets to current liabilities was 4.3 to 1 at the end of fiscal 1982.

Capital Resources

Long-term debt of $.5 million was less than 1% of total capitalization (long-term debt and shareholders' equity). Total capitalization was $165.5 million at May 31, 1982.

Inflation

The Company has dealt with inflationary pressures and maintained its profit margins through a combination of price adjustments, productivity improvement and cost containment programs.

Exhibit 5.9. Illustrated management's discussion and analysis of financial condition and results of operations (Premier Industrial Corporation). Reprinted by permission from the 1982 annual report of Premier Industrial Corporation.

Report of Management

Management is responsible for the preparation and integrity of the consolidated financial statements appearing in this Annual Report. The financial statements were prepared in conformity with generally accepted accounting principles appropriate in the circumstances and, accordingly, include some amounts based on management's best judgments and estimates. Other financial information in this Annual Report is consistent with that in the financial statements.

Management is responsible for maintaining a system of internal accounting controls and procedures to provide reasonable assurance, at an appropriate cost/benefit relationship, that assets are safeguarded and that transactions are authorized, recorded and reported properly. The internal accounting control system is augmented by a program of internal audits and appropriate reviews by management, written policies and guidelines, careful selection and training of qualified personnel and a written Code of Business Conduct adopted by the Board of Directors, applicable to all employees of the Company and its subsidiaries. Management believes that the Company's internal accounting controls provide reasonable assurance that assets are safeguarded against material loss from unauthorized use or disposition and that the financial records are reliable for preparing financial statements and other data and maintaining accountability for assets.

The Audit Committee of the Board of Directors, composed solely of Directors who are not officers of the Company, meets with the independent accountants, management and internal auditors periodically to discuss internal accounting controls, auditing and financial reporting matters. The Committee reviews with the independent accountants the scope and results of the audit effort. The Committee also meets with the independent accountants without management present to ensure that the independent accountants have free access to the Committee.

The independent accountants, Ernst & Whinney, are recommended by the Audit Committee of the Board of Directors, selected by the Board of Directors and ratified by the shareholders. Ernst & Whinney are engaged to examine the financial statements of The Coca-Cola Company and subsidiaries and conduct such tests and related procedures as they deem necessary in conformity with generally accepted auditing standards. The opinion of the independent accountants, based upon their examination of the consolidated financial statements, is contained in this Annual Report.

Roberto C. Goizueta
Chairman, Board of Directors,
and Chief Executive Officer

Sam Ayoub
Senior Executive Vice President
and Chief Financial Officer

February 14, 1983

Exhibit 5.10. Illustrated management report (The Coca Cola Company). Reprinted by permission from the 1982 annual report of The Coca Cola Company.

**Kmart
Responsibility
for Financial
Statements**

Kmart Corporation management is responsible for the integrity of the information and representations contained in this annual report. Management believes the financial statements conform with generally accepted accounting principles and have been prepared on a consistent basis. This responsibility includes making informed estimates and judgments in selecting the appropriate accounting principles in the circumstances.

To assist management in fulfilling these obligations, the company utilizes several tools, which include the following:

■ The company maintains a system of internal accounting controls to provide reasonable assurance that, among other things, financial records are reliable for purposes of preparing financial statements and the assets are properly accounted for and safeguarded. This concept of reasonable assurance is based on the recognition that the cost of the system must be related to the benefits to be derived. Management believes its system provides this appropriate balance.

■ An Internal Audit Department is maintained to evaluate, test and report the application of internal accounting controls in conformity with the standards of the practice of internal auditing.

■ The Board of Directors appoints our independent accountants to perform an examination of the company's financial statements. This examination includes, among other things, a review of the system of internal controls as required by generally accepted auditing standards.

■ The Audit Committee of the Board of Directors, consisting solely of outside directors, meets regularly with management, internal auditors and independent accountants to assure that each is carrying out its responsibilities. The internal auditors and independent accountants both have full and free access to the Audit Committee, with and without the presence of management.

B. M. FAUBER
Chairman of the Board
and Chief Executive Officer

R. E. BREWER
Executive Vice President
Finance

Exhibit 5.11. Illustrated management report (K mart Corporation). Reprinted by permission from the 1982 annual report of K mart Corporation.

Responsibilities for Integrity of Financial Statements

To the Stockholders of Northwest Industries, Inc.

The accompanying financial statements have been prepared under management's direction in conformity with generally accepted accounting principles and, where appropriate, reflect estimates based on management's best judgment. The financial information included throughout the annual report is consistent in all material respects with that contained in the financial statements. Management is primarily responsible for the integrity and objectivity of the company's financial statements.

In order to provide reasonable assurance that the company's records accurately reflect the underlying transactions, management maintains a system of internal controls which includes such safeguards as the segregation of responsibilities in organizational arrangements, the selection and training of qualified personnel, and the establishment of policies and procedures. The adequacy and effectiveness of such controls are regularly reviewed by the company's internal audit personnel.

Management believes that the company's accounting controls provide reasonable assurance that errors or irregularities that could be material to the financial statements do not occur or would be detected within a timely period by employees in the normal course of performing their assigned functions. However, inherent limitations exist in any system of internal controls, and, of course, the costs of controls should not exceed their benefits. Management believes that the company's balance between the costs and benefits of controls reasonably assures the reliability of its financial reporting at reasonable costs.

Arthur Andersen & Co., the company's independent public accountants, have examined management's financial statements, and their report appears on page 23. The auditors' report expresses an informed opinion that the financial statements, considered in their entirety, present fairly the company's financial position and operating results in conformity with generally accepted accounting principles. As required by generally accepted auditing standards, such examinations include reviewing and testing the company's system of internal controls.

The board of directors has general oversight responsibility for management's preparation of the financial statements and for engaging the independent accountants whose selection is ratified by you, the stockholders. Through the audit committee, which consists solely of directors who are not employees of the company, the board meets with the independent accountants and representatives of management to establish that each is appropriately discharging its responsibilities. In addition, Arthur Andersen & Co. have full and free access to the audit committee, without management representatives present, to discuss the results of their examinations, the adequacy of the company's internal controls and the quality of its financial reporting.

Ben W. Heineman
President

Rod Dammeyer
Executive Vice President—Finance

Exhibit 5.12. Illustrated management report (Northwest Industries, Inc.). Reprinted by permission from the 1982 annual report of Northwest Industries, Inc.

Chapter Six

Financial Reports
Filed with the SEC

INTRODUCTION

In addition to the interim and annual reports issued to shareholders, public companies are also required to file certain financial reports with the Securities and Exchange Commission (SEC). The most noteworthy financial reports are SEC Form 10-K and SEC Form 10-Q. The purpose of this chapter is to provide investors with an understanding of the SEC, its purpose and objectives, how it operates to protect investors, and the basic types of financial reports that public companies are required to file with the SEC.

OVERVIEW OF THE SEC

Objective of the SEC

Q: What is the main objective of the SEC?

A: The SEC is an independent government agency that was founded under the authority of the Securities and Exchange Act of 1934. The SEC's primary function is to provide the public with the most complete information possible concerning corporate activities and to protect the investor against abuse in the securities and financial markets.

Q: How does the SEC carry out its objective of protecting investors?

A: The SEC carries out its objective through five operating divisions, each of which is headed by a commissioner appointed for a five-year term by the President of the United States. Descriptions of these five divisions follow:

   1.   The Division of Corporation Finance is responsible for preventing fraudulent securities offerings to the public, maintaining the financial statement disclosure rules of the SEC, and maintaining and reviewing financial reports (e.g., Form 10-K and Form 10-Q).

2.   The Division of Enforcement is responsible for the investigation of all possible violations of law (e.g., securities fraud).

3.   The Division of Market Regulation is responsible for moderating the securities trading markets.

4.   The Division of Investment Management is responsible for regulating mutual funds and investment advisers.

5.   The Division of Corporate Regulations is responsible for reviewing bankruptcy claims by public companies.

Q: Does the SEC's Division of Corporation Finance look at all the financial reports that are submitted by publicly listed corporations?

A: The Division of Corporation Finance follows a selective review procedure under which some filings are automatically reviewed and others are reviewed only if they are chosen in a sampling process. For example, if a corporation is selected for a review of its Form 10-K, it is so notified by the SEC. Most of the comments made by SEC staff members on Form 10-K are based on their review and are constructive and future-oriented in nature. In this way, a reviewed corporation is expected to consider those comments for future Form 10-K filings.

Financial Reporting Rules and Regulations

Q: Does the SEC provide any rules or regulations as to the form and content of financial statements that are included within filings, such as a Form 10-K?

A: Regulation S-X governs the form and content of financial statements filed with the SEC. It consists of twelve articles that contain a number of rules. A brief description of some of the more relevant rules as they apply to financial statements follows:

Article 1, Rule 1-02 contains definitions of terms used in Regulation S-X (e.g., significant subsidiary, affiliate, audit, development stage company, and control).

Article 2 contains rules relating to the CPA's report and opinion and to the examination of financial statements by more than one independent auditor.

Article 3 contains general instructions to financial statements that are applicable to most registration and reporting forms under the Securities Act of 1933 and the Securities and Exchange Act of 1934. This article requires audited balance sheets to be presented as of the two most recent fiscal year-end dates and requires statements of income and changes in financial position to be presented for the three most recent fiscal years.

Article 3A contains the SEC's rules as to the consolidation and combination of subsidiaries in consolidated financial statements.

Article 4 contains rules of general application, such as a rule that prescribes that certain items must be disclosed in the footnotes to financial statements.

Article 5 contains the requirements applicable to the form and content of balance sheets and income statements of commercial and industrial companies, except for those companies specifically covered by other articles.

Article 5A applies to financial statements of development stage companies.

Articles 6 through 9 apply to financial statements filed for management investment companies, unit investment trusts, insurance companies, committees issuing certificates of deposit, and banks.

Article 10 covers interim financial statements.

Article 11 prescribes the content of Statements of Other Stockholders' Equity.

Article 12 sets forth the form and content of schedules required by the various rules in Regulation S-X.

Q: If SEC Regulation S-X governs the form and content of financial statements included in SEC filings, are there any SEC rules that govern the nonfinancial statement information generally found in SEC filings, such as selected financial data and the management's discussion and analysis of financial condition and results of operations?

A: SEC Regulation S-K governs the form and content of nonfinancial statement disclosures found in SEC filings. For example, Regulation S-K covers the following information generally found in a Form 10-K:

> *Description of the company's business.*
>
> *Description of the company's property.*
>
> *Legal proceedings.*
>
> *Information concerning the company's securities, such as market price and dividends, and a description of the securities.*
>
> *Specific financial information, such as selected financial data, supplementary financial information, management's discussion and analysis of financial condition and results of operations, and the nature of any disagreements with accountants on accounting and financial statement disclosures.*
>
> *Information concerning management and certain security holders, such as names of directors and executive officers, management remuneration and transactions, and security ownership of certain beneficial owners and management.*

Relationship with the FASB

Q: Does the SEC also govern the financial accounting and reporting rules issued by the FASB?

A: The SEC has the statutory authority to establish financial accounting and reporting standards under the Securities and Exchange Act of 1934. However, the SEC has relied on the private sector of business to develop appropriate standards. This was indicated by the SEC on December 20, 1973 when it issued a policy statement known as Accounting Series Release No. 150. This "Statement of Policy on the Establishment and Improvement of Accounting Principles and Standards" described SEC policy with regard to its relationship with the FASB and indicated that the SEC will look to the FASB for leadership to improve financial accounting and reporting standards.

Generally Accepted Accounting Principles

Q: Do the SEC Regulation S-X articles and related rules for the form and content of financial statements differ from the form and content of financial statements as required by generally accepted accounting principles?

A: SEC Regulation S-X articles are similar to generally accepted accounting principles. When a new financial statement disclosure requirement is issued by the FASB as a generally accepted accounting principle, the SEC usually incorporates that requirement into Regulation S-X. However, there are some disclosure requirements for SEC filings under certain articles of Regulation S-X that are more detailed for certain financial statement items than might be required under generally accepted accounting principles. In general, however, such additional disclosure requirements are minimal.

SEC FORM 10-K

Description and Purpose

Q: What is an SEC Form 10-K?

A: In order to comply with the SEC's rules and regulations under the Securities Act of 1933 and the Securities and Exchange Act of

1934, publicly traded corporations are required to file a Form 10-K with the SEC. SEC Form 10-K is basically an expanded version of a company's annual report, and it must be filed within 90 days after the close of the fiscal year. However, the additional financial statement schedules required for Form 10-K may be filed up to 120 days after the close of the fiscal year. The purpose of Form 10-K is to make current information available to the public.

Publicly Traded Companies

Q: What would happen to a publicly traded corporation if it failed to file a Form 10-K with the SEC?

A: The corporation would be suspended from trading its securities on the recognized stock exchange where its securities are registered.

Q: Are any public companies ever exempt from filing financial reports with the SEC?

A: Only those companies with fewer than 500 shareholders and less than $3 million in total assets are exempt from filing periodic and annual financial statements with the SEC. When a company that is registered with the SEC has fewer than 500 shareholders and total assets of less than $3 million at the end of the last three fiscal years, it may deregister.

Content

Q: What kind of information is included within SEC Form 10-K?

A: SEC Form 10-K consists of four parts:

Part I includes disclosures relating to a company's business, properties, legal proceedings, and security ownership by management.

Part II includes information that is also found within the annual report, such as the auditor's report; the basic financial statements and supplementary financial information; selected financial data; management's discussion and analysis of financial condition and results of operations; and information regarding the market value of the company's common stock, the markets in which the common stock is traded, and dividends paid.

Part III includes information concerning directors and executive officers and amounts of management compensation.

Part IV includes disclosure of information that is considered to be the more important financial information included in Part II, such as schedules identifying the components of, or analyzing the changes in, certain balance sheet items; the separate financial statements of the corporation's parent company or unconsolidated subsidiary companies; and other exhibits of financial statement items.

Since information in Part II is included with the annual report, a company is allowed to incorporate that information within its Form 10-K by referring to the annual report in order to save printing space and cost. Incorporation by reference to the annual report may also be made with respect to Part I of Form 10-K, if such information is included within the annual report.

Audit Report

Q: Does the independent auditor's report included within Form 10-K also cover the schedules of financial statement information included within Part IV of that form?

A: In addition to the basic financial statements and related notes found in the annual report, the independent auditor's report also covers the additional schedules of financial statement information found in Part IV of Form 10-K. The coverage is usually indicated within a separate paragraph to the independent auditor's report.

Benefit to Investors

Q: Is it essential for investors to look at a corporation's Form 10-K?

A: It is not essential, but if Form 10-K is readily available, investors might as well review it. Even though annual reports are considered to be the best vehicle for communication to shareholders and investors, Form 10-K provides some invaluable information that may not be readily available from the annual report. For example, Part I of Form 10-K provides information concerning the corporation's business. Although such information may also be found in various portions of an annual report, the business portion of Form 10-K ties it all together. Another example is Part III of Form 10-K relating to information concerning the corporation's directors and executive officers and the compensation of management. As a part owner of a corporation, an investor should be curious about who makes corporate policy, who is "minding the store," and how much money these managers are being paid to do their jobs. An investor does not have to feel obligated to conduct an in-depth analysis and review of his or her investee company's Form 10-K. But it does not hurt to have all the readily available information on hand.

Q: How would an investor go about securing a copy of a company's SEC Form 10-K?

A: Some companies provide their SEC Form 10-K within the annual report. If a company does not do so, the investor should look at the inside front or back cover, where there is usually a reference to the SEC Form 10-K indicating that it is available upon request by writing to a designated company official.

SEC FORM 10-Q

Description and Purpose

Q: What is an SEC Form 10-Q?

A: Publicly listed companies that are required to file an annual Form
10-K with the SEC are also required to file a quarterly Form 10-Q
for each of the first three quarters of each fiscal year. An SEC
Form 10-Q is basically an expanded version of the interim financial reports issued to company stockholders on a quarterly basis.
The SEC Form 10-Q must to be filed with the SEC within 45 days
after the end of each of the first three quarters of a company's fiscal
year. Like Form 10-K, the purpose of Form 10-Q is to make
current information available to the public.

Content

Q: What kind of information is included within an SEC Form 10-Q?

A: SEC Form 10-Q consists of two parts:

1. Financial information, which includes financial statements
    and the management's discussion and analysis of financial
    condition and results of operations
2. Other information, including legal proceedings, changes in
    securities, defaults upon senior securities, submission of
    matters to a vote of security holders, exhibits, and reports
    on Form 8-K

Financial information includes complete or condensed data, such
as balance sheets as of the end of the quarter and as of the end of
the prior fiscal year. Also included are statements of income and of
changes in financial position from the end of the prior fiscal year to

the date of the current balance sheet, each compared with the same period of the prior year. A statement of income for the most recent quarter compared with the same quarter of the prior year is also included.

Q: Are the notes to financial statements that are included within Form 10-Q as detailed as those included within Form 10-K?

A: No. The interim period footnotes merely highlight any significant changes since the prior year end and therefore serve to update the disclosures from the last annual report. When the management of a company prepares Form 10-Q, it presumes that readers of interim reports have read or have access to the company's last annual report or Form 10-K. Therefore, management will consider it unnecessary to repeat footnote disclosures that are essentially the same as those on the annual report.

Q: Is the management's discussion and analysis of financial condition and results of operations included within Form 10-Q basically the same as that included within the annual report and Form 10-K?

A: The discussion works in the same manner as footnotes to the financial statements in Form 10-Q. In other words, the discussion in Form 10-Q updates the discussion contained in the most recent annual report to shareholders and Form 10-K. That is, it should include material changes in financial condition and results of operations that occurred since the end of the prior fiscal year. However, inclusion of the impact of inflation is not required in the interim discussion because of the experimental nature of inflation-related disclosures.

Q: What is the nature of Form 8-K, which is included within SEC Form 10-Q?

A: An SEC Form 8-K must be filed by publicly listed companies that also file Forms 10-K and 10-Q whenever certain reportable events have occurred during the year. These reportable events include:

1. Changes in the control of either the company or its majority owned subsidiary companies.
2. Major acquisitions and dispositions of assets by the company.
3. Bankruptcy or receivership.
4. Changes in the company's CPA.
5. Other important events that are considered to be material.

The report is designed to describe the nature of the reportable event, and must be filed within 15 days after any of the events in items 1 through 4 occur and within 10 days after the end of the month of occurrence of an item 5 event. If the reportable event involves the acquisition of the assets of a business, inclusion of the financial statements of that business may also be required within a Form 8-K, provided the acquistion of those assets meets certain quantitative or numerical tests.

Review by a CPA

Q: Does a CPA perform an examination of the financial information included within Form 10-Q?

A: The CPA does not audit interim financial information within Form 10-Q as he or she would financial information included within the annual report or Form 10-K. However, the CPA generally performs inquiries and analytical review procedures concerning any significant accounting matters that relate to the financial information that is reported in Form 10-Q. For example, the CPA will inquire of company management as to (1) the company's accounting system to obtain an understanding of the manner in which transactions are recorded, classified, and summarized in the preparation of interim financial information, and (2) any significant changes in the company's internal accounting control system to determine any potential effect on the preparation of interim financial information. The CPA also applies analytical review procedures to interim financial information in order to identify any unusual relationships and trends between and among financial statement items.

Q: When a CPA reviews the interim financial information included within Form 10-Q, does the CPA also provide a report similar to that provided on audited financial statements?

A: If a statement is made within Form 10-Q by company management that a review of the interim financial information was made by the CPA, the report of the CPA must accompany the interim information. An example of a CPA's standard report on interim financial information would read as follows:

> The Board of Directors
> Name of Company
>
> We have made a review of (describe the information or statements reviewed) of XYZ Company and consolidated subsidiaries as of September 30, 19X2, and for the three-month and nine-month periods then ended, in accordance with standards established by the American Institute of Certified Public Accountants.
>
> A review of interim financial information consists principally of obtaining an understanding of the system for the preparation of interim financial information, applying analytical review procedures to financial data, and making inquiries of persons responsible for financial and accounting matters. It is substantially less in scope than an examination in accordance with generally accepted auditing standards, the objective of which is the expression of an opinion regarding the financial statements taken as a whole. Accordingly, we do not express such an opinion.
>
> Based on our review, we are not aware of any material modifications that should be made to the accompanying financial (informa-

tion or statements) in order for them to be in conformity with generally accepted accounting priniciples.

(date of report)   (signature of CPA
                                              or public accounting firm)

The report is usually dated as of the completion of the review, and each page of the interim financial information is clearly labeled "unaudited."

Benefit to Investors

Q: Is it necessary for investors to review a company's Form 10-Q?

A: It is unnecessary for investors to review Form 10-Q because the interim and annual reports issued to shareholders provide the essential information for investment decisions. However, like SEC Form 10-K, Form 10-Q is also available from a company upon request if an investor wants to review it.

OTHER SEC FORMS

Q: What is a registration statement?

A: The purpose of a registration statement is to provide information to the public regarding the company that is either selling or offering to sell a security (i.e., bonds or stock). Although the entire registration statement is available to the public, Part I of the statement, referred to as the prospectus, is essential in the sale of securities. The prospectus contains most of the significant financial and statistical data, as well as narrative descriptions concerning the business of the company, information about its products and management, and other facts that could influence an investor's decision as to whether or not to purchase the security being offered. Part II of a registration statement contains information that is not required to be included in the prospectus, such as other expenses of security issuance and distribution, indemnification of officers and directors, exhibits and financial statement schedules, undertakings (i.e., information on the underwriter), and signatures of corporate officers. Therefore, whenever an investor is interested in purchasing some new issues of securities of a particular public company, it is wise for the investor to obtain a copy of the prospectus and to review it thoroughly.

Q: What assurance does an investor have that a prospectus contains accurate and timely information?

A: The preparation of a registration statement involves the combined effort of the company and its attorneys, the independent CPA, and the underwriter and its attorney. Most important, the SEC staff always reviews a registration statement before a prospectus is issued as a selling instrument to the public.

Q: Does the form of a registration statement vary with the type of company that issues securities?

A: The SEC requires various forms for different types of companies that register securities under the Securities Act of 1933. Since the use of a particular form is primarily a legal question, the decision as to which form to use is generally made by a company in consultation with its legal counsel. Various types of forms are prescribed by the SEC for the registration of various types of security offerings to the public. The most common forms of registration statements for equity offerings are Forms S-1, S-2, and S-3. Their use by a particular company depends on certain characteristics of the company involved, such as the number of years the company has been reporting its financial position and results of operations under the Securities and Exchange Act of 1934, and minimum voting stock requirements. For example, a company would be required to file Form S-3 when it registers equity securities, provided it has been reporting under the Securities and Exchange Act of 1934 for three or more years and has at least $150 million of voting stock held by nonaffiliates. Or, if the company has $100 million of voting stock coupled with an annual trading volume of three million shares, it will be required to file Form S-3. There are other forms for registration statements that are used by companies when securities are registered for a designated or specific purpose. For example, Form S-8 is used when securities are offered to company employees pursuant to certain stock option plans, while Form S-11 is used for securities of certain real estate companies. An investor need not be well versed in the types of forms used by public companies for registering securities. The important thing is to review the related prospectus.

Q: What should an investor look for in a prospectus?

A: The format of a prospectus is difficult to read because it contains approximately 30 pages of ambiguous statements and confusing numbers. As a result, the prospectus often becomes a complex and technical treatise rather than a practical disclosure document for communicating to investors. In order to separate the proverbial "wheat from the chaff" in a prospectus, investors should focus their attention on the following:

Footnotes to financial statements. This fine print in a prospectus is an excellent clue to troubled situations within a company.

Management's discussion and analysis of financial conditions and results of operations. This will provide clues to earnings growth. Be certain that the company does not plan to sell itself on the basis of a one-time surge in earnings as compared to a more consistent growth in earnings. For example, one company tried to impress investors with a per share earnings of 93 cents over their most recently reported eight months, which was three times the company's previous annual record and exceptionally higher than its 21 cent loss for 1982.

Dilution. Find out how many shares of common stock will be outstanding after the stock is offered to the public. For example, if an investor purchases stock for $10 a share and the company has 100 million shares outstanding, it will probably take a long period of time before most of those outstanding shares of stock are *actually sold. In this type of situation, an investor needs to be certain that the company is able to compensate for that dilutive effect.*

Accounting methods. *Determine whether or not the company is using conservative rather than liberal accounting methods. For example, the LIFO method of inventory valuation is more conservative than the FIFO method, and the accelerated depreciation method is more conservative than the staight line method. In general, a company that consistently uses liberal accounting methods should be carefully examined by investors.*

Use of proceeds from the sale of stock. *Be certain that your investment in the company's stock will be used for the future growth of the company, such as investments in property plant and equipment or in research and development. Some companies often use the proceeds from the sale of stock to pay off old bank loans or salaries of corprate officers.*

Pro forma adjustments. *These adjustments occur whenever a partnership incorporates and then becomes a public company, or whenever a company acquires another company. Pro forma information may be considered to be more important than historical figures because pro forma adjustments indicate how a company might operate in the future. For example, the pro forma adjustments in a public company that was previously a partnership literally cut net income in half from $12 million to $6 million.*

Management team. *Be certain that the individuals responsible for running the company have the essential experience and plan to devote a significant amount of time in performing their stewardship functions.*

Glossary

Accelerated depreciation.   A method of depreciation that charges more of the original cost of fixed assets in the earlier year of the service life of the fixed assets than in the later years.

Accounting change.   A change from one accounting principle to an alternative accounting principle that appears to be preferable to a company.

Accounting policies.   The methodology used by a company to implement specific accounting principles that appear to be most appropriate for a particular company's operation.

Accounting principle.   A method of accounting for an event or a transaction by a company in order to meet the peculiarities or needs of its organization.

Accounts receivable.   Amounts that are owed to a company by its customers as a result of the ordinary extension of credit.

Accrual basis.   A basis of accounting that measures revenues and expenses on their incurrence rather than on actual cash receipts and disbursements.

Accrued liability.   A liability that arises because an expense occurs in a period or year prior to the related expenditure.

Accumulated depreciation.   An account that presents the total amount of depreciation of fixed assets that have been accumulated to date.

Acid test ratio.   A measure of working capital, often referred to as the quick ratio, that is determined by dividing current assets less inventory by current liabilities.

Allowance for doubtful accounts.   The amount of estimated bad debts that is subtracted from accounts receivable on the balance sheet.

American Institute of Certified Public Accountants. A professional organization whose membership is comprised of state-licensed certified public accountants.

Amortization. The process of writing off the cost of an intangible asset to earnings.

Annual report. The most common form of financial report, issued by publicly listed companies on a yearly basis to their stockholders.

Assets. Those items that are owned by a company, and have a value that can be objectively measured.

Audit. An examination of a company's financial statements by independent auditors or accountants (i.e., certified public accountants).

Audit committee. A group of nonofficer directors of a publicly listed company that is responsible for monitoring the audit function.

Auditing procedures. Tests of accounting transactions and account balances performed by certified public accountants during an audit of financial statements.

Audit report. The independent auditor's or certified public accountant's report on the examination of a company's financial statements.

Average collection period of receivables. A ratio that measures the average time in days that receivables are outstanding, which is determined by multiplying receivables by days in the year (i.e., 365) and then dividing this product by annual credit sales.

Balance sheet. A financial statement that reports a company's assets, liabilities, and stockholders' equity at a specific point in time, usually the last day of the year.

Capital lease. A lease of property that transfers many of the risks and benefits of ownership to the lessee.

Cash flow. A measure of a company's ability to generate cash to service debt, reinvest in new assets, and pay dividends.

Certified public accountants. A group of independent auditors from a public accounting firm of professional accountants who are engaged to audit or examine a company's financial statements.

Common stock. Stock that does not entitle its holders to preferential treatment with regard to dividends or the distribution of assets in the event of liquidation.

Common stock equivalents. Those types of securities that enable their stockholders to exchange or convert such securities for common stock.

Consolidated financial statements. The combined financial statements of a parent corporation and one or more of its subsidiary companies.

Constant dollar accounting. A method of accounting for the impact of inflation that adjusts certain amounts in the primary financial statements to reflect the changes that have occurred in the general puchasing power of the dollar as measured by the Consumer Price Index.

Cost of sales. The cost of merchandise or services to customers, also referred to as cost of goods sold.

Current assets. Those assets that are currently in the form of cash or are expected to be converted into cash within a short period of time, usually one year.

Current cost accounting. A method of accounting for the impact of inflation that estimates what the company's existing assets would have cost at year-end prices. Cost of goods sold and depreciation expense are also adjusted to reflect what they would have cost at the time goods were sold or used.

Current liabilities. Obligations that are due to be paid within a short period of time, usually one year.

Current ratio. A measure of working capital that is determined by dividing current assets by current liabilities.

Debt-to-equity ratio. A measure of a company's ability to obtain credit that is determined by dividing total liabilities by stockholders' equity.

Depletion. The process of writing off the cost of a natural resource, such as oil, coal, or timber.

Depreciation. The process of recognizing a portion of the cost of an asset as an expense charged to earnings during each year of its estimated service life.

Disclaimer of opinion. An audit report provided by a CPA when an opinion cannot be expressed on a company's financial statements.

Divident payout ratio. A ratio that indicates whether or not a corporation is paying enough dividends to its stockholders. The ratio is determined by dividing the amount of dividends paid to common stockholders by net income.

Dividends per share. A ratio that relates the amount of dividends received by stockholders to each share of outstanding common stock. The ratio is determined by dividing the dollar amount of dividends paid to common stockholders by the number of outstanding common shares.

Earnings. Net income.

Earnings per share. A ratio that is determined by dividing the total earnings for a given period (e.g., one year) by the number of shares of outstanding common stock.

Earnings per share—fully diluted. Earnings per share based on the weighted average number of shares of common stock outstanding during the year, adjusted for the possible dilutive effects of all contingently issuable shares of common stock, including common stock equivalents and other outstanding rights to receive or convert to common stock.

Earnings per share—primary. The relationship of net earnings for the year to the weighted average number of shares of common stock outstanding during the year, adjusted for the possible dilutive effects of common stock equivalents, such as stock options and some convertible securities outstanding.

Equity method. A method of accounting used by an investor company to record an investment in common stock of an unconsolidated company. The original investment is recorded at cost and increased (or decreased) by the investor's share of annual earnings (or losses) of the company and decreased for dividends received by the investor. The investor's share of the annual earnings (or losses) is included in its net earnings.

Extraordinary item. A gain or loss that may arise whenever an event or transaction affecting a company is unusual in its nature and occurs infrequently.

FIFO (first-in, first-out). An inventory valuation method that values the items in year-end inventory by using the most recent costs of goods purchased and manufactured. This method assumes that the costs of the oldest items are deducted from inventory and included in cost of goods sold.

Financial Accounting Standards Board. An organization that is responsible for establishing financial accounting and reporting standards.

Fixed assets. Tangible properties with a relatively long life span that are used in the production of goods and services.

Generally accepted accounting principles. The accounting principles and practices that are used for financial accounting and reporting.

Generally accepted auditing standards. Professional criteria or rules that are followed by certified public accountants in the performance of independent audits.

Going-concern concept. The accounting concept that assumes a business will operate indefinitely.

Goodwill. An intangible asset that usually comprises an amount in excess of the fair value of acquired net assets over the amount actually paid for those assets.

Income statement. A statement of revenues and earnings for a given period of time, usually one year.

Intangible assets. Those assets that have no physical existence but have value to a company because of their ability to generate revenues, such as a patent.

Interim reports. Financial reports issued by publicly listed companies to their stockholders, usually on a quarterly basis.

Internal accounting controls. The methods and procedures used by a company to insure the safe protection of its assets and reliability of its financial records.

Internal auditors. Employees of a company who perform various types of audit services and generally assist certified public accountants (i.e., independent auditors) in their examination of financial statements.

Inventories. Goods that are held for sale, and material and partially finished products that will be sold on completion.

Inventory turnover. A ratio that indicates the number of times inventory was actually sold and therefore replaced during the year, and is determined by dividing cost of sales (i.e., cost of goods sold) by the average inventory for the year.

Investments. Securities that are (1) purchased for reasons other than the temporary use of idle cash, (2) held for a relatively long period of time, and (3) classified as a noncurrent asset on the balance sheet.

Liabilities. The claims of creditors.

LIFO (last-in, first-out). An inventory valuation method that essentially charges to cost of goods sold the most recent costs of goods purchased and manufactured. Year-end inventory is valued using the costs of items included in the beginning inventory (i.e., the year the LIFO method was first used) plus costs of quantities of inventory added in that year and in subsequent years.

Market value. The amount at which an asset can be sold in the marketplace.

Marketable equity securities. Marketable securities that represent ownership shares in other companies (e.g., common stock).

Marketable securities. Securities that are expected to be converted into cash within a year.

Natural business year. That point in time at which a company experiences its lowest point of operating activity, usually at December 31 for most companies.

Net asset value. A ratio, also referred at as net book value, that indicates whether or not a company's assets are being properly managed. The ratio is determined by dividing the difference between total assets and total liabilities by the number of outstanding common shares.

Net income. The "bottom line" of an income statement, or the amount by which total revenues exceed total expenses for a given period.

Net loss. The "bottom line" of an income statement, or the amount by which total expenses exceed total revenues for a given period.

Net profit margin. A ratio that measures a company's growth rate. The ratio is determined by dividing net income by net sales.

Note receivable. An amount owed to a company that is evidenced by a promissory note.

Operating profit margin. A ratio, also referred to as gross profit margin, that measures a company's growth rate. The ratio is determined by dividing operating profit by net sales.

Operating lease. A lease that does not meet the conditions of a capital lease because most of the benefits and risks of ownership remain with the lessor. Lease payments on an operating lease are charged to rental expense by the lessee.

Operating loss. The amount by which the total cost of sales, selling, and administrative expenses exceed net sales for a given period.

Operating profit. The amount by which net sales exceed total cost of sales, selling, and adminstrative expenses.

Paid in capital. An amount in excess of the par or stated value of stock that is paid by investors.

Par value. The specific or stated amount that is printed on the face of a stock certificate.

Preferred stock. Stock whose owners receive preferential treatment regarding dividends and the distribution of assets in the event of a company's liquidation.

Prepaid expenses. Services that are purchased prior to the period during which their benefits are actually received, and treated as assets until they are consumed.

Price-earnings ratio. A ratio that is obtained by dividing the average market price of stock by earnings per share.

Publicly listed companies. Companies that have their securities traded on a recognized stock exchange and are required to file their financial statements with the Securities and Exchange Commission.

Qualified opinion. A modification to a CPA's audit report where the opinion indicates that the financial statements are presented in conformity with generally accepted accounting principles "subject to" or "except for" a certain situation or set of circumstances.

Receivable turnover. A ratio that measures the number of times receivables turn over during the year. The ratio is determined by dividing net sales by total receivables.

Registration statement. A statement required by a publicly listed company to be filed with the Securities and Exchange Commission whenever the company sells or offers to sell securities to the public.

Retained earnings. A company's profits after dividend distributions to stockholders that result in an increase in shareholders' equity and are reinvested in the business.

Return on investment. A ratio that measures a company's profitability. The ratio is determined by dividing net income and interest expense by total assets.

SEC Form 10-K. An expanded version of an annual report that must be filed with the Securities and Exchange Commission by publicly listed companies within 90 days after the close of their fiscal year.

SEC Form 10-Q. An expanded version of an interim financial report that must be filed by publicly listed companies within 45 days after the end of each of the first three quarters of a company's fiscal year.

Securities and Exchange Commission. An independent government agency that protects the investor against abuse in the securities and financial markets.

Shareholders (stockholders). The owners of an incorporated business.

Shareowners' (stockholders') equity. That portion of the balance sheet that represents the interests of shareowners or stockholders.

Segment information. A rearrangement of financial information that is included within consolidated financial statements and relates to specific business segments of a corporation (e.g., product lines, services).

Standard audit report. An audit report with a "clean" or unqualified opinion by a certified public accountant.

Statement of changes in financial position. A financial statement that explains how a company obtained and received funds, and correspondingly how such funds were used during a given period of time.

Statement of retained earnings. A financial statement that reconciles the retained earnings from the beginning to the end of a year.

Straight line method. A depreciation method that charges off an equal portion of the cost of a fixed asset over each year of the asset's useful life.

Subsidiary. A company that is owned or controlled by another company.

Times interest earned. A ratio that indicates whether or not a company is able to meet interest payments due to bondholders. The ratio is determined by dividing profit before interest expense and income tax expense by interest expense.

Treasury stock.   Previously issued stock that has been purchased back by the company that originally issued the stock.

Unqualified opinion.   The most common form of opinion provided by certified public accountants in audit reports, often referred to as a "clean" opinion.

Working capital.   The difference between current assets and current liabilities, which indicates whether or not a company is solvent.

Index